Aspects of

Rabbi Joseph Dov Soloveitchik's
Philosophy of Judaism

An Analytic Approach

Aspects of

Rabbi Joseph Dov Soloveitchik's Philosophy of Judaism

An Analytic Approach

by

Shubert Spero

KTAV Publishing House, Inc.
Jersey City, New Jersey

Copyright © 2009 Shubert Spero

　　　　　　　Library of Congress Cataloging-in-Publication Data
Spero, Shubert.
　Aspects of Rabbi Joseph Dov Soloveitchik's philosophy of Judaism : an
analytic approach / by Shubert Spero.
　　p. cm.
　Includes bibliographical references.
　ISBN 978-1-60280-125-7
1. Soloveitchik, Joseph Dov – Teachings. 2. Judaism – Philosophy.
3. Philosophy, Jewish.　I. Title.
　BM755.S6144S64 2009
　296.3092--dc22
　　　　　　　　　　　　2009018619

Published by
KTAV Publishing House, Inc.
930 Newark Avenue
Jersey City, NJ 07306
orders@ktav.com
www.ktav.com
(201) 963-9524
Fax (201) 963-0102

CONTENTS

v

Actually, I was a most unlikely candidate to do and publish a study of the thought of Rabbi Joseph Dov Soloveitchik. I never studied at Yeshivat Rabbenu Yitzchak Elchanon and so did not have the opportunity to develop the sacred personal *talmid-rebbe* relationship. In fact the yeshiva I attended was somewhat to the right of Yeshiva University, so that the positive vibes reaching us in Brooklyn concerning the famed uptown Rosh Yeshiva were limited to his brilliance in Talmud. However, after reading the Rav's *Ish Halakha* (*Talpiot Hebrew Quarterly*, vol. 1, nos. 3–4, 1944) and attending some of his public lectures, I realized I had encountered a personality of a type I had been led to believe could not possibly exist: a Rosh Yeshiva with an impeccable pedigree, familiar with general culture, and, more astonishingly, proudly going public with that familiarity. Subsequently I avidly devoured his published works as they appeared, each one deepening enormously my understanding and appreciation of those vital issues that had long been a part of my cultural baggage. But perhaps some of the very idiosyncratic elements of my personal situation have made possible and even facilitated the analytic approach I have followed. Not being able to call the Rav "my rebbe," in the full sense of the term, made for a certain distance that enabled me to approach his writings with more objectivity. My university studies in philosophy helped me to realize that the Rav was no mere name-dropper, but that every one of his references, ranging from the pre-Socratics to Heidegger, and his treatment of problems in epistemology, ethics, and aesthetics, revealed a profound and comprehensive grasp of the entire history of Western thought. Also, my familiarity with the English language and literature made it possible for me to perceive the quality of the Rav's prose with its frequent flights into exalted poetry. Thus, from a certain distance from the man has come a proximity to his thought, while worshipful reading has led to analysis. However, what has changed only in intensity is my respect, admiration, and gratitude to a towering Jew and his seminal teachings, through which Torah continues to be truly "magnified and glorified."

ACKNOWLEDGMENTS

The first stage in preparing my writing for public viewing has always been presided over by my ever reliable, most competent literary secretary, Mrs. Esther Porath, a friend I have known from Cleveland days and who by now is able to read my handwriting better than I can. Once again, I acknowledge her indispensable assistance.

A sign of the times is the fact that the immediate stimulus for this publication has come from two of my grandsons with whom I study regularly, Yitzchok Applebaum and Benjamin Silberberg, who convinced me that the public is ready and eager for some proper commentary on the teachings of the Rav. What started as mere banter has become a reality – behold the book! *Ye asher kochachem.*

Let us now pause in praise of a most cherished individual, my cousin Shmulie, Dr. Samuel Spero, oldest son of my father's youngest brother, who continues the glorious *baal tefilah* tradition of our family in a most creative way. His devotion and encouragement have accompanied me now for the past sixty years, his computer expertise, constantly at my service, has expedited this publication. May Hashem grant him and his family good health and many more years of fruitful activity.

To my wife Iris, helpmate for the past fifty-eight years, my social secretary and conscience, must go that special kind of acknowledgment, usually belated, that comes with the realization that she has been right at least half of the times we have disagreed.

Finally, of course, *kol hakavod* to my friend Bernard Scharfstein of Ktav Publishing House, whose enthusiastic reception of our publication proposal set in motion the process that has brought out this volume in record time. Much appreciation to his very efficient staff, Adam Bengal, managing editor, and Robert Milch, copyeditor.

We acknowledge with thanks receipt of permission to reprint the following articles by Shubert Spero which appeared in the following journals:

Tradition, published by the Rabbinical Council of America
"Is Judaism an Optimistic Religion?" Vol. 4, No. 1, Fall 1961
"Is There an Indigenous Jewish Theology?" Vol. 9, Nos. 1 and 2, 1967
"Rabbi Joseph Dov Soloveitchik and the Philosophy of the Halakha," Vol. 30, no. 2, 1996
"Knock, Knock, Who Is There? What Do You Want?" Vol. 39, no. 3, 2006.
"The Rav and the Tale Told by the Heavens," Vol. 4, no. 1, 2008

Modern Judaism, published by Oxford University Press
"Rabbi Joseph Dov Soloveitchik and Belief in God," Vol. 19, 1999
"Rabbi Joseph Dov Soloveitichik and the Role of the Ethical," Vol. 23, 2003
B.D.D., published by Bar-Ilan University Press
"The Role of Descriptive Hermeneutics in the Thought of the Rav," Vol. 18, April 2007

INTRODUCTION

With the passage of time, additional teachings of Rabbi Joseph Dov Soloveitchik (1903–1993) are coming to light as notes and tapes of his *sheurim* and lectures have been recovered and published. No less copious is the flow of commentary, which ranges from the uncritically effusive to the flagrantly tendentious. It may seem ironic that an individual who, during his lifetime was most hesitant to publish, continues to speak to us more than a decade after his passing. But I tend to believe that ultimately something deeply imbedded in the mechanism of Israel's providential history makes for the preservation not only of the words of the Torah but also of those words that constitute authentic explications of the Torah concepts. So, it seems, has it been with the teachings of Rabbi Soloveitchik. There seems to be a singular capacity for the well-articulated thought that bears the kiss of truth to commend itself intuitively to the human mind. As a result of this activity, references to Rabbi Soloveitchik as "the Rav," which was once characteristic only of his actual students at Yeshivat Rabeinu Yitzhak Elchanan, have now fondly become the chosen usage of the literary Jewish community worldwide.

The starting point of any attempt to understand the special

significance of the teachings of the Rav must be the purely factual observation that the appearance in modern times of an individual such as Joseph Dov Soloveitchik is unprecedented in terms of several sets of interrelated facts. The first is what you see: a Rosh Yeshiva in the Lithuanian tradition who had an earned doctorate in philosophy from the University of Berlin. Add to this an inquisitive intellect possessed of great analytic power and a retentive memory active in the service of wide-ranging interests. The result was a personality who not only mastered the entire rabbinic tradition, Halakha and Aggada, but at the same time possessed an incisive grasp of the history of Western philosophy, including recent developments in philosophy of science and the movements leading up to phenomenology and existentialism. One would have to reach back to Maimonides to find a comparable figure. Little of this, however, would have been apparent were it not for the Rav's power of expression. He was a master of the analytic, the poetic, and the dramatic use of words in at least three languages. All of this came together in a personality that exuded charisma. Rabbi Soloveitchik, however, saw himself essentially as a teacher – hence, "the Rav."

THE RAV AND PHILOSOPHY

The essays in this volume focus primarily upon the *philosophy* of the Rav rather than upon his strictly halakhic teachings as found in his *sheurim* on the Talmud. It is therefore important that we first review the general meaning of the term "philosophy" and then attempt to clarify what we have in mind when we speak of the philosophy of the Rav. There are those who see the very term "philosophy" as a foreign import, and in attaching it to Judaism an attempt to bring Judaism under alien influence. They believe that philosophy must always refer to a specific doctrine, so that anyone intending to do *philosophy* of Judaism must be trying to wed Judaism to some existing philosophical school. This, of course, is nonsense. The term "philosophy" as such, today need not refer to any particular subject matter. Essentially, the word denotes certain types of questions that may be addressed to any subject-matter. Questions, that is, which inquire as to the overriding purpose or underlying principles of any discipline or enterprise. Thus, there can be a philosophy of education, a philosophy of law, of science, of art, of entertainment, or even one's philosophy of life. In pursuit of philosophical questions, one is expected to use as method a mode of thinking that is at once critical and logical, consistent and requiring justification for any truth-claims, and that gives priority to the search for meaning before embarking upon the search for truth. (For example, before we can fruitfully discuss the question whether God exists we must first understand what is meant by the term "God.")

Assuming then, that philosophy is primarily a method of inquiry and in itself ideologically neutral, we might ask whether it has ever been applied to Judaism as a whole so that we may speak of an authentic, indigenous philosophy of Judaism. I would reply that there is both a need and a possibility for an indigenous philosophy of Judaism. Unfortunately, none yet exists as a complete and coherent system of propositions. However, I would argue that the logical implications of the givens of Judaism – its conceptions of God, man, and history, of Torah, Halakha, nature, and morality – are sufficiently clear as to enable us to judge whether any proposed theory of Judaism as a whole or any of its aspects is a *possible* candidate. I am thus suggesting that there can conceivably be more than one acceptable philosophy of Judaism or aspect thereof. (For further discussion of this point, see below, Chapter 1.)

Admittedly, the phrase "philosophy of the Rav" means different things to different people. To many in the yeshiva world, any and all of the writings of the Rav which are not of a strictly halakhic nature are designated "philosophy of the Rav." Often this includes material which is not philosophy at all but rather interpretations of biblical and rabbinic texts that would more properly qualify as *midrash aggada*. My own intention in using this phrase is as an abbreviation for "aspects of the Rav's *philosophy of*

Judaism." Consider this: could there be in this context any other meaningful interpretation of this phrase? Could it mean the Rav's own personal philosophy? Hardly! As a committed observant Jew, the Rav's understanding and acceptance of the full range of the rabbinic tradition certainly provided him with a religious world-view that included substantial beliefs about God, man, nature, and history. Actually there never was much of a question about the Rav's philosophy in the broad sense. Most of what he says in his writings takes place within the frame of reference of traditional Judaism, which is the subject matter he starts out from and to which he returns. Therefore when we find teachings of the Rav in response to *philosophical* questions in the sense described above, unless there is clear evidence to the contrary, we may assume that the Rav is expounding what he believes to be an aspect of the philosophy of Judaism.

There is, however, an important exception to this generalization, and that is the Rav's work *The Halakhic Mind.* The bulk of this essay consists of a philosophy of religion in general worked out by the Rav on the basis of currently accepted epistemology. It is not based on Judaism, nor does the Rav claim that it is. However, in the last few pages, the Rav attempts to apply his theory to Judaism and attempts to explain by its means the role and importance of the Halakha. It is these aspects of the Rav's teachings, aspects of the *philosophy of Judaism*, which are the focus of the essays in this volume.

Before we proceed to examine the substance of the teachings in which the Rav presents a philosophy of some aspects of Judaism, let me comment upon an issue that has been repeatedly raised. Many in the yeshiva world are prepared to forgive the Rav for having attended the University of Berlin and even for having excelled in his studies. However, they are disturbed by the Rav's many detailed references to scores of strange philosophies and theologies, particularly in his first and now famous essay *Halakhic Man* (first printed in Hebrew in 1944), which deals with such an intimately Jewish theme as the Halakha! Does this mean that the

Rav derived his views from these foreign sources? Was he influenced by them?

In view of the fact that no other major Orthodox rabbinic scholar has seen fit to refer in his writings so openly and in such detail to so broad a range of philosophers and theologians, we are compelled to ask why the Rav did so and what effect all this "outside" reading may have had upon his teachings? Is there justification for saying, for example, that his philosophy is Neo-Kantian or that it is a form of religious existentialism, and what does that mean?

Let us try to imaginatively reconstruct the attitude with which the Rav at age twenty-three might have entered the University of Berlin. Here is a young man with a brilliant, questing mind, master of the entire rabbinic tradition, including the medieval Jewish philosophers, with the equivalent of a secular *Gymnasium* education, who has an opportunity to study at a prominent German institution of higher learning. What is he seeking? Judging from the areas of general philosophy dealt with by the Rav, I would retrospectively put it this way: He was seeking what the Jewish tradition was not able to provide. To begin with, clarification of a vital philosophical question: the nature of human cognition. What *do* we know? *How* do we know? What is the status of our knowledge of God as compared to the knowledge discovered by science? The Rav knew what Maimonides said. But what had men discovered since? The second, verification of a deeply seated apprehension. Exposed to Hasidic teachings in his youth, with their emphasis on inwardness, and immersed in a religious culture saturated with God-consciousness, and having tasted Russian literature, this young man, with his penetrating power of introspection, had concluded that the most direct medium we have to God is by way of our own consciousness, which each of us experiences in our individual subjectivity.[1] Therefore, another of his main objectives was to further explore the nature of the religious consciousness. In this last area, however, the Rav did not arrive empty-handed but with considerable baggage culled from his own introspection as well as with insight from biblical and rabbinic teachings. Both of these areas, the nature of cognition and the nature of religious consciousness, were beyond the ken of traditional Jewish thinking and were generally outside their sphere of interest.

In terms of the first question, the Rav learned with great excitement that a tectonic shift had taken place in the relationship between science and philosophy. As the Rav tells it, twice in the history of philosophy was the scientific world-perspective of its day accepted as the model of knowledge in general, so that philosophy did its theorizing about the world as presented to it by science. The first was the Aristotelian natural science and metaphysics, which held sway up to and including the medieval period. The second was the Galilean-Newtonian view of reality, based on mathematical, mechanistic physics, which was accepted until very recently. Throughout this long stretch of time, the presumption was that scientific knowledge obtained by the scientific method was "exclusive," that is, "eliminating any other cognitive approach to reality."[2] As a result, philosophy, including philosophy of religion, was subservient to science. Today, however, for reasons the Rav explains in detail, it is generally acknowledged that the picture of reality given to us by science is partial and incomplete. Hence a cleavage has developed between scientific empiricism and philosophic speculation, so that today it is reasonable to believe that there can be an independent philosophical methodology; that aside from the quantitative universe, there is a qualitative universe, a private one which can be known or intuited. The Rav called this revolutionary new discovery *epistemological pluralism*, that is, there is more than one way to know the reality in which we exist. The Rav believed that for the religious person this was a "propitious turn of events."[3] And indeed it was.

The Rav arrived at this conclusion after having digested the entire complex history of modern science and philosophy since Kant. This, of course, was quite necessary, since the Rav's objective was to determine the conventional wisdom regarding epistemology in his day, and to show that the view he proposed had by then become the standard view. I find nothing in the writing of the Rav that would support the notion that he was influenced by or particularly attached to the philosophy of Hermann Cohen or to the Neo-Kantians in general. His references to these philosophers are usually in connection with some particular point and hardly constitute a general endorsement. The following remarks of the Rav seem to dissipate claims that his philosophy, as such, can be characterized as especially Neo-Kantian.

> I desire only to elucidate the nature of Halakhic man by drawing upon the philosophical understanding of mathematics as an a priori science with ideal constructs. This view is prevalent not only in all the doctrines that have been influenced by the Kantian and neo-Kantian philosophy but also within the circles of great contemporary mathematicians and physicists.[4]

Having made the discovery of epistemological pluralism, the Rav went on to formulate an alternative epistemology upon which he built his own general philosophy of religion, which he judges to be an adequate account of Judaism in general and the Halakha in particular (see further Chapter 6).

In his search for insight into the contents of the religious consciousness, in which, as we have indicated, the Rav saw the main theater for the God-experience, he found a number of kindred souls. Among them were psychologists, theologians, and philosophers, but primarily a school of thought roughly called existentialism.[5]

In those of his essays which deal with the nature of man and the conflicted religious consciousness ("The Lonely Man of Faith" and "Confrontation"), the Rav states his view very clearly, concisely, and tellingly, giving exegesis of the Bible as his source without referring to other philosophers.

> The role of the man of faith whose religious experience is fraught with inner conflicts and incongruities which oscillates between ecstasy in God's companionship and despair when he feels abandoned by God and who is torn asunder by heightened contrast between self appreciation and abnegation has been a difficult one since the times of Abraham and Moses.[6]

The Rav made it very clear that his belief in the conflicted nature of the religious consciousness was based on individual experience which once discovered can be read back as insightful explanation of the creation account in Genesis, other scriptural descriptions of biblical figures, as well as the structure of certain halakhot concerning prayer, mourning, and repentance.

What remains to be explained, however, is why, precisely in an essay that purportedly deals with phenomena of the Halakha, the Rav feels the need to review in such impressive detail the history of the religious consciousness.[7] The answer lies in the innovative nature of his method for describing the personality of the man of the Halakha. As is well known by now, the Rav held that halakhic man is an uneasy combination of two ideal types, religious man and cognitive man. But in order for the Rav's thesis to be taken seriously, his description of *homo-religiosus* must be one that is recognized as valid by contemporary thought and not some aberration peculiar to the Rav. Hence it is precisely here, in the opening section of *Halakhic Man*, that the Rav must convincingly demonstrate that there is substantial opinion supporting the notion of the religious consciousness as conflicted: "in the light of modern philosophy homo-religiosus in general has come to be regarded as an antithetical being fraught with contradictions and struggle."[8] Saying so is not enough, and so the Rav finds it necessary to provide the sources in *modern philosophy* that support the description. It would seem, therefore, that the Rav arrived in Berlin with his view of the conflicted nature of the religious personality already in hand.

The issue of the nature of the religious consciousness is not simply a matter of depth psychology, of interest only to contemplative soul-searchers. It is, rather, an issue that touches upon the very character and function of religion. In the 1950s and 1960s in the United States, a serious debate was being waged on this very question, with the dominant view being that the function of religion was to provide peace of mind rather than peace of soul.

The Rav was very explicit on this point: "Those that are inclined to portray religion as a poetic Acadia, a realm of simplicity, wholeness and tranquility that enables you to achieve a comfortable psychic equilibrium – this ideology is intentionally false and deceptive."[9]

It was this sort of theology that was then being preached by certain liberal Protestant groups and was being used to justify the practices of Reform and Conservative Judaism and to discredit Orthodoxy. The Rav, therefore, wished to seek support among contemporary theologians in order to uphold his view of the conflicted nature of the religious consciousness .

Anyone familiar with the writing of Kierkegaard will be struck by its similarity to the sentiments expressed by the Rav, particularly when speaking of the human condition. There is also no question that the Rav was thoroughly familiar with the writing of Kierkegaard. This should come as no surprise inasmuch as both were deeply religious figures acutely aware of the profound struggles going on within themselves and convinced that the rationalism of naturalistic philosophy as well as the speculative idealistic philosophy were of little help in accounting for individual human existence and the significance of intersubjective relationship. There were obviously vast differences between Kierkegaard, a religious Christian, and the Rav, a religious Jew, in terms of the solutions they offered.[10] However, there is a shared vocabulary in their respective diagnoses of many aspects of man's predicament, a vocabulary the Rav had no compunction in using and, when appropriate, attributing to Kierkegaard when needed to clarify a point.

It should be remembered that existentialism started out as a literary trend in France and Germany after World War II, with a message of alienation, anxiety, and loneliness. Thus a basic "existentialist" approach had become popular parallel with the appearance of systematic existential philosophies such as those of Jaspers and Marcel.[11] However, early on it had been noted that the philosophic trend called existential had many characteristics and emphases that were recognized as biblical and Hebraic. In short, what we had was simply a confluence of the teaching of the Rav on the question of religious consciousness with a postwar trend known as existentialism. It was not an adoption by the Rav of "modern packaging" for ancient doctrines, but rather an awakening and recovery by postwar man of the wisdom of biblical categories.

It is interesting to note that when reports of the existentialist trend, both in literature and philosophy, reached America, Reform and Conservative leaders came out sharply against it as irrational and not in accordance with Judaism. The fact that the Rav was the only major rabbinic figure to perceive aspects of biblical and rabbinic teachings in existentialism testifies to his deep understanding. In fact, the word "existential" (meaning an emphasis upon individual experience) has today become so denuded of any doctrinal content that to characterize the Rav's philosophy as existential does nothing more than point up his emphasis on the human condition.

THE FAITH EXPERIENCE

We find a similar disclaimer in the Rav's introduction to his essay "The Lonely Man of Faith" in which he describes the inner religious experience of a man of faith:

> Whatever I am going to say here has been derived not from philosophical dialectics, abstract speculation or detached impersonal reflections but from actual activities and experiences with which I have been confronted.... My interpretive

gesture is completely subjective and lays no claim to representing a definitive Halakhic philosophy.[12]

Once again, the Rav seems to be making a sharp distinction between doing *philosophy* or *theology* of Judaism, on the one hand, and analyzing and describing the inner religious consciousness, which is fraught with "inner conflicts and incongruities." This consciousness in its varying moods is always in the background of the mind of the man of faith because it is part of his very being. By emphasizing that this is his *personal* experience, the Rav is saying that it is not his view that all men of faith actually have these experiences or that they should have them, but only that some do and that they are authentic. By drawing this complex anthropology from the first two chapters of Genesis, the Rav is saying that this view is not only compatible with the biblical view of man but suggested by it. The question "What is man?" is indeed a major philosophical/theological issue that has been treated within the framework of Judaism. The single biblical statement that man was "created in the image of God" is in itself a rich source for a Jewish anthropology. It already implies that man has been given contra-causal freedom of will which imposes moral responsibility, that man can achieve knowledge of himself and his environment, that man can and should be creative. This is part of the basic philosophy of man that is a given for every believing Jew. However, a religious consciousness fraught with inner conflicts and incongruities need not be a necessary component of that philosophy.

In one of his essays, the Rav explicitly asks "What is man?" in the context of Judaism, and his immediate answer is "Man is a solitary (בודד) creature and it is this isolation (בדידות) which characterizes his uniqueness."[13] He goes on to explain that man is alone in the universe in a double sense. First, humankind as a species is in many ways different from all other forms of life. Second, each individual person is different from all others, with a unique sense of personal identity. Stated thus in objective language, these observations are factual statements and can be accepted as additional parts of Judaism's philosophy of man (תורת האדם). However, the Rav, as always, sees this from the point of view of the subject, of his personal religious consciousness. Thus, to be בודד or לבד means not only physically alone or theoretically unique but could imply the complex psychological state of feeling lonely with all of its existential offshoots, such as feeling alienated or like a stranger. The Rav sees this as one of the consequences of being "in the image of God." For haven't we been told that "the Lord our God, the Lord is One" (*echod*). God's oneness *means* His uniqueness, His total transcendence and otherness. To have been created in His image, therefore, means that man too is unique in nature and subjectively experiences it as existential loneliness.[14]

However, to talk about the religious consciousness or the religious experience as if it were a stable, identifiable entity is extremely misleading. Since entry to it is only by means of introspection by the individual, our "data" consist solely of snatches of personal memory. Therefore, even comparative studies of the reports of different individuals may not yield information about the religious consciousness as such. In any case, this seems more a matter of psychology than of philosophy.

It has sometimes been argued that the primary commands of Judaism, to both love and fear God and to be both just and merciful, create the conditions for a conflicted, tension-filled religious consciousness. It seems to the present writer that such tension and antithetical sentiments are indeed inherent in the very nature of man, in his position in the cosmos and in his relationship to God. However, precisely how each person resolves these conflicts, balances these emotions, and what outlook he adopts toward his own condition is a matter of personality. In regard to the issue of the religious consciousness, who is to say which is the more authentic, the more preferable, the more appropriate in the eyes of God?

Critics have pointed to the Rav's emphasis on the darker side of the religious consciousness, on loneliness, defeat, and anxiety, as evidence of the alien influence of existentialism and as tending to ignore the Jews' ability to achieve an integrated personality with its resultant joys. Chapter 2 (which appeared four years before the Rav's "Lonely Man of Faith") traces the background in classical Judaism for the Rav's approach.

MORAL PHILOSOPHY

By virtue of his family background and early training, the Rav was eminently qualified both intellectually and temperamentally to be a Rosh Yeshiva. However, his powerful intellect and wide-ranging interests impelled him to reach far beyond the conventional limitations of a Rosh Yeshiva in his search for self-understanding as a committed Jew living in a changing world. The Rav had never set himself the task of constructing a coherent systematic philosophy of Judaism, one that would encompass Halakha and Aggada and include explications of God and man, history and nature, creation, revelation, and redemption. Most of his philosophy came about "incidentally" in the course of expounding various texts on halakhot or delivering lectures on the festivals or on special occasions, or on particular subjects, such as mental health, the aging process, or marriage and family.[15]

Striking evidence of the sporadic nature of the Rav's philosophic endeavors is his treatment of the subject of the ethics of Judaism. Of course, throughout his lectures and writings, the Rav constantly refers to ethics, morality, the moral mitzvot, and moral values. Thus, for example, in one discussion he points out that "the Decalogue contains nothing cultic. It is throughout an ethical code. Its realization constitutes the basic relationship between God and Israel as a nation, as a community of the committed."[16]

In some recent publications of the Rav's early lectures there are tantalizing statements about morality that are of great philosophic significance but somehow have never been conjoined and developed.

However important the intellect, the crowning head of human accomplishment, is a very sensitive moral will which is capable of deciding freely, of choosing the deed and carrying out its decisions.[17]

Judaism has maintained that the aboriginal discovery of the moral law and ideal was made by the heart, by the feeling not by the intellect or the will, although the latter two are needed to decode, interpret and implement the message.[18]

Judaism believes that the emotional experience is suffused with ethical-moral meaning. Axiological structures and moral ideas are intuited through our emotional experiences.[19]

…the basic moral norm is contained in the idea of *imitatio Dei* which we derive from the verse והלכת בדרכיו (Deuteronomy 28:9) or from זה אלי ואנוהו (Exodus 15:2). This desire to be like Him, to fashion our deeds after a Divine design is understandable if it is seen against the background of a relationship based on passionate love. This emotion expresses itself in an overpowering longing for the complete identification of the lover with the beloved – the inner striving for identity and unity.[20]

Because of the intrinsic importance of morality to Judaism, it is instructive to review the Rav's approach to the subject (see Chapter 3).

PHILOSOPHY OF PRAYER

The difficulty in sorting out the Rav's philosophy, in the sense of its being a philosophy of some aspect of Judaism, from the remainder of his teachings can be seen in his approach to the subject of prayer. Prayer, of course, is a major component of Judaism, as it is of most religions. In terms of the demand of the Halakha to pray formally three times a day, observant Jews are well aware of its impact upon one's personal life. Regarding its halakhic development, from the sixteenth-century codifications and extending into contemporary responsa literature, prayer has enjoyed as much attention as any other area. In the modern period, the history of the texts of Jewish prayer and the origins of different customs have been a subject of extensive and fruitful scholarship. Indeed, it has been rightly noted that "no other book in the whole range of Jewish literature...comes so close to the life of the Jewish masses as does the *Siddur* – the Jewish prayer book."[21] Yet surprisingly, the subject of the *philosophy* of prayer in Judaism has not received comparable attention. Few of the medieval Jewish philosophers treated the subject at length. Those who did, dealt with it primarily as related to the theological issue of Divine Providence.[22] Surprisingly, for the Rav (generally perceived as the intellectual talmudist *par excellence*) prayer (usually seen as an emotional expression) constituted a vital part of Jewish religious life to which he devoted a great deal of thought. As has been pointed out, "prayer with its intricate interplay of legal, liturgical and experiential motifs, provides an extraordinarily fertile demonstration of the Rav's method."[23]

How then shall we understand the following words of the Rav that we find in the opening section of the recent splendid publication entitled *Worship of the Heart*: "...when I speak about the *philosophy of prayer* or Shema, I do not claim universal validity for my conclusions. I am not lecturing on *philosophy of prayer*, as such, but on prayer as understood, experienced and enjoyed by an individual" (emphasis added).[24]

I take the Rav to be saying that in what follows he will be speaking about what people might popularly call philosophy of prayer but actually is not *philosophy* of prayer as such. What we *can* infer from these statements is that, while the Rav is prepared to claim "universal validity" for his pronouncements on the Halakha (of prayer), this is not the case in the area he calls "the *experience* of prayer." This stems from the Rav's general view that the mitzvah of prayer, which in its formal practical aspects is treated by the Halakha, is integrally tied to its inward subjective side. And it is precisely here, in analyzing in depth and in describing so lucidly the various emotions, the dialectical tensions, the subtle nuances of the experiential side of prayer, that the Rav is at his peerless best. But because the Rav derives most of this by means of introspection from his own inner individual experience, he disclaims that it has "universal validity," although he invites the reader to compare his own prayer experiences. However, since the Rav is able to demonstrate how his analysis is reflected in different parts of the prayer texts, his teachings are an important contribution to *iyun tefilla* – "thinking deeply about our prayer" – but not yet a *philosophy of Jewish prayer*. Nevertheless, while the Rav may insist that he is not lecturing on philosophy of prayer as such, from what he has said we can extract (mostly in his own words) what can credibly be called an outline or at least a prolegomenon to a philosophy of Jewish prayer:

> Prayer in Judaism, as set forth in the Halakha, is one of the modes of expression or objectification of a person's inner subjective religious experience. Other modes being the intellectual (*limud hatorah*) and the volitional (deeds). Designated "Worship of the Heart" (*avoda she-ba-lev*), the inner prayer experience partakes of the sum total of man's relationship to God in all of its dialectical tension-filled aspects. While in this sense, the prayer experience can be called "the quintessence of Judaism," prayer as such is by no means central to Judaism (there being the other modes). Prayer is dialogical and constitutes fellowship with God. Whereas in prophecy God speaks and man listens, in prayer, man reaches out to God and God listens. By designating prayer as "worship of the heart" we are underlining its emotional character in which love, awe, reverence and gratitude, and even anxiety and despair, can find expression. While praise of God for His bounty abounds in Jewish prayer, the concept of petition is central because it reflects a feeling (both of the community and the individual) of unqualified dependence upon God.

One would be hard pressed to find a more concise and comprehensive formulation of the philosophy of Jewish prayer which takes into account its distinctive features in so balanced a manner, which accords so well with its texts, halakhic rules, and rabbinic pronouncements, and so clearly delineates its proper role within Judaism as a whole

A PHILOSOPHY OF THE HALAKHA

While the Rav's treatment of the man of the Halakha seems to have focused upon analysis of the personality of a particular type of individual, included therein are important teachings regarding the Rav's understanding of the Halakha as such. This question of the Halakha as a whole, how it is to be regarded and studied and its place and role in Judaism, was the central goal of the Rav's intellectual quest and the starting point of much of his philosophy. This can be seen in the titles of his earliest works, *The Halakhic Mind* and *Halakhic Man*, but most clearly in his biography. His entire Jewish intellectual heritage and upbringing was tied to the Lithuanian talmudic tradition. As the Rav states in his conclusion to *Halakhic Man*, "My sole intention [in writing this essay] was to defend the honor of the Halakha and Halakhic man." Here again, as he had done in connection with prayer and faith, the Rav disclaims that his analyses have serious philosophical value: "This essay is but a patchwork of scattered reflections, a haphazard collection of fragmentary observations.... It is devoid of scientific precision, of substance and stylistic clarity."[25]

However, whether intended or not and perhaps only incidental to his main purpose, the Rav *has* given us a philosophy of the Halakha. Before we take this any further, let us take a look at *The Halakhic Mind*, which, as we have already indicated, is a philosophical work of a general nature in which the Rav works out a general philosophy of religion. After applying this to Judaism, the Rav concludes that "the Halakha is the objectifying instrument" of our religious consciousness, and thus by analyzing the Halakha one can gain insight into the "living, historical religious consciousness" which is the true meeting ground between man and God. Here we have a key statement as to the nature of the Halakha, its importance, and its relationship to the religious consciousness – in short, the beginning of a philosophy of the Halakha. The Rav, however, sees this as warranting a further, rather sweeping principle: "To this end there is only a single source from which a Jewish philosophical *Weltanschauung* could emerge: the objective order – the Halakha."[26]

The Rav seems to be saying that only from the Halakha can we generate an authentic philosophy of Judaism. Can this view be maintained? Additional elements for a philosophy of the Halakha are to be found in the Rav's comparison of the halakhic conceptual system to the *a priori* mathematical model of reality employed by the science of physics today.

The essay *Halakhic Man* has generated much discussion as to whether the Rav saw himself as a man of the Halakha as he is described in this essay. The question has also been raised as to whether his idealized *ish ha-halakha* is a truly admirable figure to be imitated today. While interesting, these questions are irrelevant to our present study. What is of great significance, however, are the elements of a philosophy of the Halakha that we have found in the two works. It should be noted that the *need* in Jewish life for a philosophy of the Halakha is far greater than, for example, the need for a philosophy of prayer. From his very first appearance on this planet, man has turned to the transcendent, beseeching out of fear and need or praising out of gratitude.[27] And he continues to do so, whether Jew or non-Jew, with or without a philosophy. The Halakha, however, is a comprehensive system of ritual laws as well as moral rules and principles designed to be applied and practiced in real life. Fortunately, it has come down to us with a method showing how the rules and laws are to be interpreted for practical application in ever novel situations. This method is internal to the Halakha. However, here the question of one's philosophy of Halakha is of paramount practical significance to every observant Jew today: *How* is the Halakha to be studied? How much time is to be devoted to its study? Is one to seek out the more strict or the more lenient view? The answers to these very

practical questions in large measure depend upon one's philosophy of the Halakha.

The reader is invited to join us in considering whether the
approach suggested by the Rav is "adequate" in the sense that
it takes into account all of the primary relevant items we know
about the Halakha and the way it functions in Jewish religious
life. Hopefully, the reader will see himself challenged to consider
that philosophy of the Halakha which is most in accord with his
understanding of the other components of Judaism. (For further
discussion, see Chapter 4.)

BELIEF IN GOD

There is a statement by the Rav which has made some people
wonder whether in the light of the many issues that *do not* trouble him, his teachings can be truly relevant for the modern Jew. I
have reference to the following statement:

> I have never been seriously troubled by the Biblical problem
> of the doctrine of creation vis-à-vis the scientific story of evo-
> lution at both the cosmic and the organic levels, nor have I
> been perturbed by the confrontation of the mechanistic in-
> terpretation of the human mind with the Biblical spiritual
> concept of man. I have not been perplexed by the impossi-
> bility of fitting the mystery of revelation into the framework
> of historical empiricism. Moreover, I have not even been
> troubled by the theories of Biblical criticism which contradict
> the very foundations upon which the sanctity and integrity
> of the Scriptures rest.[28]

How unfortunate! Not that I wish upon the Rav more problems,
but it surely would be helpful to read what this towering intellect
might have said about these issues. However, on the particular
question of the rational demonstration of the existence of God,
the Rav elaborates somewhat, and in a footnote he points out its
futility and insists that belief in God is based on a living primal

experience which is "to apprehend God *in* reality rather than *through* reality."[29] Does that constitute a rational basis for belief in God? I believe that questions of this kind entail some of the more important philosophical issues confronting Jews who have had a liberal arts education. In studying the teachings of the Rav, I was pleased to find what I take to be an important contribution to this subject (see Chapter 6).

THE RAV AND HISTORY

One of the surprising events in the Rav's biography, given his family background, was his move into the Zionist camp to become the leader of the Mizrachi (Religious Zionist) organization in America. Over the years there has been intense interest in the nature of the Rav's Zionism, some describing it as non-messianic Zionism, as compared to Rav Kook's messianic Zionism. The Rav's personal practices regarding some halakhic observances, such as the saying of Hallel on Yom Ha'atzmaut and the prayer for the State of Israel with its phrase *reishit tzmichat geulatanu*, "the beginning of the flowering of our redemption," were scrutinized and discussed. However, in order to grasp the Rav's Zionism, we must first understand his approach to history as a whole.[30]

From our description of the Rav, both as a traditional Rosh Yeshiva, giving regular *sheurim* in Talmud, and as a scholar immersed in the complexities of modern philosophy, one might think of him as the proverbial ivory-tower pedant, locked into his private world of abstract theory. Actually, the Rav was very much a man of the larger public world, highly aware of his surroundings and endowed with what has been called practical wisdom. The Rav paid close attention to history, not only of the antique past as recorded by *Tnach*, but also to all of the real, relevant, and often painful events of the recent past, particularly as they impacted upon the condition of the Jewish people. Thus, the chief motivating factor in the Rav's espousal of practical Zionism was his fear for the Jews in Europe, for he grasped the deadly menace of the increasing black clouds of anti-Semitism that were gathering.

Another basic insight of the Rav was his appreciation of the radical changes that were taking place in Western civilization in terms of science, technology, and, yes, philosophy. This brought him to realize that Jews must open themselves to the full range of the culture of modernity as filtered through Torah values, so as to provide Jewish youth with access to the highest levels of general education.

Thus, two of the most distinctive features of the Rav as a traditional Rosh Yeshiva and as a grandson of Reb Chaim Brisker, namely his practical Zionism and his embrace of general culture, were the logical consequences of his deep understanding of recent history. The Rav realized that profound changes had taken place in our world, changes so radical that they had shattered the framework within which Jews had been thinking and living for millennia. Man's new potential for evil and destruction had grown enormously even as his knowledge of "what is above and what is below," i.e., particle physics and deep-space cosmology, began to show signs of built-in limitations. The physical dangers facing the Jewish people were now much greater. At the same time, certain strains in modern philosophy tended to make man more humble and more open to the transcendent. Jews, urged the Rav, must become more sensitive and responsive to the opportunities afforded by a Jewish state in Eretz Yisrael and to the education of our young, keeping them in tune with the cutting-edge of man's intellectual development. (It will be remembered that according to the Rav, Adam, the first human involved in creative interaction with the world, possessed *dignity* and *majesty*, which were aspects of the image of God within him.)

The Rav greeted the declaration of Jewish statehood with pretty much the same mixture of joy and apprehension as did much of Jewry. Born amidst the violence and the dislocations of the Holocaust, with its physical survival dubious, it was too early for anyone to grasp the religious significance of the state or to foresee its effects on world Jewry. On Yom Ha'atzmaut 1955, with dangers mounting from neighboring Arab countries and changes

taking place in international relations among the European powers, the Rav delivered an address known as *Kol Dodi Dofek* which
has become a classic of Religious Zionism and a window into the
Rav's views on several philosophical subjects, including the role
of God in history. In 2006 the editors of the journal *Tradition* invited a number of rabbis to share their personal responses to *Kol
Dodi* and give their perceptions of the extent to which the Rav's
work provided a satisfactory framework for what might be the approach of Jewish theology to history and particularly to the State
of Israel.[31] My response is printed below in Chapter 7.

It has been said that the enduring importance of the Rav lies
more in the enlightened type of rabbinic scholar he represents
than in his actual teachings. I would tend to disagree. Quite the
contrary. It is precisely the depth and grandeur of his teachings,
with their subtle blending of philosophic thought and Halakha,
that testifies to the propriety of his method and the integrity of
his personality.

It is probably too early to attempt an overall judgment of the
Rav's oeuvre, because all of it has still not been published. In my
article "The Rav and the Tale Told by the Heavens" (see Chapter 8),
I dealt with what appeared to be some new material of the Rav's on
the role of the aesthetic in Jewish theology. Perhaps this is a proper
note upon which to conclude our introduction. For, in truth, the
aesthetic is one of the more important lenses through which to
view the Rav as writer. To read Joseph Dov Soloveitchik is to read
literature, that is, writing whose value lies also in the emotional
effect of the beauty of its language. To listen to his formal lectures
is to hear poetry and to be lifted by the sheer lyricism of his words
to lofty emotional levels.[32] The Rav's word-pictures of his sense of
the Presence of God, of the beauty of nature, the anguish of the
mourner, and of his childhood memory of overhearing his father
defend the views of the Rambam, are themselves works of art.[33]
However, even in the small amount of material published so far
in which the Rav speaks of the aesthetic, there is a most impor-

tant contribution to our understanding of the approach of Jewish theology to this vital subject (see Chapter 9).

In Chapter 6 we discuss whether it would appear that the profound teachings of the Rav cannot be attributed to the use of some special method. If that were the case, he would long ago have had successful imitators. We can follow the moves of the Rav, understand what he is doing, and stand in awe before the finished product. Yet somehow the connections he makes, which appear so reasonable after we hear them, would probably never have occurred to us. If indeed, as some have suggested, the philosophic work of the Rav is to be seen as a form of *derush*, which the Rav employs not only as a methodological tool but as a substantive component, then it must be granted that never before has this mode of thought reached such profound depths or been expressed with such literary beauty. For, after all, what is *derush*? It is the encounter of a human mind with the word of God "as a hammer that breaks up the rock," and the sparks that fly are the product of both the hammer and the rock. Of course, the word of God remains what it always has been, but the caliber of the sparks depends upon the caliber of the individual mind involved in the encounter. In the case of the Rav, it has never been higher.

ENDNOTES

1. One of the Rav's most distinctive and influential teachings is his belief that human existence as experienced by the individual is, by its very nature, ultimately and inescapably filled with tension and contradictions. While there are all sorts of psychological devices by which people may for a while delude themselves into thinking otherwise, maturity requires that the individual confront his true condition. There is a remarkable passage in *Out of the Whirlwind* in which the Rav describes in detail his personal experience when confronted by sickness and an impending operation. He tells us how "sickness initiated me into the secret of non-being. I suddenly ceased to be immortal: I became a mortal, able to confront nihility" (pp. 131–132). But affliction and suffering, says the Rav, also opened to him the domain of being different, singled out, utterly alone, and a feeling of loneliness that for the Rav has multiple states. Two points are to be

noted here: (1) He describes the experiences that he calls "non-being" and "loneliness" in a nonreligious context. They are experiences that occur to every human being at some time or another, are quite normal and natural, and are part of the human condition. (2) These experiences are not to be shunned but welcomed. They are "a great experience," one in which "one finds peace of mind and relief from other worries." *Out of the Whirlwind*, pp. 132, 134.

2. *The Halakhic Mind*, p. 5.

3. Ibid., pp. 12–22.

4. *Halakhic Man*, p. 146, n. 18.

5. Early on, the Rav realized that the movement known as religious existentialism constituted an historic shift in the focus of philosophical attention. In the past, philosophy and religion had directed their research primarily toward the world, the demands of God, and what it would take to afford man happiness and salvation. Rarely had the focus been upon the individual, his feelings and his view of things. Yet, observes the Rav, Judaism had always been in the paradoxical position of being, on the one hand, theocentric (i.e., God is our be-all and end-all), and yet on the other, the Torah is essentially about man – that is, a religious anthropology. It is therefore to be expected that the Rav would see religious existentialism, with its emphasis on the human condition, as a movement of great interest to Jewish thinkers (see *Ha-Adam ve-Olamo*, pp. 13–14).

6. "The Lonely Man of Faith," *Tradition*, vol. 7, no. 2 (1965) p.6.

7. See notes in *Halakhic Man*.

8. Ibid., p. 1.

9. *Halakhic Man*, notes on pp. 140–141.

10. See *Out of the Whirlwind*, pp. 206–207.

11. In considering the meaning of the term "existential," one must distinguish between currents of thought that appeared after World War II in essays, plays, and novels in France and Germany that were basically a dramatic presentation of a mood and an emotion, and the modes of thought that had characterized earlier philosophers such as Pascal, Nietzsche, and Kierkegaard, which later blended into systematic philosophies such as those of Jaspers, Marcel, and Heidegger. What they had in common is a concern about individual human existence, intersubjective human relations, and the conditions and quality of that existence. Both these movements were, in their time, rebellions against the regnant wisdom. The philosophers were rebelling against the excesses of speculative idealistic philosophy and the rationalism of naturalistic philosophy. The artists after World War II had seen the vaunted values of Western civilization drowned in a blood bath of war, dictatorship, and genocide, and scientific achievement turned to mass destruction. They experienced

a sense of alienation, of being strangers in an uncaring world, a feeling of disillusionment and pessimism. If in the past it was believed that scientific knowledge and objective information, that is, penetrating to the essence of things, was the key to man's salvation and hopes, it was now understood that existence must come before essence, and that the reality of existence is to be found in the subjective experience of the individual.

Here are some of the general characteristics of existentialism as propounded by David E. Roberts in *Existentialism and Religious Belief* (New York: Oxford University Press, 1957), pp. 6–9: (1) Existentialism is a protest against all forms of rationalism which assumes that reality can be grasped primarily or exclusively by intellectual means. (2) It is a protest against all views that regard man as if he were a "thing," i.e., an assortment of functions and reactions only. (3) It makes a sharp distinction between objective and subjective truth, giving priority to the latter, particularly in connection with ultimate questions, and thus the impassioned concerns of the human individual must be considered. (4) It regards man as fundamentally ambiguous, filled with tensions and contradictions. This is the result of his being both free and finite. He knows that he is bounded in time and moving inexorably toward death, yet through memory and imagination he can relate to the past and the future and thus can rise above the present. Viewed objectively from the outside, the individual is but an episode. From the inside, each man knows himself to be a universe.

12. See "Lonely Man of Faith," pp. 5, 10.
13. *Ha-Adam ve-Olamo*, p. 20. See also *Halakhic Man*, n. 115, for rabbinic sources for dualism in man.
14. See "Lonely Man of Faith," pp. 6–7.
15. Except, of course, for *The Halakhic Mind*.
16. *Worship of the Heart*, pp. 9–10.
17. Ibid., p. 9.
18. *Out of the Whirlwind*, p. 197.
19. Ibid., p. 197.
20. Ibid.
21. Joseph H. Hertz, *Daily Prayer Book* (New York: Bloch, 1961), introduction.
22. Joseph Albo, *Sefer ha-Ikarim* (Philadelphia: Jewish Publication Society, 1929), 4:16–24.
23. *Worship of the Heart*, introduction, p. ix.
24. Ibid., p. 2.
25. *Halakhic Man*, p. 137
26. *The Halakhic Mind*, pp. 100–101.
27. See Genesis 4:3–4.
28. *Lonely Man of Faith*, pp. 8–9.
29. Ibid.

30. See Shubert Spero, *Holocaust and Return to Zion: A Jewish Philosophy of History* (Hoboken, N.J.: Ktav, 2000).
31. *Tradition* 39, no. 3 (Fall 2006).
32. For anyone who has any doubt about the Rav's sensitivity to aesthetic elements, I herewith submit some recently published writing of the Rav which, in this particular case, is incidental to his main theme (*Out of the Whirlwind*, p. 17; see also *Halakhic Man*, n. 114, pp. 157–158):

   "That is why the Jewish service distinguishes itself by its utter simplicity and by the absence of any cultic-ceremonial elements. It lacks the solemnity and magnificence of the Byzantine Greek Orthodox service, the moment of awe-struck wonder of the Roman Catholic Mass of transubstantiation, and the rhythm and streamlined quality of the Protestant church ceremony. It is nothing but a dialogue between God and man, a conversation—ordinary in its beginning, simple in its unfolding and unceremoniously organized at its conclusion. There was never an attempt to use architectural designs (like vaulted halls, half-dark spaces, and lofty gothic sweep), decorative effects (such as the stained glass through which light filters, losing its living brightness and mingling with a magical darkness, or tonal effects (from the hardly perceptible soft *pianissimo* to triumphant hymn singing), in order to suggest to the worshipper on the one hand the great mystery, and on the other hand the heavenly bliss, of the God-man encounter.

   "Judaism sees in all these esthetic motifs, which are designed to intimate the greatness and ineffability of God, merely extraneous means of creating a fugitive mood which will disappear with the departure of the worshipper from the cathedral into the fresh air and sunshine. Instead, Judaism concentrates on feeling which flows not from the outside, but from within the personality, on emotions which are exponents of much more deep-seated experiences, enhanced not by external stimuli but by the inner existence awareness."
33. "Lonely Man of Faith," p. 17 (top of page); *Out of the Whirlwind*, pp. 36–37; "U-vekashtem Misham," pp. 230–231.

CHAPTER 1

▊▊ Is There an Indigenous
▊▊ Jewish Theology?

I wish to defend the claim that there is an indigenous Jewish theology. Of the several words that comprise this assertion, the most
misleading is the two-letter word "is" in the sentence "There is an
indigenous Jewish theology." For while "indigenous" and "Jewish"
and "theology" might be vague, the word "is" is systematically
ambiguous. No single word has given rise to more confusion and
discussion in contemporary philosophy than this simple copula.
There are, to name a few, the "is" of predication and the "is" of
identity, and the is of existence, of which our own sentence is an
instance. Bertrand Russell once said that "it is a disgrace to the
human race that it has chosen to employ the same word 'is' for so
many entirely different ideas."[1]

In what sense, then, am I asserting that there is an indigenous Jewish theology? Consider the question: Is there a prime
number greater than one hundred? Clearly the answer to this

This chapter originally appeared, in slightly different form, in *Tradition* 9
(1967).

question is not to be found by empirical investigation based on observation, but by logical analysis based on the rules for the introduction of new expressions in the system of natural numbers.

Analogously, when I claim that there is an indigenous Jewish theology, I do not mean that it necessarily exists as an explicitly formulated system of propositions, suitably labeled, to be discovered in a book of some sort. What I am asserting is that, given a commitment to the beliefs and practices of Judaism and an acceptance of the Bible and the Talmud, there follows by logical entailment a commitment to certain theological propositions. The individual adherent of Judaism may never have reflected upon the theoretical presuppositions of his faith or, if he has, may never have taken the trouble to articulate these propositions in an explicit manner. But that is of no consequence for this question. Jewish theology is there. It is implicit. It is logically entailed by the beliefs and practices of Judaism, by the assertions of the Chumash and the expressions of the Midrash. It is there, waiting to be unpacked, to be drawn out, to be formulated in a systematic way. And, as I will indicate later, for many areas of Judaism this has already been done. If an individual Jew, confronted by the articulated implications of his commitment, chooses to ignore them, refuses to recognize them, or rejects them he does so at the cost of forfeiting his claim to coherence, consistency, and rationality. While the Ravad may have been right in his acerbic stricture against Maimonides that many greater and better people than he believe the One God to have corporeal attributes, he was right only in the sense that perhaps we cannot say of them, that they are to be considered heretics or unworthy of a share in the world-to-come. On the other hand, Maimonides was undoubtedly correct that logically the unity of God implies His incorporeality, and that to affirm one and deny the other is a self-contradiction. The others referred to by the Ravad may have been greater and better than Maimonides, but they were certainly less logical.[2]

What is theology? I use the word interchangeably with the

phrase "religious philosophy." There is one distinction between the two that is not really relevant for our purposes, namely, that the theologian operates from within the faith, from a posture of commitment, while the philosopher of religion may be a professional thinker who examines religion from the outside, with no personal attachment. However be it, theology or religious philosophy, one is engaged in it as soon as one becomes reflective about one's religious beliefs and puts into words, either for one's own benefit or in order to communicate to others, what it is that one believes in or why one is engaged in certain religious practices.

When Rav said: "The mitzvot were given only for the purpose of refining mankind,"[3] he was laying the groundwork for a philosophy of the mitzvot.

When Rabbi Akiva said, "Everything is foreseen [by God] but free will is given [to man],"[4] he was pointing up a profound paradox resulting from two opposed religious principles.

When the schools of Hillel and Shammai for two and a half years debated the question of whether a man would have been better off if he had not been created,[5] they were debating a theological issue with great existential candor.

But even the Bible itself is a mine of Jewish theology. The simple answer to Rashi's opening question of why the Torah did not begin with the words "this month is to you…" is obviously and precisely, as pointed out by Nachmanides, that the Torah is not merely a halakhic code but is concerned to impart a theology, an anthropology, a philosophy of history, and that is indeed the material to be found in these early portions.

In fact, the case for Jewish theology seems to me to be so strong and so indubitable that perhaps we should ask why it became a question in the first place. Why should anyone have thought that Judaism does not have a theology?

A number of pertinent considerations come to mind:

(1) We erroneously learned to equate philosophy and theology with the style of Greek thought which was systematic,

speculative, and formal. Because our people "did" their theology in a different key and with a different style, we sometimes failed to recognize it as such. Jewish theology was enunciated spasmodically, more by impulse, and never, in our primary sources, worked into a formal system.

(2) Judaism's emphasis upon deeds, the Halakha, and external behavior weakened concern with theology. As Schechter put it so aptly: "With God as a reality, revelation as a fact, the Torah as a rule of life and the hope of redemption as a most vivid expectation, they felt no need for formulating their dogmas into a creed – which is repeated – not because we believe but that we may believe."[6] In short, Judaism apparently believed that it is the sign of a healthy religion to have a theology and not to be aware of it.

(3) There were some technical objections to the assertion that Judaism had a theology. Strictly speaking, theology means "the science of God." Traditionally, however, Judaism has always had little to say about God other than that He exists, that He is One and His acts are recognized in history, and that He requires certain things of His creatures. Maimonides developed this indigenous Jewish approach in his doctrine of negative differentiation with the well-known paradoxical consequence that the more you assert of God, the less you know about Him. In fact one recent thinker insists upon regarding the Bible as "God's anthropology" (i.e., God's view of man) rather than man's theology.[7] Another writer who sees the Halakha as central likes to believe that rather than a theology what we have is a "theonomy," a Divine Law.[8] In a current review of Rabbi Soloveitchik's work, his theology is respectfully referred to as a "Misnagid phenomenology."[9] But all of these different names merely help to point up emphases or an approach. In the larger sense with which we are concerned, these are *all* theology.

(4) Another reason why theology was never encouraged in Judaism is that certain aspects of theology were considered dangerous to Judaism. For example, dogmatics is a part of theology. There were always many who feared the reduction of Judaism to

thirteen principles (of Maimonides) or three principles (according to Rabbi Joseph Albo), with the implication that all else is perhaps not important. It is the same psychology that is behind the warning to be as careful with a minor mitzvah as with a major one.[10] It was the same fear that prompted the Chatam Sofer, when asked how many basic principles Judaism has, to answer, "613"! Another integral part of Jewish theology has always been an investigation of the reasons for the mitzvot. Here, too, tradition has always sensed a danger. King Solomon is held up as the paradigm of one who used his understanding of the purpose behind the mitzvah to reason his way to a personal exemption.[11] In this connection Maimonides's presentation of the reasons for the mitzvot *did* indeed confirm the fears of the traditionalists. The worst fear of all, however, was based on the association of theology with rationalism as a philosophic school. For many, the inevitable result of theologizing was to end up with religious beliefs based on fickle reason rather than unswerving faith. And the proof of the weakness of the former was seen in the large-scale defection of Jews to Christianity in Spain during the massacres of 1391. In France and Germany during the terrible persecutions of the thirteenth and fourteenth centuries, the Ashkenazic communities stood firm. In Spain at the end of the fourteenth and early fifteenth centuries a large proportion succumbed. The crucial difference, such was the verdict of tradition, was to be found in the weakening of simple faith before the insidious reasoning of theology and philosophy.[12]

From the historical perspective it can be granted that there was justification for the fears I have just outlined. Someday, some historian of ideas is going to draw a distinction between the value of an idea itself and the use to which the idea is put by certain social groups.

Suffice it to say, then, there are historical reasons why Judaism never developed a systematic, explicitly formulated theology. The point I wish to make now, however, is that today, when the Jewish community has lost its insularity, when the atmosphere is saturated with the spirit of science, the hallmark of which is skepticism of everything nonempirical, when Orthodoxy must demonstrate its superiority over rival Jewish theologies, one cannot have an intelligent, reflective Judaism either for oneself or for others without developing some kind of theology, some kind of religious philosophy in the broad sense. Once modern man has tasted of the fruit of the tree of philosophic sophistication, he cannot go back to the Eden of simple faith. Once man becomes aware of his epistemological nakedness, God Himself must help him to fashion a conceptual garment. Even in our classic age we were told that we must know what to answer the heretic.[13] The heretic by definition was never interested in mere information. His questions required a *justification of* Judaism. To answer him one had to know theology. Today the questioning aspect of the heretic has been internalized. The demand for justification is within each of us. And the knowledge of what to answer must be built into our educational agencies if Judaism is to have a future.

As far as the dangers are concerned, most of the ones I have outlined can, I believe, be avoided by the new approach to theology which contemporary philosophy makes possible and whose main characteristics I shall outline later.

What specifically is to be expected from a Jewish theology?

(1) Theology is needed to *explicate* various principles of Judaism that are not at all clear from the Bible and Talmud. For example, medieval Jewish philosophy focused upon the concept of God, His unity, and His attributes, what we can know about God and what we cannot. This was of permanent value and is quite relevant to the crisis in contemporary Jewish thought. An example of something still needed, however, is a clarification of our *eschatological* concepts – Messiah, world-to-come, and resurrection – not an anthology of relevant passages but a systematic working through of these principles showing their meaning and implications.

(2) Theology is needed to show the *relationship* between various principles of Judaism. For example, I once attempted to

show how the kabbalistic thinkers alone preserved the dynamic characteristics of the concept of God's unity and that it is within *this* concept that one is to find the impulse and the origin of the concept of ultimate and inevitable redemption.[14] *Achdut*, unity, implies *malchut*, kingship, and, as Rabbi Moshe Chaim Luzzatto points out, there is the notion of an *achdut bishlitah* which is implicit in Rashi's comment on the Shema. It happens that neither Saadia nor Maimonides nor Yehuda Halevi emphasized this point. Why is it important to know this? First, so that when we say the Shema we can concentrate on the full meaning of this important principle. Second, so that when we hear a prominent scholar saying that the Jews invented the messianic vision because they had a lackluster origin, we will be able to supply the correct explanation.[15] Another illustration of an outstanding relationship with important practical bearing is the problem of ethics and its relationship to God. Is something good because God wants it that way, or does God want it that way because it is good? Our whole understanding of the Akeda (the binding of Isaac) depends upon how we resolve this issue.

(3) A third task for theology is to reconcile apparent conflicts between various principles, such as between human freedom and divine omniscience, or between God's justice and God's mercy. This task is too well known to require further elucidation.

I wish to draw your attention to the fact that the three aforementioned tasks are of an *internal* nature arising out of the *inner needs* of Judaism. None of these functions can be thought of as motivated by an unholy desire to reconcile Judaism with anything foreign. None of these inquiries comes about through forbidden questions of the category "what is above and what is below, what is before and what is after." They come to the surface simply because a Jew reflects about his Judaism. And that a Jew *may* reflect about his Judaism – nay, *ought* to reflect upon his Judaism – was long ago demonstrated by a Saadia, a Maimonides, a Bachya.

The Jew, however, no matter how pious, does not simply sit and contemplate his Torah. We live and move in history, and the theoretical principle, clarified or not, sooner or later comes into abrupt confrontation with the jagged and indifferent edge of experience.

There is the problem of evil – the problem of the suffering of the righteous and the good fortune of the wicked – which has vexed and tortured believers from Job onwards. There is conflict with science regarding the origin of species and the age of the earth, with pertinent historical findings, with widely held psychological theories. Under the pressure of these confrontations we are sent back *both* to reexamine our principles and to apply our critical faculties to the findings of science – and out of this intellectual ferment more Jewish theology is born. But how can we neglect to mention the challenge to Jewish thought presented by the unique and awesome historical experiences of our own day. Nothing so pointedly illustrates at once *the need for* and *our lack of* a Jewish theology than our failure to grapple on a theological level with the meaning of an Auschwitz, the State of Israel, and the implications of the space age, and to deduce from them their meaning for our people and a direction for the future.

But over and above all these considerations, there is an even more basic necessity for theology, a fundamental dependence upon philosophy which, it seems to me, no thinking Jew can avoid. One must be able to give a rational answer to the question "Why am I an Orthodox Jew?" One must be able to give reasons, not causes. Causes are: "Because I was brought up Orthodox," "Because my parents were Orthodox." A reason would be: "I am Orthodox because I choose to believe that the Creator of the world revealed Himself to my forefathers at Mount Sinai." And then one must be able to give reasons justifying that belief. If you reply that your commitment is based upon faith about which you do not reason, you must nevertheless explain why it is that this faith needs no reasons and why it is that you choose to have faith in Judaism but not in Christianity or in Buddhism! Aristotle once said, "You say one must philosophize, then you must philosophize. You say one should not philosophize. Then to prove your contention you must philosophize. In any case you must philosophize."

Consider Yehuda Halevi, who in many ways is the most Jewish of our philosophers. He attempted to do away with natural theology to ground Judaism upon its true epistemological basis – historical experience. "We know these things first from personal experience and afterwards through uninterrupted tradition which is equal to the former."[16] Now all this is true, but having taken a position as to the epistemological grounds of our religious belief, we must be prepared to defend them should someone challenge the veracity of the experience or the authenticity of the tradition. Once again we are in the midst of theology. The same answer has to be given to Samson Raphael Hirsch when he says:

> The basis of your knowledge of God does not rest on be-lief, which can after all allow an element of doubt. It rests solidly on the empirical evidence of your own senses…on what you have yourselves experienced…. Both the Exodus and the Revelation are completely out of the realm of mere believing or thinking and are irrefutable facts which must serve as the starting points of all our other knowledge with the same certainty as our own experience and the existence of the material world we see about us.[17]

These words are true when directed to the generation of the Exodus. They are not if directed to us. These events *cannot* serve as starting points to be accepted without question. Their acceptance is a matter of believing and thinking, and Hirsch himself attempts elsewhere to justify rationally the acceptance of the Oral Tradition.[18] Once again we are in the midst of theology.

More recently, Heschel attempted to distinguish between theology and depth theology. According to him, the former deals with the content of believing, while depth theology "is a special type of inquiry whose theme is the act of believing; the substratum out of which belief arises."[19] But upon analysis we find that this is only a confusing way of saying what has been known for a long time: that theology, as such, is never to be equated with the inwardness of faith, the experiential intimacy of the believing heart, the so-called fact of faith.[20] Indeed, theological theories can never have the sanctity nor the epistemological status of the basic facts of faith. A few pages later Heschel himself admits that the "insights of depth theology are vague and often defy formulation and expression, and that it is the task of theology to establish the doctrines, bring about coherence and find words compatible with the insights." If so, we are better off to forget this misleading talk of theology and depth theology and speak only of the facts of faith and the attempt to talk about them which is theology.

Up to this point I have attempted to argue that (1) there is a Jewish theology, albeit largely implicit, and (2) that in our day, no thinking Jew can escape theologizing. I now wish to make a few brief remarks about the question of an indigenous Jewish theology. Can there be such a thing?

I think it is quite clear that the perennial stumbling block encountered by all who would attempt to develop a Jewish theology has been the invariable intrusion of contemporary philosophical categories or presuppositions in terms of which the theologian would formulate, organize, and interpret his Jewish material. The inevitable result was an Aristotelian Judaism or a Neoplatonic Judaism or a Neo-Kantian Judaism, or even, as someone recently maintained – although wrongly I think – that he saw in S.R. Hirsch a Hegelian exposition.[21] In the same vein, some traditionalists today might dismiss the work of Rosenzweig and Buber as an existential version of Judaism and, as such, impure and a distortion. This is not to say that every concept so treated necessarily becomes distorted. Quite the contrary, I think that it can be shown in many instances that the employment of foreign philosophical categories can sometimes bring out the truly Jewish content of an idea.

Nevertheless, when this occurs, the theological enterprise

in question is at least open to the *charge* of no longer being an indigenous Jewish theology. Often, these philosophical assumptions are not recognized by the thinker himself, who, being a child of his age, believes his presuppositions to be the dictates of reason itself and quite self-evident.[22] If we were to examine the origin and source of philosophical categories, it appears doubtful that we ever had, or could have, an indigenous Jewish theology. Berkovits, in a perceptive article in *Tradition*, seems willing to accept this condition and suggests that perhaps each generation needs to formulate its own Jewish philosophy in the light of the philosophical categories of its day.[23] The criterion of authenticity as a bona-fide Jewish philosophy will be its "acknowledgement of God, Israel and the Torah as historic realities" and the success of its attempt "to provide the meta-physical corollary to the facts and events for which they stand."

I think this criterion is a good one as far as it goes and is certainly a *necessary* condition of any Jewish theology. However, I cannot accept the distinction made by Berkovits that these three – God, Israel, and Torah – are the constants of Judaism, because they are *events*, whereas once we conceptualize them we are already in the realm of variables. It is clear from philosophical analysis that there is no absolute distinction between facts and theories, and that facts rarely if ever speak for themselves. Certainly, it must be granted that "events" such as God, Israel, and Torah, from the very moment they are apprehended by the Jew, are not simple discriminated elements in sense perception, but are already shot through with interpretation and conceptualization. The givenness of Judaism is not merely that an actual communication occurred between the living God and Moses, but that this living God cannot be represented by anything visual, that He is merciful and that He is a jealous God, that He is One. These are already ideas. Torah is not only an event – it has conceptual content. Israel is not merely a people that historically was the recipient of a divine revelation – it is a concept in whose givenness there is already an attachment to a land, a messianic future, a promise of eternity. All of these ideas, vague as they may be, are already part of the *constant* of Judaism, denial of which makes any theology suspect.

I am, however, more optimistic about the possibility of an indigenous Jewish theology for two reasons.

(1) We are more aware today than ever before of the possibilities of extraneous influences upon our theologizing and of the tentative nature of philosophical systems, and we are not ready to accept any as final. We are much more conscious today of the many-faceted nature of Judaism, of its rationalism as well as its mysticism, of its Halakha as well as its inwardness, and we will not easily accept a theology which does not, in some serious sense, account for all aspects of historic Judaism. This awareness, this sophistication, puts us on our guard, makes us highly critical, and enables us to come ever closer to a truly Jewish theology. An analogous problem exists in the philosophy of history, where it is sometimes claimed that there cannot be an objective writing of history, since each historian brings to the task his biases, his prejudices, and his particular principle of interpretation.[24] For example, does he see economic forces as crucial, or ideas as the causal factor? But here, too, the answer can be that once we are aware of the sources of subjectivity, we can watch for them and work toward a balanced view.

(2) There has been a radical change in our understanding of the task of the philosophic enterprise. Contemporary philosophy in both its empirical and linguistic aspects is suspicious of metaphysical systems. Gone are the ambitious expectations that philosophy, through its own royal road to truth, can illuminate for us what *ought* to be or tell us about the world of *noumena*. The dominant conception of philosophy today is a sort of anti-philosophy consisting of a critical examination of the ultimate presuppositions, the notions of explanation, the logics of belief of the various disciplines. Contemporary philosophy is only concerned to ask what kind of situations theological and religious language talk about and how.[25] Philosophy only supplies the tools of linguistic analysis and the rules of deductive and inductive logic.

Thus philosophy itself, employed critically, can help us to detect our prejudgments and purify our theology of extraneous elements. Many of the dangers which rationalism, in its attempt to prove the existence of God, posed for the faith of Judaism, are not factors in the type of philosophy current today.

In a recent symposium on the directions for contemporary Jewish philosophy, Michael Wyschogrod – a professional philosopher and an Orthodox Jew – confirms this judgment. "We are living in the post-enlightenment period and Jewish Philosophy can therefore return to its own sources instead of validating itself by criteria foreign to it."[26] This realization has cut across denominational lines, and three years ago at the annual meeting of the Central Conference of American Rabbis, three papers were read urging their colleagues, in the words of S.R. Hirsch, "to forget inherited prejudices and opinions concerning Judaism…to go back to the source…to know Judaism out of itself." The program of S.R. Hirsch, the development of a *"sich selbst begreifendes Judentum"* can be achieved today. The tools are not Jewish. But they don't have to be. They are universal, as they should be.

How would one recognize an indigenous Jewish theology? What are the conditions of adequacy for such a conceptual structure? In the space of this paper we can only present the barest outline. Useful at this point is an analogy to the relationship that holds between scientific theories and empirical facts. A scientific theory may be considered confirmed if (1) it explains or accounts for all the relevant facts in terms of the theory, and (2) when compared to other theories that may do the same thing, it accounts for the facts in the simplest and ontologically most economical way.

So it is with our Jewish theology. The "facts" or givenness of our faith are not only God, Israel, and Torah in a general sense, but the specific teachings found in our Torah – our sense of history and God's role within it, our messianic expectations, our understanding of man as image of God, the role of the nations, the meaning of anti-Semitism, the place of the land of Israel, the power of prophecy, the function of the Halakha. All must, in some significant sense, be explained and analyzed, and the results shown to correspond with the *representative* utterances of the Midrash and the Aggada on the subject.

I am fully aware of the imprecision of the word "representative." However, I am convinced that, given sufficient attention, we can develop a set of criteria which will win general agreement. For example, groups of jointly sufficient conditions for calling a saying of our sages representative can be formulated that might perhaps include location, stature of author, frequency with which it is repeated, attention given it by *rishonim*, and general consistency with other midrashic utterances.

But most significant, a viable Jewish theology must develop a justificatory apparatus showing the sense in which it is reasonable for the Orthodox Jew to make his commitment to God and to tradition on the basis of the evidence available.

I said that Jewish theology must, among other things, account for the Halakha. In light of the many confused and confusing statements that have been made about the relationship between Halakha and theology, a few remarks are indicated.

An Orthodox scholar wrote recently, "The Theology of Judaism is contained largely in the Halakha...it is in the Halakha therefore that the philosophy of Judaism is to be sought."[27] I do not believe this is true. The main sources of Jewish theology are still the non-halakhic portions of the Bible, and the Aggada. Let not our partisan desire to work out a favored position for Orthodox theologizing blind us to the patent facts. This does not mean that Halakha is not relevant for the concerns of the theologian. Quite the contrary. It is the necessary condition for an adequate Jewish theology. But what does philosophy of the Halakha mean? Here we must disentangle several different strands and distinguish several different meanings.

(1) An authentic Jewish theology must account for the Halakha in the sense that it must make a place for it; must show it to be integrally related to the concept of revelation on the one hand and to the needs of man on the other. Jewish theology must show

how the entire structure of the Halakha is in a sense required by, and is coherent with, the other principles of Judaism. This is the kind of "accounting for" that Gershom Sholem and Alexander Altman claim medieval Jewish philosophy never achieved with the Halakha, while Kabbalah did.[28]

(2) Another task of Jewish theology, and this is another sense of the term "philosophy of the Halakha," is to subject the Halakha *itself* to philosophical analysis. This would give us a philosophy of Halakha in the same sense in which we have a philosophy of law, a philosophy of history, and a philosophy of science. Its purpose would be to analyze the methods of Halakha, its special concept of "truth," its theological and anthropological presuppositions, the relationship between law and equity and to extract from the relevant Halakha its philosophy of society and its relationship to the individual, its philosophy of punishment, responsibility, and so on. It is to be expected that for *those* aspects of Jewish theology which deal with the law, society, and justice, one is primarily dependent upon the Halakha. However, our concept of God, for example, does *not* come *from* the Halakha, as such. It comes from the Bible, the divine record of what is essentially Jewish historical experience but, to be sure, it is *reflected* in the Halakha. Similarly, our concept of man as the bearer of the divine image, derives from Genesis 2:27. Once we know what we are looking for, we can approach the Halakha and there find manifestations, reflections, expressions of these fundamental concepts. However, one cannot expect them to be *derived* from the Halakha. Moreover, the *details* of the Halakha must be consulted in formulating any philosophy of the mitzvot. The classic example of this is the contention of S.R. Hirsch that the purpose of the Sabbath is not merely for its physical rest. Since an examination of the Halakha reveals that the Torah forbids *melekhet machshevet* (purposeful work), the purpose of the Sabbath is to teach man that he may not create, that he is only a creature, a "steward of [God's] estate," and only God is the creator.

(3) There is a third intersection between theology and

Halakha. This is where purely theological principles have become crystallized into Halakha. So, for example, the Halakha legislates that if a person does not subscribe to belief in *Torah min ha-shamayim* (divine revelation of the Torah) he is classified as a heretic with various halakhic consequences. There are several "duties of the heart" which, once prescribed, fall into the area of the Halakha. Now these are best described as instances where theology has become part of the *content* of the Halakha and as such these principles are truly authoritative. In fact, one could properly argue that in many instances they came to be embodied in the Halakha because they were principles in Albo's sense – that in their absence, Judaism is not viable.

(4) Now as a result of doing philosophy of Halakha in the sense of (2) we may come up with certain theological principles that may be called *presuppositions* of the Halakha – what Rabbi Walter S. Wurzburger, in a recent insightful article, calls "meta-halakhic propositions."[29] Now I cannot agree that *all* the propositions that Rabbi Wurzburger chooses to call meta-halakhic are indeed so. He fails to distinguish, if I read him right, between what I have called "theology crystallized into Halakha" (my number three), which is merely halakhic propositions, and Halakha subjected to philosophical analysis, all of whose conclusions can legitimately be called meta-halakhic (my number two). Hence, even if one should hold with Chasdai Crescas that belief in God cannot be a mitzvah and is thus not Halakha, nevertheless this principle *can* qualify as a *meta-halakhic* proposition, since it is unquestionably presupposed by the entire structure of Halakha.

It is not clear to me what significance Rabbi Wurzburger places upon these meta-halakhic propositions. If, as it sometimes appears, he merely wishes to show that the "Halakha is not devoid of all theological and philosophical presuppositions" and these are *necessary* conditions for any authentic Jewish theology, I quite agree. On the other hand, if he wishes to claim that "it is feasible to construct a philosophy of Halakhic Judaism [read Orthodox Judaism] out of the Halakhic data available to us,"[30] I cannot agree.

It has yet to be demonstrated that a philosophy of the Halakha is the equivalent of a philosophy of Judaism.

In the latter part of this paper I have argued for the feasibility today of an indigenous Jewish theology and the conditions of adequacy that such a theology would be required to meet in order to be so judged. I think it should be clear on the basis of what I have said that there can be more than one indigenous Jewish theology. There are areas where more than one alternate belief may fit the facts of faith. For example: Can a Jew believe that God may reveal another Torah? What does Judaism involve in terms of psychological theory or self-theory? Is beauty an objective value in Judaism?

I would also like to suggest that we cease accepting and rejecting theologies as wholes. It is not necessary to accept or reject Rambam *in toto, or* Moshe Chaim Luzzatto *in toto.* Every concept in Judaism must be examined critically and individually. It is by no means obvious that accepting any one part of Rambam's philosophy necessarily entails a commitment to the whole.

We must also learn to do our theology piecemeal and to build slowly toward a picture of the whole. Instead of first conceiving an over-all grandiose scheme as to the purpose and character of Judaism and then trying to force the individual concepts into the pattern, we must reverse the process. Before writing books on Judaism we must first write monographs. Let us concentrate first upon an analysis of specific concepts, special areas with as few presuppositions as possible. Only after the result of such work is before us can we go on to synthesize our conclusions and join the fragments together.

There is today a great need for, and an interest in, Jewish theology. The editors and sponsors of such journals as *Tradition* and *Judaism* are to be commended for providing both a stimulus and an outlet for work in this area. It is true that the word "theology" has had a bad press and bad associations for traditional Jews in the past. I believe, however, that the term *can* be reinstated if we remember that "we can admit that religious truth arises in the heart and all that theology asks is that it come out through the head.

ENDNOTES

1. Bertrand Russell, *Introduction to Mathematical Philosophy*, 2nd ed. (London: Allen & Unwin, 1920), p. 100.
2. *Mishneh Torah,* Hilchot Teshuva 3:7.
3. *Bereshit Rabba* 44.
4. Avot 3:16.
5. Eruvin 13 b.
6. Solomon Schechter, *Aspects of Rabbinic Theology* (New York: Schocken Books, 1961), p. 12.
7. Abraham Joshua Heschel, *Man Is Not Alone* (New York: Farrar, Straus & Young, 1951), p. 129.
8. Isaiah Grunfeld, *Horeb* (London: Soncino Press, 1962), vol. 1, p. xiv.
9. Eugene Borowitz, "The Typological Theology of J.B. Soloveitchik," *Judaism* 15, no. 2.
10. Avot 2:1.
11. Sanhedrin 21b.
12. See Yitzhak Baer, *A History of the Jews in Christian Spain* (Philadelphia: Jewish Publication Society, 1961), esp. vol. 2.
13. Avot 2:14.
14. Shubert Spero, "Unity of God as Dynamic of Redemption," *Perspective* 2, no. 1.
15. Julius H. Greenstone, *Messiah Idea in Jewish History* (Philadelphia: Jewish Publication Society, 1906), p. 24.
16. Yehuda Halevi, *Kitab al-Khazari*, trans. Hartwig Hirschfeld (New York: Bernard & Richards, 1927), p. 47.
17. Samson Raphael Hirsch, *Commentary on Exodus*, trans. I. Levy (London, 1958), 19:4.
18. *Gesammelte Schriften*, ed. N. Frankfort, 1908–12, vol. 1, p. 97.
19. Abraham Joshua Heschel, *The Insecurity of Freedom* (New York: Farrar, Straus & Giroux, 1966), p. 117.
20. See John Hick, *Philosophy of Religion* (Englewood Cliffs, N.J.: Prentice Hall, 1963), pp. 76–77.
21. Noah H. Rosenbloom in *Historica Judaica* (New York), 22, no. 1.
22. On the role of presuppositions, see R.G. Collingwood, *An Essay in Metaphysics*, pts. I and II (Oxford University Press, 1940).
23. "What Is Jewish Philosophy?" *Tradition* 3, no. 2, p. 121.
24. See William H. Walsh. *Philosophy of History* (New York: Harper Torchbooks, 1960), chap. 5.

25. I.T. Ramsey, "Contemporary Philosophy and the Christian Faith," *Religious Studies* 1, no. 1.

26. In *Judaism* 2, no. 3, p. 196.

27. Samuel Belkin, *In His Image* (New York: Abelard-Schuman, 1961), p. 16.

28. Gershom Scholem, *Major Trends in Jewish Mysticism* (New York: Schocken Books, 1941), p. 28.

29. "Meta-Halakhic Propositions," in *Leo Jung Jubilee Volume* (New York, 1962).

30. Ibid., p. 212.

CHAPTER 2

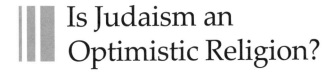

Is Judaism an Optimistic Religion?

Two intellectual currents have been the favorites of Jewish theological surf riders in recent years. One is the existentialist wave of pessimism, the sense of human helplessness and the futility of human reason, ridden mainly by estranged intellectuals returning to Judaism. The second is the "know thyself" current of depth psychology and psychiatry ridden mainly by leaders of Liberal and Reform Judaism. Presumably, Orthodoxy can get to the beach on its own motive power and needs the help of neither current. Certain interesting issues, however, have arisen as a result of the conflicting views on Judaism emerging from the two aforementioned groups.

Ever since the publication of *Peace of Mind* (1946), publicists of Liberal Judaism have not tired of pointing out the affinity between the counsels of psychiatry and the insights of Judaism. The secret of happiness, it is asserted, lies completely within the

This chapter originally appeared, in slightly different form, in *Tradition* 4 (1961).

human being and his ability to accept a new morality which will overcome inner anxieties, teach us how to love, accept death with courage, and become mature, responsible adults. God is to be encountered in a "good friend, a wise father, a loving mother, and in general in the love, sympathy and relationships of the world."[1] Man is a responsible co-worker with God who must persist in his confidence in eternal progress and social victory. Peace of mind, so understood, seemed to have primarily therapeutic value, i.e., the ability to accept life's disappointments, rejections, and death without becoming inwardly tormented, emotionally unhappy, or developing any recognizable neuroses or anxieties.[2] The underlying premise peculiar to this entire tendency is the notion that with the eradication of all mental illness and social evils, life in its "natural healthy state" justifies itself and will itself generate fulfillment and satisfaction.

Related to this view, and indeed presupposed by it, is the oft-repeated notion that Judaism is an optimistic religion. Speaking of the exaggerated pessimism of the existentialists, a leader of Liberal Judaism tells us that "this is diametrically opposed to Judaism, which does not build God's absolutism on man's nothingness. Man can, to a large degree, make it."[3] And again, we are told, "Judaism's faith is suffused with optimism and therefore reactions against tendencies towards varieties of asceticism among Jews were bound to set in, for they were not at heart native or intrinsically Jewish. The life-loving and optimistic spirit of Judaism was certain to resist it."[4]

It appears to the present writer that much of the discussion on this subject has failed to maintain the distinction between optimism as the quality of metaphysics and optimism as the subjective state of an individual temperament. There can be no question that Judaism as a system of thought is metaphysically optimistic. Our view of the unity of God, the doctrine of creation *ex nihilo*, the perfectibility of man, the relative character of evil, and the promise of a messianic future all reflect an overall view which pronounces "good" upon the world and promises ultimate victory for the forces of divinity. However, it does not necessarily follow from this that the individual Jew, the devout believing Jew, is therefore endowed with a sustained optimistic mental attitude. The very contrary can be shown to be the case.

I disagree with the thesis which holds that historical lapses from "natural Jewish optimism" are to be explained in terms of persecution and suffering which darkened the cheerful Jewish spirit. ("Bruised spirits in dark hours might give way.") If persecution and suffering make for pessimism, then it would be more correct to say that by now pessimism has become "natural" for the Jew. Moreover, pessimism has more often been the result of repletion and satiety than of want and deprivation. Koheleth was written by Solomon and not by Bar Kochba!

What I wish to assert is that any attempt to take God and Judaism seriously must involve profound, life-long anxieties and not peace of mind in any usual sense of the term; that metaphysical optimism notwithstanding, the more accurate description of the Jewish religious temperament is probably pessimism; that in spite of the fact that the Torah does not forbid us to enjoy life, it does not follow that the thinking Jew therefore necessarily does enjoy it. The origins of Liberal Judaism's bias in the direction of optimism is to be found in a weakness traditionally associated with the liberal position.[5]

It would be futile to attempt to demonstrate the optimistic or pessimistic character of Judaism solely by an appeal to appropriate passages in Scripture and in the Talmud. Let us assume that one could amass an impressive collection of references in support of either view. Of course, the very ability to do this would suggest a rather comfortable hypothesis. Perhaps Judaism *qua* Judaism is "beyond pessimism and optimism" and is something which lends itself to free will, to the determination of individual temperaments and historical epochs.[6]

Indeed William James, in one of the earliest analyses of the psychology of religion, distinguishes between what he calls "the religion of healthy-mindedness" and "the religion of the sick soul."[7]

The former is an expression of a religious sentiment which is happy, optimistic, and usually extroverted. It sees the good in all things, looks upon evil and misfortune as an "accident," and greets the dawn of each new day with cheer and joy. The latter road is the opposite of all this. The religion of the "sick soul" is pessimistic and is given to periods of melancholy and depression. This type of religious sentiment senses the dark side of things, suffering and death, and sees little in life to be cheerful about. As students of the psychology of religion have pointed out, it is doubtful whether the majority of individuals fall into the categories represented by the extreme poles of these two approaches. More likely, one is apt to discover a continuum of characteristics.[8] However, if these categories are in any way descriptive of basic human types, then one can maintain that Judaism in its rich modal variety lies before the devotee and that the "sick soul" opts for those elements conducive to his temperament, while the "healthy-minded" appropriates those aspects suitable to his emotional structure.

While one may find occasional references which appear to support this approach, nevertheless, I believe that a careful examination of the sources will reveal a structured view which leans in the direction of pessimism. Of the two broad outlooks on life, pessimism and optimism, the former represents the more realistic and the more Jewish view. Elsewhere, James rejects the view that answers the question "Is life worth living?" with the rejoinder "It depends upon the liver!" and casts his vote in favor of pessimism. Says he, "We are bound to say that morbid-mindedness ranges over the wider scale of experience. The method of averting one's attention from evil and living simply in the light of the good is splendid as long as it will work. But it breaks down impotently as soon as "tragedy comes."[10] Of course, asserts James, there are the lucky few who live their years unscathed and appear to escape the frustrations and the failures, the catastrophes and the sudden death. However, even the most healthy-minded of men must surely know what life can have in store.

The fact that we can die, that we can be ill at all, is what perplexes us; the fact that we now for a moment live and are well is irrelevant to that perplexity. We need a life not correlated to death, a health not liable to illness, a kind of food that will not perish, a good that flies beyond the goods of nature.[11]

As James astutely observed, "The luster of the present hour is always borrowed from the backgrounds of possibilities it goes with." Once a person's eyes are opened to the radical contingency of human life, the breath of the sepulcher will forever be present. Hence, "they [the morbid experiences of life] may be after all the best key to life's significance and possibly the only openers of our eyes to the deepest levels of truth."

From another direction, Freud, too, confirms the basic unfriendliness of life to the program of the pleasure-principle. From three pervasive quarters there constantly arise experiences which run counter to happiness construed in its narrow sense: from our own bodies, where anxiety and pain are danger signals of decay and dissolution; from the outer world with its forces of destruction; and from our relations with other men. Concludes Freud, "the intention that man should be 'happy' is not included in the scheme of 'creation.'"[12]

I should like to call this realistic view, which sees much of man's existence as characterized by suffering, anxiety, and frustration, as "first-order pessimism." This type of pessimism has been incorporated in the philosophies of despair cultivated by the Stoics and Epicureans. As James rightfully observed, Stoics and Epicureans should be considered not merely as historical schools, but as a "typical attitude marking a definite stage in the development of the sick soul."[13] One can clearly see this kind of attitude reflected in the writings of many thinkers today who adopt the sober position of naturalism. While committed to a transcendent pessimism, they nevertheless advocate a philosophy which possesses at least courage and dignity. Sidney Hook, for example, recently pointed out that "pragmatism is an attempt to make it possible for men to live in a precarious world of inescapable tragedy...by the arts of intelligent social control.... It may be a lost cause. I do not know of a better one."[14]

These views represent what James calls "the highest flight of purely natural man."

Let us examine the claims of the advocates of Jewish optimism and the Jewish love of life and attempt to comprehend how this is achieved. The thesis has been suggested that the Jewish way of life, with its Sabbaths, holidays, and ceremonials, gives the Jew a "zest for life" by simply developing his faculty "to get more joy than sorrow out of life." "Although the cup of Jewish suffering was virtually always running over, the cup of Jewish joys was yet fuller."[15] This is a rather strange notion. Does the concept of *simcha shel mitzvah*, and the fact that the Jewish tradition bids us to enjoy life, imply that the resulting joy to the Jew is so intense that he will, to a greater degree than others, affirm life and tenaciously cling to it, "never be gloomy even in the most tragic periods," and "savor life as long as there is breath in one's nostrils"? What shall we say of Rabbi Judah the Prince, who, at his death, called upon heaven as witness that he did not enjoy this world even to the extent of his little finger?[16]

An alternative explanation is one which shifts the grounds of the Jewish will-to-live from an egotistic, subjective hedonism to the concept of a transcendent happiness. That is to say, Judaism as a system of values, irrespective of the joys it may give or not give, is considered meaningful and worthwhile. "Judaism fills the Jew rooted in the traditions of his people with the certainty of significant self-fulfillment before which even the harshest sufferings pale."[17] This is, of course, something entirely different. Such a view of the Jewish affirmation of life simply draws the implications of its metaphysical optimism and assigns to life values and meaning which are beyond the reach of the vicissitudes of our worldly existence. But then, what is unique about this? There are countless philosophies of life, including the classic formulations of ancient

Greece, which equate man's happiness with the fulfillment of his particular *telos* or end, each differently conceived. Such abstract happiness, however, does not necessarily entail cheerfulness rather than sadness, joy rather than depression.

Upon consideration, it appears that the initial effect of a religious consciousness upon the outlook and feeling tone of an individual is in the direction of pessimism. James, for example, maintains that pessimism is essentially a religious disease. "It consists in nothing but a religious demand to which there comes no normal religious reply." On the basis of mere animal existence, the expression of first-order pessimism can perhaps be overcome by the resignation and courage of the Stoic approach. Man is a small part of a cosmic process. This is life and there is no more. Let us make the best of it.

But if, as a result of a religious orientation, man encourages attitudes which attribute a supreme worth to the human spirit and to certain values, and which see a Spirit beyond reality and posit intrinsic good, then the sheer contradiction between the religious evaluation of things and the harsh reality of existence plunges him into a nightmarish pessimism of a far deeper nature. Precisely because life is good, intrinsically good, transcendentally good, is its negation bad. To the extent that the religious outlook invests life with tremendous spiritual opportunities, to that extent must it look upon every frustration of these opportunities with increased horror and a heightened sense of tragedy. Thus we arrive at a "second order of pessimism" which has, as its reflective source, religious sentiment.

Whenever Judaism has been taken seriously, this element of pessimism has been apparent. Perhaps its clearest expression is to be found in the Talmud, wherein is recorded an issue debated for two and one half years between the House of Hillel and the House of Shammai. The House of Hillel maintained, "Better would it have been for man to have been created than to have been created." The House of Shammai maintained, "Better would it have been for man not to have been created than to have been created." The issue was called to a decision, and it was concluded, "Better would it have been for man not to have been created, but now that he has been created, let him examine his behavior."[18] What we have here does not contradict the accepted view of the metaphysical optimism of Judaism. "And the Lord saw everything that He had made, and behold, it was very good." Creation gives man an opportunity he would otherwise not have. Nevertheless, looked at existentially, as part of my own individual, personal being, the possibility (no matter how small) of not achieving the goal, the possibility that my fate might be "death and evil" can well engender the reaction "Neither thy sting nor thy honey," better that I not be given this crushing responsibility, better not to have been created!

Indeed, the truly righteous person will constantly question and be critical of his own deeds and behavior and will be forever anxious about the state of his relationship with God. Does not the Bible itself record that Jacob, in his hour of peril, "was sorely afraid" lest his sins be the cause of a suspension of God's providence?[19] Does not the Talmud stipulate that hints of the esoteric wisdom may be revealed only to him "whose heart worries inside of him?"[20] There can be no question but that the individual who takes the absolute demand of his religion seriously will develop profound anxieties of guilt concerning the quality and validity of his religious response. The modern Musar movement in particular stressed the need for constant vigilance and constant tension on the part of the God-fearing person. Rabbi Israel Salanter taught: "Man may be compared to the bird. It is within the power of the bird to ascend ever higher on condition that it continue to flap its wings without cessation. If it should stop flapping for a moment, it would fall into the abyss. So is it with man."[21]

Psychologists have observed the conditional quality of even the most ego-bolstering of Jewish concepts. One of them remarks rather perceptively, "The Jews have very often been in situations which have caused them to doubt...the love of their God.... All their trials and tribulations have been regarded as sent by God as punishment for their sins, but also as special proof of His love, since only through suffering could they be made worthy of a Covenant with Him…. the Jew's self-esteem has none of the serenity of certainty. It is restless and based on doubts."[22] A recent sociological study of the shtetl finds evidence of "intense and unremitting anxiety" in spite of strict observance of the law. The very elements which Liberal Judaism sees as making for optimism are seen here as conducive to anxiety:

> The combination of the two concepts, free will and predestination, discourages fatalism and fosters anxiety. God has decreed the circumstances of each man's life but the individual alone is responsible for what he does with them. There are so many opportunities for failure in fulfillment of the commandments, in the amount of effort one expends on earning a livelihood, in all one's activities and relationships. Ignorance of circumstances may be an excuse, but ignorance of the Law is not, and there is no excuse for ignorance due to oversight or negligence. Obligations are so many, opposite God, family, and fellows, that no matter how much one does, it is never really enough. There is always the burden of un-discharged duty.[23]

There is yet another aspect to this issue. The existentialist analysis of man as a creature beset by a natural anxiety stemming from his awareness of his own finitude affords us an opportunity to restate the authentic Jewish view on a metaphysical level. Existentialist literature abounds with analyses of man's growing anxiety and sense of alienation. To call our time an age of anxiety has become almost a truism. Alienation is a fact. Undoubtedly all of the sociological explanations are relevant – the breakdown of the family, the impersonalism of modern industry, the uncontrollability of political events, the element of infinitude in the new cosmological image. Alienation is a multidimensional phenomenon. Religious thinkers, however, have asked whether modern man's estrangement is merely "the itch of personal neuroses" to be overcome by the wisdom of the Fromms and Peales, or whether it is perhaps revelatory of human existence as it really is. The latter view holds that there are forms of anxiety which belong to existence as such and are to be distinguished from an abnormal state of mind, as in neurotic anxiety. This notion is already implicit in the account of Genesis, where man is described as having been created in a condition of freedom – a condition of sheer possibility in which he can negate as well as affirm, destroy as well as create. This condition of indeterminate potentiality with its awful responsibilities is already a condition of anxiety. Finitude, temporality, selfhood, and sexuality are aspects of the grandeur of creation. But we rarely encounter them in this unspoiled condition. "Sin lieth at the door and its desire is unto thee, but thou canst rule over it."[24]

Kierkegaard and Tillich after him raised the phenomena of guilt, fear, despair, the prospect of one's own death, and the prospect of salvation, beyond the sphere of purely psychological considerations into aspects of metaphysical thought, which is what they have always been for traditional Judaism. Kierkegaard maintains that the self is a synthesis of the infinite and the finite, the eternal and the temporal, freedom and necessity.[25] Man is thus not self-sufficient and can achieve true selfhood only by being related aright to God. Whether man is aware of it or not, God is both the criterion and the goal of selfhood. Hence, whoever has no God has no self, and who has no self is in despair, which is a specific illness of man as a spiritual being. Despair, to Kierkegaard, is any imbalance in the relationship of the self to itself. Any attempt by man to separate himself from the power which created him, or to neglect what is eternal in him, or to fight his spiritual nature, will result in despair. Kierkegaard goes on to analyze the different types of despair, such as the "despair of weakness" and the "despair of defiance," which correspond to well-known types in the Jewish gallery of the godless. There is little here that Jewish theology could not agree with. Even Tillich's formulation of the basic types of anxieties[26] – the anxiety of death, the anxiety of meaningless, and the anxiety of guilt – is implicit in traditional accounts of repentance.[27]

Another approach, also not without interest to traditional Jewish thinking, sees as basic in current analyses of the dynamics of anxiety a positive urge that is somehow frustrated.

This view maintains that the experience of anxiety has a certain constant structure. Whether described by Catholic mystic, agnostic existentialist, or atheistic psychoanalyst, it exhibits a specific character. "That character is anxious longing. The experience itself is constituted by a polar tension between fear and longing. Anxiety is desire aware of a threat to its fulfillment."[28]

Could we not therefore understand anxiety as the consequence of a genuine desire for God, a longing for the elements of goodness and divinity and at the same time a reflection of the impediments faced by this finite creature in responding to this call? The anxiety of the sinner is thus his tendency to erect false gods and encounter inevitable frustration as he seeks to satisfy the soul's thirst for God with imperfect substitutes of things of this world.

Psalms do not lack for expressions of the soul thirsting after God. Rabbi Joseph Albo taught, "Everything has a desire for that which is of the same nature as and similar to itself...so the mind desires to fulfill the will of God because it is natural to do so"[29] Rabbi Nissan ben Reuben adds the thought: "Just as man's sense of touch fears the fire because it is contrary to its nature, so does the mind fear to violate the commands of the Almighty because its very nature requires compliance."[30] It remains for us to draw the implications and with them formulate a hypothesis in explanation of the empirical phenomena of anxiety and alienation. Indeed, Saadia already saw this as an intimation of the world-to-come:

> I find furthermore that none of God's creatures known to me feel secure and tranquil in this world, even when they have reached the most exalted ruling position and the highest station therein. Now this feeling is not something natural to

the soul. It is due, rather, to its consciousness of the fact that there is reserved for it an abode that is superior to all the excellence of its present dwelling. That is why its eyes look forward longingly to it. Were it not so, the soul would have felt secure and have been at rest.[31]

It appears, therefore, that traditional Judaism possesses all the ingredients making for a doctrine of human nature which could incorporate the phenomenon of existential anxiety and offer an explanation for man's growing sense of alienation.

We stated that the initial effect of the religious outlook is in the direction of pessimism. The religious person is in a position to develop a fuller recognition of the terror and insecurity of ordinary human life, of the blackness of sin and, as far as one's own strength goes, of the possibility of slipping back into evil and nothingness. Indeed, it has been rightfully said that the religious outlook does not give peace of mind but simply substitutes the right anxieties for the wrong anxieties. This is reflected in a teaching of Rabbi Nachman of Bratslav: "Man is afraid of things that cannot harm him and he knows it, and he craves things that cannot be of help to him and he knows it; but in truth the one thing man is afraid of is within himself and the one thing he craves is within himself."[32]

Is this, however, the ultimate condition, or can we perhaps find in Judaism some final turn, some higher level of feeling which bespeaks joy? I believe that the key to the teaching of Judaism on this point lies in the phrase "serve the Lord with fear and rejoice in trembling."[33]

Thinkers as diverse as Rabbi Joseph Albo and Rabbi Judah Loew of Prague are one in their understanding of this passage.[34] Both agree in describing man's initial awareness of himself as a creature subject to contingency and temporality in terms of fear and sadness which cause the heart "to tremble and grieve." Rabbi Loew specifically points to what we have called the first-order pessimism of the creature as he faces death and also the second-order pessimism which takes hold of man as he contemplates the rigors of ultimate judgment. This is the fear of God, which is not only the beginning of wisdom but the ultimate salvation. This state of fear and trembling is prior to any other and constitutes "the fundamental spirit of service." As a more recent thinker has put it,

> All religious reality begins with what biblical religion calls the "fear of God." It comes when our existence between birth and death becomes incomprehensible and uncanny, when all security is shattered through the mystery. This is not the relative mystery of that which is inaccessible only to the present state of human knowledge and is hence in principle discoverable. It is the essential mystery, the inscrutableness of which belongs to its very nature; it is the unknowable.[35]

However, once man reaches the state of fear of God he can, as he contemplates his trembling, find cause for joy "because he realizes that he fears that which is deserving of fear – an indication of spiritual perfection and health on his part."[36] This "joy in trembling" is neither the hedonistic zest of life described above nor the healthy-minded optimism which believes it can, by positive thinking and talking, blind itself to the grim realities of life. This Jewish joy is instead a tempered optimism, a "holy insecurity" which recognizes that existence has meaning under God not in spite of its tragedies and sufferings, but perhaps through its tragedies and sufferings, by means of the trivial and the prosaic. Kierkegaard observed with great sensitivity that Abraham, who attained the level of faith, unlike one who has merely achieved the level of resignation, does not lose the finite but rather regains it.[37] "After passing through the dark gate, the believing man steps forth into the everyday which is henceforth hallowed as the place in which he has to live with mystery."[38] The believing Jew has looked sadness in the face. He knows that wife, the family, career, the daily tasks are not the ultimate answer. But precisely because he has accepted their contingency can they have for him freshness and be a source of tempered joy. We can indeed experience the simple joys of life if we know their limitations beforehand. The cry of "vanity of vanities, all is vanity" comes as no surprise because we did not strain the simple joys with a burden they are not equipped to bear. We did not ask them to justify life for us. "Serve the Lord with fear, and rejoice in the trembling."

In summation: Judaism as a metaphysical system is optimistic, yet it recognizes fully the tragic character of human existence. On the existential level, it fosters sobriety and shifts the locus of anxieties to the areas that count – concern for the state of one's soul and one's relationship to God. Those who repress their thirst for the spirit expose themselves to futile frustrations and suffer the unmitigated consequences of man's naturally anxious condition. The mature religious personality who fixes his gaze on the infinite can, however, regain the finite in tempered joy.

ENDNOTES

1. Joshua Loth Liebman, *Peace of Mind* (New York: Simon & Schuster, 1946), pp. 165, 171.
2. Ibid., p. 202.
3. Abba Hillel Silver, *Where Judaism Differed* (New York: Macmillan, 1957), p. 179.
4. Ibid., p. 210.
5. Walter Houston Clark, *The Psychology of Religion* (New York: Macmillan 1958), p. 159.
6. H. Rose, "Beyond Pessimism and Optimism," in *Judaism*, Spring 1957.
7. William James, *The Varieties of Religious Experience* (New York: Modern Library), pp. 66, 77–163.
8. Clark, *Psychology of Religion*, p. 155.
9. William James, *The Will to Believe* (New York: Dover, 1956), p.32.
10. James, *Varieties of Religious Experience*, p. 160.
11. Ibid., p 137.
12. Sigmund Freud, *Civilization and Its Discontents* (London: Hogarth Press, 1930), chap. 2.
13. James, *Varieties of Religious Experience*, p. 141.
14. Sidney Hook, "Pragmatism and the Tragic Sense of Life," *Commentary*, August 1960.
15. Trude Weiss-Rosmarin, *Jewish Survival* (New York: Philosophical Library, 1949), p. 207.

16. Ketubot 104a. See commentaries of Rashi and Tosafot.
17. Rosmarin, *Jewish Survival*, p. 210.
18. Eruvin 13b.
19. Genesis 32:8.
20. Chagigah 13a.
21. Dov Katz, *Tenuat ha-Musar* (Tel Aviv: Beitan ha-Sefer, 1946), p. 269.
22. Rudolph M. Loewenstein, *Christians and Jews* (New York: International Universities Press, 1952), p. 139.
23. Mark Zborowski and Elizabeth Herzog, *Life Is with People* (New York: International Universities Press, 1952), p. 411.
24. Genesis 4:7.
25. Soren Kierkegaard, *The Sickness unto Death* (New York: Doubleday, 1954), pp. 182–207.
26. Paul Tillich, *The Courage to Be* (New Haven: Yale University Press, 1952), p. 35.
27. Despair of weakness is the unwillingness to be oneself which results in the life of pure immediacy. In this condition, the person looks at others in order to discover what he himself is and "recognizes himself by his dress." He becomes "an imitation, a number, a cipher in the crowd." He flees reflection, plunges into the outgoing, active life, and takes his cue from external circumstances. If he ever experiences self-reflection, it is thrust into forgetfulness or attributed to the instability of youth. In despair of defiance, man will to be himself but tries to overcome finitude on his own power. He attempts to create his self to his own specifications by sheer assertion of will. This is "the despairing abuse of the eternal in the self to the point of being despairingly determined to be on oneself." In its final desperate form, this defiance turns into demoniac rage in which the despairer wills to be himself with his torment, which he believes constitutes a proof against the goodness of existence, and thus he revolts and protests against the whole of existence. He will not hear of any help, because comfort now "would be the destruction of him as an objection against existence and would rid him of his justification for being what he is." From this psychological analysis, Kierkegaard moves forward to theological considerations and asserts that "sin is the potentiation of despair before God."

These analyses apply quite readily to well-known types in our own literature. The despair of weakness may well explain the disciples of Balaam with their "evil eye, haughty spirit, and excessive desire" (Avot 5:22), or even he who "blesses himself in his heart saying, I will have peace" (Deuteronomy 29:18), or the *kesil*, who has all the knowledge but is lost in his "immediacy" (see commentary of Malbim on Proverbs 1:22), or those "whose stomachs have become their gods, and their clothing their Torah" (*Chovot ha-Levavot*, Shaar ha-Perishut 2). Those afflicted with the despair of defiance have a recognized niche in Jewish thought. This genre starts with Nimrod, who "knows his Master but deliberately revolts against Him" (see Rashi on Genesis 10:9) and continues with the stiff-necked ones who persist in their ways though there be proof to the contrary" (see Sforno on Deuteronomy 9:6), and concludes with the "wicked ones who refuse to repent even on the threshold of Gehinnom" (Eruvin 19a).

According to Tillich, man's ontic self-affirmation as a created being is threatened from three directions by nonbeing. Awareness of this threefold threat is anxiety appearing in three forms: threat of death, threat of emptiness or loss of meaning, threat of condemnation or guilt. In all of these the anxiety is existential, i.e., it belongs to man's nature. If we accept this analysis, then making man aware of his anxieties and the sources of his anxieties can perhaps bring him to the realization that he can overcome these anxieties only by grounding himself in God.

It is not difficult to see that the rabbis have consistently appealed to these three kinds of anxieties in attempting to bring about the experience of repentance. The entire Book of Koheleth is an appeal to the emptiness of man's existence if it is lived only "under the sun" (see R. Jonah Gerondi, *Shaarei Teshuva* 2:19–20). Remembrance of the day of one's death is suggested as a most potent stimulus for *teshuva* (Berachot 5), while the constant theme of the prophets is to point to Israel's obligation, both collectively and individually, to God as "liberator from Egypt," as "Father and as Master," as "the Rock that begot thee," and "the God who made thee," and the ingratitude with which Israel has responded. The purpose of all of this is, of course, to generate a sense of guilt and remorse, which is the first step toward repentance (Maimonides, Hilchot Teshuva 2:2).

It is quite plausible that these three anxieties are implied in the dictum of R. Akavya ben Mahalel: "You come from a fetid drop" – your existence, due essentially to egotistic sexuality, is thus meaningless. "You are going to a place of dust and worms" – the anxiety of death. And "Before Whom are you destined to give judgment and reckoning? Before the Almighty" – the anxiety of guilt (Avot 3:1).

28. Fred Berthold, Jr., *Fear of God* (New York: Harper, 1959), pp. 75, 90, 92.
29. Joseph Albo, *Sefer ha-Ikarim* (Philadelphia: Jewish Publication Society, 1930), vol. 3, p. 301.
30. Rabbenu Nissim, *Shneim Assar Derushim* (Jerusalem: 1955), *derush* 10, p. 69.
31. Saadia Gaon, *The Book of Beliefs and Opinions* (New Haven: Yale University Press, 1948), Treatise IX, chap. 1, p. 324.

32. Martin Buber, *The Tales of Rabbi Nachman* (New York: Horizon Press, 1956), p. 37.
33. Psalms 2:11.
34. Albo, *Ikarim*, p. 308; Judah Loewe, *Netivot Olam* (Tel Aviv: Pardes, 1956), Netiv Halizanut, p. 167. See also the discussion in Berachot 30.
35. Martin Buber, *Eclipse of God* (New York: Harper, 1952), p. 50.
36. Albo, loc. cit.
37. Soren Kierkegaard, *Fear and Trembling* (New York: Doubleday, 1954), p. 46.
38. Buber, loc. cit.

CHAPTER 3

▌▌▌ The Role of the Ethical

Amidst the plethora of scholarship devoted to the work of
Rabbi Joseph Dov Soloveitchik there is little that focuses on his
view of ethics.[1] This is probably because the Rav never made ethics,
as such, a subject for philosophical inquiry, although there are, of
course, countless oblique references to ethics (musar) in a variety
of contexts throughout his written and oral teachings. The casual
reader may therefore assume that the Rav has nothing "new" to
say on the subject, and that in this matter he goes along with the
traditional view. Such an assumption, however, is doubly confusing, because there has never been much agreement on what the
traditional view actually is.[2] Thus, not only do we remain with an
incomplete understanding of the teachings of the Rav, but we are
no closer to achieving clarity in what is surely a core area of Jewish philosophy: the role of the ethical in Judaism.

The Rav himself stated that the special relationship between
the ethical and the religious was a unique insight of Judaism.

This chapter originally appeared, in slightly different form, in *Modern Judaism* 23 (2001).

If I would be asked to explain my view as to Judaism's unique contribution to the world, I would reply as follows: It is well known that Judaism has contributed to the world the belief in one supreme God: monotheism...(although sparks of belief in a supreme deity appeared here and there among other religions). Judaism can also pride itself in an additional great contribution to mankind and that is the connection between religious experience and ethical action. Judaism was the first religion to place the service of God at the center of its concern where service of God included social ethics.[3]

However, there is a fundamental difficulty at the heart of our subject which must be grasped if we are to make any progress in our inquiry. It is not at all obvious that Judaism in its biblical and talmudic expressions recognizes the special type of human experience that we call *moral* experience or the special type of commandment that we call *moral* commandments. For in the vocabulary of classical Judaism there is no term that uniquely denotes what we call morality or ethics."[4] Involved here is not merely a matter of classificatory nomenclature but whether there is any special significance to experiences or commandments of this type. I have shown elsewhere that the account of the early history of mankind in the first ten chapters of Genesis suggests that the principles of righteousness and justice (*tzedek umishpot*) obligate the human being as such, and that their denial or systematic violation by man brings into question his entire *raison d'etre*.[5] This says, in effect, that principles such as *tzedek umishpot chesed v'rachamim* (righteousness and justice, kindness and mercy) qualify as moral in precisely the same sense that we use these terms today. "Judgements using approval/disapproval terms such as good, right or ought, bad, evil, wrong, ought-not, are to be deemed moral when they are thought to be judging individuals simply as human beings, qua human beings."[6]

It follows, therefore, that even after the Sinaitic revelation with the giving of the *taryag* (613) commandments, there remains an implicit recognition of the difference between moral principles and commandments (*mishpatim*) and ritual commandments (*chukim*). This distinction was further deepened by the prophets, who, in the name of God, rejected observance of the ritual when not accompanied by observance of the moral injunctions.[7] Thus the category of the ethical as such is indeed indigenous to Judaism. However, its precise role and significance within Judaism were never explicitly defined. It remained for the talmudic sages and later Jewish thinkers to explore the precise relationship of ethics to God, man, and the Torah.

It was therefore not necessary for the Rav to define what he meant by the term "ethical" or "moral" (or its equivalent in modern Hebrew, *musar*) either when referring to aspects of Judaism or when speaking within the context of general philosophy. For there is general agreement as to the kind of material being referred to. We see this clearly when the Rav refers to "you shall love your fellow man," "thou shalt not murder," and "thou shalt help thy fellow man" as "ethico-religious norms," "the ethical ought."[8] Or, when he describes a person "wanting in any ethical passion" as "bereft of *mitzvah* performance, good deeds and meritorious acts."[9]

We can similarly understand the Rav's use of hyphenated terms such as "ethico-Halakhic."[10] He employed this when he wished to refer to the practical, prescriptive content of the Torah. While much of Jewish morality is included in the Halakha, the rabbinic distinction between *din* (law) and *befnim mishurat hadin* (beyond the line of the law) suggests that there may be supererogatory moral injunctions in Judaism that fall outside of the Halakha.[11] Thus the term "ethical," when used by the Rav in the contexts of Judaism and the Halakha, refers to those normative principles, such as *tzedek, mishpot, chesed, yoshair, rachamim,* and *nedivut* (righteousness, justice, loving-kindness, equity, mercy, generosity), and to the many specific commandments they generate.[12]

*   *   *

There is another nuance of meaning to the word "ethical" or "moral" which sees the word "good" as primary and implies a more generalized sense of ethical value rather than particular duties or prescriptions. On occasion the Rav uses the term in that sense. Consider the following:

> The creation of the world is a moral act (*p'ula musarit*) that finds its perfection in the Sinaitic revelation. The materialization of the revelational-ethics command constitutes a creative act. Mending reality constitutes a moral act (*ma'aseh musari*). In creating the world, the Creator materialized the highest ethical purpose (*tachlit musarit*). The source of morality (*makor hamusari*) is God, and its revelation is the creation. The fact of existence is the embodiment of the ethical will (*ratzon hamusari*). Ethical action is action that creates and renews. The highest ethical good (*hatov hamusari*) is full existence. The entire cosmic process is the revelation of the divine ethics (*musar elohi*) out of the remoteness of separation and isolation. The moral law in itself (*chok musari*) is the law of reality, and moral action is action that is interwoven in the web of the great creation.[13]

These citations are exceedingly important not only for the light they shed on the Rav's use of the word "moral" but for understanding his views on the nature of the relationship between creation and morality. First, in what sense is God the "source of morality"? To begin with, our *knowledge* of good/evil comes from divine revelation, and the *authority* of moral law is rooted in God. But also the goodness that we encounter on the human level and our experience of ethical value has its counterpart in the transcendent God: "Give thanks unto the Lord, *for He is good*."[14] We wish to say that God is a moral God not only in the sense that were His actions to be performed by a human we would call them moral, but that in some special sense which respects God's unity and transcendence, ethical value is an integral part of His essence.[15]

God moves out of His splendid isolation to create the cosmos in response to His own goodness. For to be good is to do good for others. Thus with Creation, God brings into existence conditions that make possible further good. Also, by creating the cosmos, moral values (which until now subsisted in some transcendent form as "goodness" in God) now have an opportunity to take on "existence" in the human realm, first as moral principles so recognized by man, and then become truly "real" as moral actions in the social context and as moral virtues in building individual character ("The highest ethical good is full existence").[16]

Thus God's creation of the world is a moral action in a double sense: (1) that which is created is good ("And the Lord saw everything that He had made, and behold, it was very good"; Genesis 1:31); and (2) the *intention* is ethical, i.e., the creation is an expression of God's goodness ("The creation of the world took place on account of God's goodness").[17]

Now, in what sense can it be said that the cosmos, a largely material phenomenon created by God, is good? Ethical values in their primary sense can only have persons (including God) as their bearers. To say that the material universe is good means, minimally, that it is better that this world should exist than that there should be no world at all. Here the Rav introduces the concept of teleology (*tachlit musarit*). Since the ultimate purpose of creation involves man, who as moral agent is given the tools necessary to create a just society and create for himself a virtuous personality, the entire cosmos, which provides conditions for the materialization of this purpose, takes on a derivative moral value.

∗ ∗ ∗

Ever alert to cross-reference insights of Judaism to problems in general philosophy, the Rav makes a bold claim for Judaism's understanding of the relationship between ethics and nature. Recalling that "philosophical ethics from the days of Kant until the present" has been seeking "the road that leads from ethics to physics and metaphysics," the Rav proclaims that Judaism has made that connection:[18]

> Judaism declared that there is no difference between revealed law and ontological law but by human perception. The ontological law demonstrated in the existence of creation makes itself known to man as a revealed ethical commandment.[19]

When and where did Judaism make such a declaration, and what does it mean? According to Judaism, God is indeed the source of all reality, of all intelligibility, of all value, and transcends the distinctions between them. In terms of their origin, therefore, one might say that ontology and revealed ethics are related.[20] But surely this in itself contributes little to solving the philosophical problem. At least since David Hume, philosophy has been cognizant of the gap between fact and value, between the "is" and the "ought." Judaism finds this gap quite congenial, as it explains the need for a revelational ethics. The gap tells us that had the "ought" not come from Sinai, it could not have been generated from the "is." Indeed, the Rav explicitly states that "the moral law cannot be legislated by human reason in absolute terms."[21] In the human search for God, the Rav points out quite clearly the limitations of natural theology and of the possibility of successfully finding God in nature. While "the heavens declare the glory of God," the "tale they tell is not a personal one...the message of the heavens is at best an equivocal one."[22]

If this is so in regard to the existence of God, how much more so in regard to the ability of nature to generate an "ought"; on our being able to deduce a norm from the material cosmos?

And yet one finds the Rav making the following strange statement:

> But what is the tale of the heavens, if not the proclamation of the norm? What is the recitation of the firmament if not the declaration of the commandment? All of existence declares

the glory of God – man's obligation to order his life according to the will of the Almighty…. We can know God's ways
only through studying the cosmos.[23]

But as we have seen, a norm is precisely that which the heavens
do not declare![24] Perhaps overwhelmed by the sublimity and intelligibility of the cosmos, one can indeed feel humbled at seeking
one's own place in all of this, can feel some vague sense of "obligation" to whosoever is responsible for the cosmos. But in no way
can the heavens declare what is truly the will of the Almighty and
what it is that He demands of man. It should perhaps be noted
that in that section the Rav speaks only of the "echoes" of the
norm and of "traces of the norm" rather than the actual content.
It should also be remembered that the above is attributed by the
Rav to the idealized *homo religiosus* who does not always reflect
the views of Judaism.

*   *   *

There is another use and, therefore, meaning to the terms "ethics/
morality/*musar*," and that is in particular relation to the perceived
nature of man. Since morality in its broadest sense is conduct that
is appropriate for the person as person, the next important question is, *who* and *what* is a person? Once we know that, the right
and the good become that which enables the person to realize his
nature or potential, to fulfill his purpose and destiny. Thus, for
example, if according to Aristotle man is a rational animal, then
the ethical is that which brings man's unique quality of reason to
fruition.

One of the most important and unique teachings of the Rav
is that man was created by God as a dialectal creature with conflicted tendencies reaching deep into his very being.[25] This cleavage is not, as Christianity would have it, the result of man's rising
in sinful rebellion against God, but is something willed for man
by God, and reflects different aspects of God, His majesty and
His humility. The Rav variously describes man's dual capacity as

the cosmic explorer versus a man seeking his roots, or as Adam i, who is creative, worldly-minded, and sees control over his environment as the source of human dignity, versus Adam ii, who seeks the answer to "why" questions, is preoccupied with God and redemption, and sees human dignity as submission to the will of his Creator.

In describing dialectical man, the Rav makes the following comments:

> It is self-evident that dialectical man is not capable of committing himself to a unitary monochromatic ethics. If man is dialectical so also his ethical actions. The ethical person strives towards two goals.... He is attracted to two opposing norms, by two sets of values....
>
> The two-fold religious experience of God in the splendor of His majesty and God in His humility imprinted its seal upon the ethics of Judaism. There are two systems of ethics: the ethics of majesty and the ethics of humility. In the one case, man seeks to rule, to dominate, to achieve victory. In the other, man must be ready to withdraw, to retreat, and accept defeat.[26]

It should be obvious that the Rav is not stating that Judaism contains two contradictory systems of ethics in the prescriptive sense of the term, i.e., two different rulings on what is morally right and morally wrong in a particular situation.[27] By *maarachot shel musar* (systems of ethics) the Rav here is referring to different values in the sense of personality goals and a general orientation to life. These sets of values are opposed to each other in the sense that they both cannot be cultivated by the same individual at the same time. However, they are not contradictory in a logical sense. According to the Rav, Judaism affirms both sets of values as legitimate and proper, i.e., the individual Jew can cultivate either one as a model by which to structure his personality and as a lens by which to highlight aspects of the activity of God. It is part of the Rav's method of typological analysis to sharply differentiate the dualities. However, while he initially implies that this split in man "is final and almost absolute" and not given to "synthesis,"[28] ultimately, when it comes to practical decisions, "the Halakha paves the way, permitting the individual to respond to the two calls at once."[29]

Evidence that the Rav did not at all intend to supplant the prescriptive content of Jewish ethics with this concept of a pluralism of values is provided by the following caveats:

> Man is destined by his God to rule and be victorious. In the most important sense of sovereignty, it is an ethical purpose and man's efforts to acquire it is an ethical effort *so long as he will be supplied with the appropriate tools.*[30]
>
> We are speaking of "triumph" which does not confine itself to subjugation of nature in order to satisfy human needs, but also involves the *establishment of a just and truthful society and the building of a fair economic order.*[31]

Thus we see that no matter what set of values the individual may choose in regard to Adam I or Adam II, the way he goes about achieving this must be in accordance with Judaism's deontological morality.

*   *   *

What is the place of ethics in Judaism as a whole? The Torah itself contains a variety of literary forms. Among them are many of the most noble ethical rules and principles. But there are even more ritual laws, historical narratives, epic poems, and theological principles. There is no explicit indication as to whether one element is more important than any other. The text of the Pentateuch strives mightily to maintain a balance as to the relative importance of the ethical to the ritual. Thus, if *mishpatim* represent the ethical commandments, and *chukim* the ritual, the usage of the text sends a message that both are equally authoritative, both come from God, and therefore both merit meticulous observance.[32]

Among the teachings of the Rav we find a number of sweeping observations that seem to suggest the centrality of the ethical:

> Every story in the Torah comes to teach us a great principle in the ethics of Judaism, and what is the principle of all principles in the ethics of Judaism if not to imitate the ethical attributes of the Holy One, blessed be He.[33]

And in speaking of the theological principles of Judaism:

> In Judaism every one of the principles serves as a sort of ethical challenge. There is no principle that is solely abstract. Everyone of our thirteen principles of faith which ostensibly is only a declaration, "I believe" – theoretical, brings with itself a challenge and an obligation for ethical action.[34]

On the subject of knowledge of God (*da'at hashem*) the Rav says:

> The knowledge of God, which is of primary significance in Judaism, is not to be regarded abstractly as something by itself. The value of this knowledge is that it brings the individual to acts of kindness, justice, and righteousness.[35]
>
> At the center of Jewish thought stands a knowledge whose purpose is essentially ethical. The knowledge of God is proper ethical understanding in order to "walk in His ways."[36]

However, the Rav not only *declares* the centrality of ethics but *demonstrates* it by revealing a new dimension to an old rabbinic teaching: the concept of *imitatio Dei*, the obligation to imitate God. This teaching was formulated by the sages primarily as an interpretation of the oft-repeated commandment to "walk in His ways."[37]

It appears in two versions:

"To walk in all of His ways" (Deuteronomy 11:22). These are the ways of the Holy One, blessed be He, as it is written "The Lord, the Lord, God, merciful and gracious" (Exodus 34:6). As the Omnipresent is called "merciful and gracious, so shall you be merciful and gracious, as the Holy One, blessed be He, is called holy so shall you be holy.[38]

"After the Lord your God shall you walk" (Deuteronomy 13:5). Walk after the traits of the Holy One, blessed be He. As He clothes the naked, so shall you clothe the naked; as He visits the sick, so shall you.[39]

"The Lord your God has multiplied you, and behold, you are this day as the stars of the heavens for multitude (*la rov*)" (Deuteronomy 1:10). He [Moshe] said to them, "Today you are like the stars, but in time to come you will be *la rov*, like (*domin*) unto your Master."[40]

"This is my God and I will glorify Him (*anvei hu*)" (Exodus 15:2). Abba Shaul said, "Be like (*domeh*) Him; as He is merciful so shall you be merciful." Rashi explains the derivation, *anvei hu* is to be read as *ani ve hu*, "I and He," that is to say, I must make myself like Him to cleave to His ways.[41]

The injunction to walk in God's ways seems to refer to behavior of a certain kind: "to walk" denotes a particular action. And, indeed, the second source describes a series of ethical deeds performed by God which we are commanded to emulate. Whereas, the third and fourth sources speak of the duty to "be like" (*domeh*) God in some particular way. Of these two formulations, the latter would seem to be the more daring doctrine. For in what way can man be said to be like God, which implies similarity in some sense? Yet there are two additional biblical texts which quite literally, without the help of homiletic interpretation, suggest the possibility of *imitatio*

Dei: "You shall be holy, for I the Lord your God am holy"[42] and "Let us make man in Our image and in Our likeness."[43]

The Leviticus text implies that man can share in a certain quality called holiness which in some sense also characterizes God. Genesis suggests that man, as a created being, is already like God, in some sense (*demut*, "likeness"). However, according to the first and fourth sources it would seem that being like God is the responsibility of the individual: to *become* something that at present he is not (*hevei domeh* lo). "Be [or become] like unto Him," or *af ata hevei*, "You too shall be." Unlike the second source, in which imitating God requires that one do something for the other, the first and fourth sources require that the individual do something for himself, i.e., make himself into a personality in whom mercy and compassion are resident characteristics.

Taken together, these teachings conjure up a concept of *imitatio Dei* that obligates the individual to a twofold program of deeds and self-improvement, all of which are in the realm of the ethical. Clearly, it is the latter which is much more difficult and more significant. For once the individual has been transformed into an ethical personality, the deeds can be expected to follow.

At this juncture the Rav points out that the entire process that is demanded of the individual is in itself, in some far deeper sense, an instance of *imitatio Dei*. For in attempting to become merciful and compassionate, man is transforming himself into an ethical being. And by this very act of *creation* man is acting like God. As the Lord God created and continues to create, so must man become a partner with God in Creation. However, man's role as creator is an ethical one in a double sense.

(1) God's world seems impaired and unfinished in many ways. This was to provide opportunities for man to participate in God's creation by repairing its flaws and by ridding the world of hunger, violence, and disease, and by controlling the forces of nature. This, says the Rav, is an ethical task because in any way that the void can be filled with plenitude of being, chaos replaced by order, and violence by law, goodness in the world is being increased.

(2) When man engages in self-creation, as in the process of *teshuva*, when he creates his own "I," that which is being created is a human-self whose very substance is what we call *character* or *virtue* which is moral value.[44] In the words of the Rav:

The most fundamental principle of all is that man must create himself.[45]

The peak of religious ethical perfection to which Judaism aspires is man as creator.[46]

After all, the very possibility of self-creation by man, in this sense, is ongoing testimony to the fact that man was indeed created in the image of God.[47] For selfhood is both the possibility and the result of ethical action which is brought about by the will and intellect acting together.[48] An act of moral self-creation is the realization of individuality, autonomy, uniqueness, and freedom, and enables man to break out of the limitations of causality and species-dependence.[49]

* * *

The question has been raised as to the Rav's treatment of holiness (*kedusha*) insofar as it relates to the ethical. It appeared to some that the Rav emphasizes the centrality of the ethical to the point where it is "the ultimate purpose and supreme value of the entire Torah."[50] If so, it would be expected that holiness, the highest religious category, should be considered identical with the ethical. But, of course, precisely because holiness is a supreme *religious* category, it cannot be said to be identical with the ethical, which, as such, has nothing to do with the transcendent. The Rav says as much quite clearly:

The idea of Holiness according to the halakhic world view does not signify a transcendent realm completely separate and removed from reality. Similarly it does not denote the complete actualization of the ethical ideal, of the supreme good which is not grounded in a transcendent realm but in the domain of norms and values.[51]

According to the Rav, holiness is some "mysterious transcendence" which man is capable of experiencing at certain times and in certain places.[52] However, as a phenomenon which in some sense has its source in God and yet can be generated by man, it can be expected to answer to diverse descriptions. The Rav cites an ancient commentary on the threefold repetition of *kadosh* ("holy") in Isaiah that recognizes three different realms for the appearance of holiness.[53] There is the holiness that is with God in the highest heavens, then there is the holiness that will come at the end of days when history will have reached fruition. Mediating between the two is the holiness generated by each individual as he lives his biological life and actualizes the ethical and ritual commandments in the empirical world.

The Rav's insistence upon including the biological and ritual in order to generate holiness is based upon the Holiness Code as formulated in Leviticus 19 and 20. There, all of the diverse commandments, ritual as well as ethical, are sandwiched between explicit calls for holiness, implying that holiness is achieved only by observance of both types of injunctions: "You shall be holy, for I the Lord your God am holy" (Leviticus 19:2); "And you shall be holy unto Me, for I the Lord am holy" (Leviticus 20:26).

It is clear, therefore, that while the ethical is not a sufficient condition for holiness in man, it is certainly a necessary condition.[54] Evidently, in the making of the religious personality, the different types of mitzvot have their respective roles, although we may not know exactly what they are. The rabbinic distinction between commandments between man and man and those between man and God is not very helpful. For, in truth, both the ethical and the ritual reflect and affect our relationships to God and man, if not directly then indirectly.[55]

Let us go on to the holiness that is ascribed to God. A careful study of the occurrence of the words *kedusha* and *kodesh* throughout the Torah, in reference to God, yields the conclusion that the only recognizable element therein is moral value.[56] Consider the following:

> But the Lord of hosts is exalted through justice,
> And God the Holy One (*hakadosh*) is sanctified (*nikdash*)
> through righteousness (Isaiah 5:16).[57]

Every concept analyzed so far, be it *imitatio Dei*, knowledge of God, or holiness, has shown its active ingredient to be the ethical as experienced by man. If from every angle it appears that it is moral value that leads to God, should we not now inquire as to whether moral value is, in some sense, a quality or aspect of God Himself? Indeed, can we speak at all of qualities of God's personality without impinging upon His unity?

*   *   *

Before we can deal with this question we must examine another concept called *devekut*, loosely translated as "communion with God," which is counted by Maimonides as a separate commandment.[58]

> For if you shall diligently keep all this commandment which I command you to do, to love the Lord your God, to walk in all His ways and to cleave unto Him (*ledavka bo*).[59]

Coming as it does at the end of a series of the most exalted religious states, after "love of God," and after "imitating His ways," the command to "cleave unto God" would appear to be the Torah's expression for the state of ultimate proximity of man to God. The Hebrew word *devekut* suggests a state of attachment of some sort. According to the Rav we are dealing here with stages in religious development. Just as in an earlier stage fear and awe of God gave way to an intense love, so too man can ascend from the level of walking in God's ways to the more intense level of clinging to

God.[60] Coming closer to God begins with *imitatio Dei* and is sealed with *devekut*.[61] While this suggests some sort of mystical relationship, the Rav points out that in Judaism there can be no thought of union with God in the sense that the individual loses his self-identity.

However, *imitatio Dei* is not merely a condition that precedes *devekut* but is actually constitutive of it. That is to say, the individual who has been "walking in the ways of God" has become a fully developed ethical person, active in the social sphere and constantly molding his personality in the direction of character and virtue, and must remain so as he ascends to the level of *devekut*. For Judaism this is the highest religious experience attainable by a living person,[62] one that is *sui generis* and in some way partakes of the experience of the world-to-come described as "enjoying the splendor of the Divine Presence."[63]

In explicating the mechanics of *devekut*, the Rav introduces a metaphysical concept which has complex historical and philosophical roots. This is known as the doctrine of "the union of the knower and the known."[64] Maimonides explained that unlike human knowledge, God knows the world because He knows Himself, so that, in a sense, God, who is the knower, and all that is known are One. Now, the relationship between God and His creation are such that the entire cosmos has being and continues to exist only because God constantly gives it being by constantly remaining conscious of it. Therefore, when man knows the world, apprehending its structure and laws, he is, in a sense, uniting with God the Creator. For they both have something in common: consciousness of the world! If this is true of the material cosmos, it should apply even more meaningfully to the Torah, which is the revealed word or thoughts of God that reflect His will and wisdom. Thus, he who immerses himself in the study of Torah achieves a certain contact with God by means of this shared cognition.

The idea of the union of the knower and the known had great attraction for Maimonides because it enabled him to say something significant about divine knowledge without compromising his position about the unknowability of God. For the Rav, this idea, first of all, provided a reasonable way to conceptualize the mystical notion of *devekut*.[65] If two completely different centers of consciousness think about the same thing, they may be said to be united in some sense. The Rav compared it to the mathematical-logical principle: "If A is equal to B, and C is equal to B, then A may be said to be equal to C."[66]

Somehow, to the traditional Jew who prays three times a day, the notion of *devekut* seems strange! Particularly today, when many of the activities of thinking are done better by a computer, it is difficult to feel religiously inspired by the idea that it is by thinking that I am most like God! One would expect *devekut*, as the highest level of human proximity to God, to involve more distinctive aspects of the self. Yet the mechanism of the union of knower and known calls upon intellectual activity only: thinking, cognizing, knowing. As to *what* you are knowing, i.e., the *content* of your thought, the idea of the cosmos seems too broad to arouse religious significance. Moreover, as applied to the study of Torah, it would restrict the road to *devekut* to an elite capable and willing to concentrate their religious devotion on the *study* of Torah. What of the others not so capable?[67]

There is another puzzling aspect. We have seen that the ethical is the significant element in *imitatio Dei*. Is it reasonable to suppose that to reach the higher level of *devekut* the decisive element is intellectual activity? Surely moral value seems a more substantive link with God than thinking the same thing? However, in his major essay "*Uvikashtem misham*" (And From There You Shall Seek), the Rav proceeds to introduce what I would call a *holistic* interpretation. "Man must seek not only identity of knower and known but also identity of thought, will, and action."[68] "The God of Creation is not a God who is thought thinking thought." Judaism has always connected "And God said" with "Let there be." There is with God the thought that accompanies the word and the actualization that follows both. God's knowledge, as expressed in creation, is a mysterious unity of thought, will, and action.

Therefore to truly achieve *devekut* man must go beyond thought and attempt to integrate thinking, volition, and creative activity. The activity, says the Rav, must be those that result in *chesed, mishpot, tzedaka* – loving-kindness, justice and righteousness. So we are really back to the ethical.

> True thought is also ethical. Thought equals volition. The moral will is the essential quality of consciousness. When man knows the world, he directs his knowledge toward higher moral purpose. He unites with the world, which has become known through him, and by means of the world does he cleave unto God. For the very existence of the world is rooted in the thought of the Holy One, blessed be He, as absolute truth and infinite ethical will that is all creative action.[69]

How is man to realize all this?

> Realization comes by means of the working of consciousness charged with will and action. In other words, by means of man's identification with the revealed Supreme will that comes to expression by means of the Halakha which translates the cognitive-volitional to the willed activity.... Contemplation of the work of creation that is not accompanied by submission to the divine halakhic and ethical law will bring neither love nor *devekut*, nor the union of the knower and the known.[70]

Having so expanded the concept, it would appear that precious little remains of the original theory. There is no longer any special emphasis on the intellect as such. We are simply talking about a consciously positive and inquiring orientation of the individual toward the world as God's creation with the aim of actualizing the commandments of the Torah.

What then is the crucial element that unites the individual with the divine, making possible the experience of *devekut*?

I wish to suggest that just as in *imitatio Dei* it all turns on the ethical, so too the ultimate experience of *devekut* consists essentially of the mysterious attachment of two conscious personal beings: one in whom moral value *is* always constitutive and the other in whom moral value has *become* constitutive.

Am I distorting the Rav's position? If the Rav intended to retain the ethical as the key to *devekut*, you may ask, why didn't he explicitly say so? Why introduce the idea of the union of knower and known altogether? The answer lies in the Rav's commitment to intense and prolonged study of the Halakha. He quotes approvingly the following statement by R. Hayyim Volozhin:

> The primary purpose of Torah study is not to study simply for the sake of cleaving to God, but to comprehend the commandments and laws and to know each and every matter clearly, both its general principles and its particulars. Even though at the time of study a person does not have the fear of God in mind, nevertheless the study itself is for the sake of the unification of the Holy One, blessed be He.[71]

Here we have a clear enunciation of the doctrine that intellectual immersion in the minutia of the Halakha, regardless of the particular subject matter and even in the absence of any specific thoughts or emotions pertaining to God, is in itself actual communion with God. It would thus appear that the Rav introduces the idea of the union of the knower and the known in order to provide philosophical justification for the type of Torah study practiced and highly regarded in the yeshiva world. The overwhelming emphasis on study and understanding of the Halakha required a theory that would show how intellectual apprehension leads to the state of *devekut*.[72]

* * *

Elsewhere I have examined the general question of why classical Jewish thinkers did not pick up on the implications of the prophetic and rabbinic literature as to the centrality of the ethical in Judaism.[73] It is first in the work of the Maharal of Prague (d. 1609) that we find a clear statement that it is moral value that provides the link between man and God, and serves as the basis for *devekut.*

> The commandments of the Torah purify the soul and bring man closer to God until he cleaves unto Him. And by doing all these good things like charity, righteousness, and justice, man achieves ultimate salvation because these things relate him to God and make him like unto Him, since these are the attributes of God, who is kindness and justice and righteousness. And it is precisely by being in such relationship that one might be said to cleave unto Him.[74]

Thinkers like Crescas and Halevi believed that disinterested love of God was the key to *devekut.* Indeed, why not a theory of the union of the lover and the beloved?[75]

Can it be that I am exaggerating the importance of the ethical? Consider the following statement: "Morality is God's known essence."[76] I would put it another way: "The only positive things we can know about God is that He is good, just, and kind." The principle of God's unknowability is firmly rooted in the idea of God's transcendence, of His being completely other and of the limitations of human language to express that which by definition is beyond our experience.[77] Also, the principle of God's oneness precludes any ascription of positive attributes that might imply compositeness. Hence, Maimonides's program to reduce biblical descriptions of God to either action predicates or negative attributes served a vital philosophic need. However, in light of the absolute demand made upon man to be moral and the repeated attributions of moral qualities to God in the most intimate of terms which are found in all parts of the Torah and rabbinic literature, we must, at least in this area, reject philosophical straitjacketing.[78] If love of God is to mean anything a human being can recognize, then the word "God" must refer to something more than a cloud of total unknowability! The believer must be able to sense that the goodness of God is a real part of God, that goodness and kindness, love and justice characterize the personality of God in a substantive way.[79] So then, *devekut* comes about when a self-created moral self responds in joyous love to the loving goodness of the living God.

Is there a way to assert this so that it does not compromise God's complete otherness?

> If we could know the life of God, we should see in it something which human love really resembles, so that to call it love would be the best way of saying what it is in human language. Thus, conduct which flows from the belief that God is love is not only the best kind of conduct, judged by the scales of human ethical values, but is also the kind of conduct which corresponds best with reality. If you are unable to imagine what the reality is, you can know at any rate that it is of such a character that the right reaction to it in conduct and feeling is the reaction which follows upon your thinking of the ground of the universe as a loving God.[80]

*   *   *

In discussing the Rav's outlook on the role of the ethical, Shalom Carmy wonders, without attempting an answer, what might have been the response of the Rav to the persistent question "why be moral?"[81]

While this question remains a favorite of teachers of moral philosophy, it is doubtful that the Rav would have warmed to the subject. And as a matter of fact, nowhere that I am aware of does he explicitly address this question.

However, I doubt that the Rav would have responded as perhaps other traditional thinkers might have, with a dismissive, "Because it is a mitzvah like other mitzvot." I am confident that the Rav, fully sensitive to its philosophical subtlety, would not only have analyzed the question in a manner reflecting his own stated views on the ethical as described above, but also would have drawn upon elements implicit in the sources.

To an analytic philosopher the question "why be moral?" is an extremely challenging one and may very well be unanswerable. What is our understanding of "moral" as we ask the question? According to the philosophically neutral definition given earlier, "moral" refers to actions and principles that are appropriate to persons and *obligate* them as such. If so, to be moral, i.e., the duty to behave in accordance with particular criteria and values, is already entailed by the very recognition that something *is* moral. Moral value is generally regarded as an intrinsic good, so that one does what is good and right for its own sake. "I *do* the good and right because it *is* good and right." No other answer is available or needed. To answer, "because it will help you get ahead in business" is to reduce the entire enterprise of morality to an adjunct of self-interest and to destroy its autonomy.

I believe the Rav would concur up to this point. However, a second question would immediately follow: How do you know what is moral? How do you distinguish between good and evil?

Here is where the philosopher and the Rav would have a parting of the ways. At this point, the Rav would place the entire category of the ethical within the context of Judaism. That is to say, within a world-picture that includes a Creator-God, man formed in His image, and a revealed Torah. In this Torah man is told of his origins and of the way of God which he is to imitate, the way of justice and righteousness, mercy and kindness.

Now let us return to the question: why be moral? Everything we said earlier about the intrinsic value of morality remains the same. Only now we can point to the significance of morality within the larger framework. Man is a moral agent as a consequence of having been created in His image. He is therefore able and obligated to create for himself a moral personality, so that in this he becomes "like" God and fulfills his humanity. While moral value in human life remains an intrinsic good, we now know *why* that it is so. It is because moral value is in some sense a quality of God Himself.

The Bible hints that man has a natural apprehension of moral value and can intuit the moral ought in particular situations.[82] What Sinai did was to confirm the basic validity of these intuitions and to provide a method by which to apply moral principles to concrete situations.

For the Rav, in terms of origin and ultimate significance, the ethical connects with God. The ethical is not identical with the Halakha but comprises a large portion of it.[83] If the centrality of the ethical is not always apparent in his writing, it is because of the vestigial effects of Maimonidean intellectualism and the Rav's abiding commitment to intensive study of the Halakha.

Almost everywhere that the Rav mentions the Halakha, ascribing to it sweeping significance, he is sure to insert the term "ethics."[84] For, while the ethical is only part of the Halakha, it is always its active ingredient, the operative element that transforms "image" into "likeness" and makes possible the daring and sublime experience of *devekut*.

ENDNOTES

1. Two articles that deal directly with the ethical are Shalom Carmy, "Pluralism and the Category of the Ethical," in *Exploring the Thought of Rabbi Joseph D. Soloveitchik*, ed. Marc D. Angel (Hoboken, N.J.: Ktav, 1997), pp. 325–346; D. Statman, "Aspects of the Ethical Views of Rabbi Soloveitchik," in *Faith in Changing Times*, ed. Avi Sagi (Jerusalem, 1996), pp. 249–264 (Hebrew). Carmy explores the Rav's writings to determine his position on the issue between what he calls the "identity thesis" equating ethics with Halakha and the "pluralistic theory" in which the two are held to denote distinct realms of value. His efforts are inconclusive: "Some of the Rav's texts point one way, some the other" (p. 347). I submit that Carmy confuses two different questions: one is the relationship between the ethical and Halakha, and the other between the ethical and the religious. I will comment on the first in the course of this article. As to the second, I will show that for the Rav the ethical is a religious

category throughout. The religious, while interpenetrated by the ethical, is not identical with it. Carmy's assumptions about the phenomenology of the ethical experience are overstated. Not many will agree that "ethical obligation has something sacred, inviolable and unutterably exalted by it" (p. 328). The most you can hope for is agreement that recognition that act X is moral carries with it the notion that X ought to be done by all persons in similar circumstances.

Statman deals primarily with the Rav's attempts to demonstrate the ineffectiveness of secular moral systems, the inability of human reason to legislate moral norms, and the superiority of a revealed ethic.

2. See Shubert Spero, "Towards an Ethical Theory of Judaism," BDD: *Journal of Torah and Scholarship* 4 (Winter 1997): 55–75.

3. *Man and His World (Ha-Adam ve-Olamo)*.

4. The word *musar* appears once in the Pentateuch (Deuteronomy 11:2) and there, as in all of its occurrences in Proverbs and elsewhere, means "instruction" or "chastisement" in general. The term *mishpatim* includes moral norms but much else of civil law. The rabbinic term *bain adam le-chavero* ("between man and his fellow man") is too narrow, as it does not include man's relations to animals. The term *derech eretz*, while including moral norms, could also refer to practical skills and cultural customs.

5. See my "Towards an Ethical Theory of Judaism," p. 56.

6. Ibid.

7. Ibid., p. 61.

8. *The Halakhic Mind*, p. 69.

9. *Halakhic Man*, p. 127.

10. Ibid., pp. 105, 137.

11. See A. Lichtenstein, "Does Jewish Tradition Recognize an Ethic Independent of Halakah?" in *Modern Jewish Ethics*, ed. Marvin Fox (Columbus: Ohio State University Press, 1975), p. 68.

12. See also "U-bekashtem Misham," pp. 182–183: "Halakhic ethics focuses and encompasses man's relationship to the other, to creatures of nature, and to the creations of man."

13. "Ibid., pp. 223–225.

14. Psalm 136.

15. Note that the Rav speaks of *ha-musar ha-elyon* (divine ethics) which is *al enoshi* (superhuman) ("U-bekashtem Misham," p. 225). Although we can have no understanding of what *musar* means as part of God, the Rav uses the same term. I return to this question further on.

16. "U-bekashtem Misham."

17. *Halakhic Man*, p. 50.

18. "U-bekashtem Misham," p. 225.

19. Ibid.

20. In Hasidic thought this idea is expressed by saying that the Ten Plagues in Egypt transformed the Ten Statements by which the world was created into the Ten Commandments. That is to say, prophetic intervention converts ontology into ethics.
21. *Divrei Hagut ve-ha-Arakha*, pp. 251–252.
22. "The Lonely Man of Faith," pp. 30–31.
23. *Halakhic Man*, p. 64.
24. This difficulty is noticed by Aviezer Ravitsky in "Rabbi J.B. Soloveitchik on Human Knowledge," *Modern Judaism* 6, no. 2 (May 1986): 187, n. 109. He comments: "It would seem that a change took place in Soloveitchik's conception concerning the nature of cosmic experience and cosmic knowledge." This article is a brilliant analysis of the philosophical background of the entire problem of human knowledge and how it influenced the thinking of the Rav. Ravitsky works his way from Aristotle to Maimonides via Solomon Maimon and Hermann Cohen. However, Ravitsky points out quite correctly that in the last analysis what seems to have governed the Rav's choices in this matter was his understanding that the Halakha is essentially an intellectually creative activity which requires realization in the material universe for its completion.
25. See *Ha-Adam ve-Olamo*, pp. 279–300.
26. *Divrei Hagut*, pp. 212, 219.
27. It is not clear whether Carmy understands this. See p. 336.
28. *Divrei Hagut*, p. 211.
29. Ibid., p. 213. Elsewhere the Rav puts it this way: "I have the distinct impression as if the Halakha considered the steady oscillating of the man of faith between majesty and covenant not as a dialectical but rather as a complementary movement. . . . Accordingly, the task of the covenantal man is to be engaged not in dialectical surging forward and retreating but in uniting the two communities." "The Lonely Man of Faith," p. 51.
30. Ibid., p. 219.
31. Ibid.
32. See Shubert Spero, *Morality, Halakha and the Jewish Tradition* (New York: Ktav, 1983), pp. 21–31.
33. *Yemei Zikaron* (Jerusalem: World Zionist Organization, 1986), pp. 85–87.
34. *Ha-Adam ve-Olamo*, p. 226.
35. Ibid., p. 128.
36. Ibid., pp. 90–91.
37. Deuteronomy 28:9, 11:22, 13:5, 8:6, 10:12.
38. Sifri, Deuteronomy 11:22.
39. Talmud Sota 14a.
40. Midrash Deuteronomy Rabba 1:10.
41. Talmud Shabbat 133b.

42. Leviticus 19:1.
43. Genesis 1:26.
44. It has been well said that what we call character is the coming together of certain properties: (1) moral discipline: the inner capacity for restraint, the ability to inhibit oneself in one's passions, desires, habits; (2) moral attachment: the affirmation or commitment to a larger ideal or community; and (3) moral autonomy: the capacity to freely make ethical decisions. James Davison Hunter, *The Death of Character* (New York: Basic Books, 2000), p. 20.
45. *Halakhic Man*, p. 101.
46. Ibid., p. 109.
47. While the announced plan was to create man in God's image (*tzelem*) and likeness (*demut*) (Genesis 1:26), the description of the actual creation speaks only of "His image" (Genesis 1:27). Perhaps it can be said that the image of God endows every human being with the potential to be a moral agent. That is, he is given power of conceptual thought, power of speech, self-consciousness, self-identity, freedom of will. If man realizes his potential and exercises his freedom to live a moral life, then he becomes "like God" and acquires His *demut* – "His likeness."
48. "The full definition of someone's identity usually involved not only his stand on moral and spiritual matters but also some reference to a defining community." Charles Taylor, *Sources of Self* (Cambridge, Mass.: Harvard University Press, 1986), p. 36.
49. *Halakhic Man*, p. 112.
50. Statman, "Aspects of the Ethical Views of Rabbi Soloveitchik," p. 259.
51. *Halakhic Man*, pp. 45–46.
52. Ibid., p. 46.
53. Isaiah 6:3.
54. The *kedusha* that man achieves must be the kind of *kedusha* appropriate to man; that is to say, he must not overreach himself. The Torah stresses, "And you shall be holy men (*anshei kodesh*) unto Me" (Exodus 22:30), which has been interpreted to mean a human holiness.
55. See Spero, *Morality, Halakha and the Jewish Tradition*, pp. 36–39, where it is shown that the ethical is of intrinsic value, whereas the ritual possesses only instrumental value.
56. David S. Shapiro, "The Meaning of Holiness in Judaism," *Tradition* 7, no. 1 (Winter 1964–65): 48.
57. Isaiah 5:16; see also Psalm. 17:15.
58. *Devekut*, from the root *davak* ("attached") has also been translated as "cleaving unto God" and "clinging to God."
59. Deuteronomy 11:22.
60. "U-bekashtem Misham," p. 187.

61. Ibid., p. 195.
62. While the level of prophecy may appear to be higher, it is, in the last analysis, dependent upon God and therefore cannot be considered entirely an achievement of the individual.
63. Talmud Berachot 17a.
64. See the article by Ravitsky for the historical background.
65. "U-bekashtem Misham," p. 194.
66. *Ha-Adam ve-Olamo*, p. 211.
67. In *Ha-Adam ve-Olamo*, which is a collection of lectures and talks given by the Rav, there is an important section in the chapter entitled "Holiness and Humility." There the Rav asserts that "proximity and contact with God are possible, according to Judaism, only by means of the study of Torah" (p. 20) and explains it on the basis of the doctrine of the union of the knower and the known. But then the Rav poses the question of whether this restricts the possibility of *devekut* to an intellectual elite. Amazingly, the Rav asks the following: "We are therefore in need of another doctrine to explain the unity of man and his Creator...and that is on the basis of 'the lover and the beloved'" (p. 213). Since both God and the pious Jew love the Torah, that becomes the basis of their *devekut*. But if love can unite two individuals, why not speak directly of man's love for God and of God's love for Israel and for the righteous individual? Unfortunately, the date of these talks is not given. Perhaps "Holiness and Humility" represents an earlier stage in the Rav's thinking, which reaches its fullest development in "U-bekashtem Misham."
68. "U-bekashtem Misham," pp. 202–203.
69. Ibid., p. 203.
70. Ibid., p. 204.
71. *Halakhic Man*, pp. 88–89.
72. Note the explanation of the Rav at the end of *Halakhic Man*: "My sole intention was to defend the honor of the Halakha and Halakhic men" (p. 137), which seems to imply that he did not consider himself one of the "Halakhic men"!
73. See Spero, "Towards an Ethical Theory of Judaism."
74. Rabbi Judah Loeb ben Bezalel, *Tiferet Yisrael*, chap. 9.
75. See n. 67 above.
76. Hermann Cohen, "The Character of Maimonides' Ethical Theory," in *Selected Essays from "Judische Schriften"* (Hebrew) (Jerusalem, 1977), p. 41.
77. The Bible clearly hinted at this. See Exodus 33:20, Isaiah 40:25, 55:9.
78. See Spero, *Morality, Halakha and the Jewish Tradition*, chap. 2.
79. Shubert Spero, "Is the God of Maimonides Truly Unknowable?" *Judaism* 22, no. 1 (Winter 1973): 66–78. See Eliezer Berkovits, *God, Man and History* (New York: Jonathan David, 1959), chaps. 6 and 7.

80. Quoted by Edwyn Robert Bevan, *Symbolism and Belief* (New York: Macmillan, 1938), pp. 332–333.
81. Shalom Carmy, "Pluralism and the Category of the Ethical," pp. 331–332.
82. See Spero, *Morality, Halakha and the Jewish Tradition*, chap. 3.
83. Conflicts can arise between the methods of the Halakha and the demands of the ethical. See ibid., chap. 6.
84. For example, in *Halakhic Man*, see pp. 91, 78, 105, 121, 137; in "U-bekashtem Misham," pp. 183, 204, and many others.

 The Philosophy of Halakha

The Halakha,[1] while probably the most distinctive component of Judaism and most instrumental in the survival of the Jewish people,[2] has also been philosophically the most problematic. At the beginning of our history, to outsiders looking in, the Halakha appeared as a set of misanthropic superstitions.[3] Later, to groups within Judaism with a sectarian bent, Christians, Karaites, and classical Reform, the Halakha embodied all that was objectionable both in content as well as in methodology. However, even within the living environment of Talmudic Judaism which produced the Halakha, there arose philosophical issues which were never resolved and which impinged upon the theoretical grounds of the Halakha: Which is greater, study or action,[4] wisdom or deeds?[5] Are there reasons for the *chukim*?[6] Are some commandments more important than others?[7] But even more significant was the fact that from the very beginning of the use of the term

This article originally appeared, in slightly different form, in *Tradition* 30 (1966).

Halakha one finds the opposite term, Aggada, so that it is clear that Halakha was never meant to encompass all of Judaism. Thus, the conceptual stage was already set for comparisons between the two as to their relative roles and significance.[8]

While the Halakha itself, from the talmudic period until the present, has experienced remarkable development in almost every area – talmudic commentary and translation, codification, responsa, history of the Halakha – there has been a lacuna in the systematic treatment of the philosophy of the Halakha.[9] As for the medieval period, long considered the Golden Age of Jewish philosophy, conventional wisdom is wont to accept the summary judgment of Gershom Scholem, "of the two reflective movements in Judaism, the mystical [Kabbala] and philosophy [rational] the latter failed to establish a satisfactory and intimate relation to the Halakha."[10]

Our generation, however, has been blessed with the presence and creative productivity of Rabbi Joseph Dov Soloveitchik, eminent talmudist, halakhic authority, and charismatic teacher, whose writings are characterized by a modern philosophic approach. The Halakha and its role in Judaism as a whole is a central focus of the Rav's writing, as evinced by the titles of two of his major essays: *Halakhic Man* and *The Halakhic Mind*.[11] Indeed, he has been justly called "the philosopher of Halakha."[12] As the teacher and mentor of the modern Orthodox rabbinate, the Rav has been enormously influential in increasing awareness of the centrality of the Halakha in theory as well as in practice, to the point where for many the term "Halakhic Judaism" has come to replace "Orthodox Judaism." Since in *Halakhic Man* the Rav worked with ideal types, it is extremely difficult to determine whether the views of the Halakha attributed to Halakhic Man are to be considered normative for Judaism. I shall therefore begin with his more philosophic work, *The Halakhic Mind*, and consider a single although obviously sweeping claim made by the Rav on behalf of the Halakha which is presented as the conclusion of the theory he outlines in that essay.

H_1...there is only a single source from which a Jewish philosophical *Weltanschauung* could emerge: the objective order – the Halakha.[13]...Out of the sources of Halakha, a new world view awaits formulation.[14]

Others have paraphrased the Rav's views thus: Religious and philosophical accounts of Jewish spirituality are sound and meaningful only to the extent that they derive from the Halakha. The deepest religious emotion, the subtlest theological understanding can only be Jewishly authentic to the extent that it arises from reflection on matters of Halakha.[15] Philosophy is always to be derived from the realm of the Halakha, and not vice versa.[16] Halakha is the visible surface of a philosophy: the only philosophy that could legitimately claim to be Jewish.[17]

I shall consider proposition H_1 in three different contexts: (1) as an independent assertion about Jewish theology; (2) as the logical conclusion of a theory developed by the Rav in *The Halakhic Mind*; (3) as a working principle employed by the Rav in the articulation of his own philosophy.

Let us note at the outset that the real problematic in the Rav's assertion is his claim that the Halakha is the only source of Jewish philosophy. Certainly it must be acknowledged that the Halakha may serve as a source for philosophy, although even this is not immediately obvious. Halakha is essentially material which takes the form of norms and practices obligatory upon the Jew.

Thus, as imperatives and nonpropositional, Halakha as such cannot qualify as philosophy. However, one can conceivably infer a philosophical proposition from a specific rule of halakha. Assuming there to be a halakhic rule that one who has sinned is obliged to repent, one might infer that since "ought" implies "can," the Halakha presupposes the psycho-philosophical principle of human freedom of the will. As another example, one might argue that since the content of the Halakha is regarded as "commandments," there is the implication of the existence of a "commander." Hence the theological principle of the existence of God as Divine

Commander is inferable from the Halakha. There is also the case of a purely theological principle having crystallized into Halakha. So, for example, the Halakha rules that if a person does not subscribe to belief in the divine revelation of the Torah (*Torah min hashamayim*) he is classified as a heretic, which has specific halakhic consequences.[18]

Can we, however, insist that Halakha is the only source of Jewish philosophy? From where did Jewish thinkers in the past draw their philosophy? If we examine the works of the classical Jewish philosophers, Saadia, Judah Halevi, and Maimonides, we find that the proof-texts they offer are mainly from the Bible and, if rabbinic, are generally aggadic in nature.[19] Even if one should disagree with some particular philosophic tenets of these thinkers, one cannot accuse all of them of having looked in the wrong place! Certainly many of the talmudic rabbis perceived the Aggada rather than the Halakha as the appropriate place to find philosophic insights. "If you wish to know He-who-spoke-and-the-world-was-created, study Aggada."[20] Particularly if we believe with Yehuda Halevi that the God of Israel manifests Himself more tellingly in history than in nature, then we should get ourselves to Aggada. For it is the Aggada and not the Halakha that deals with the significance of history.

Consider, for example, that most crucial of theological questions: Shall a Jew seek to justify his religious faith by means of proofs and rational arguments? Bachya ibn Pakuda found the answer in the biblical verse "Know this day and lay it to the heart, that the Lord He is God in heaven above and upon the earth beneath; there is none else."[21] A fundamental question of this kind touches upon the very nature of human knowledge, and of religious knowledge in particular. Bachya reads this biblical verse as a mandate to engage in whatever rational methods of investigation are available in order to demonstrate the doctrine of the unity of God. Others did not read the verse in the same way. But the issue was not one of midrash Halakha but hinged upon an *a priori* understanding of religious knowledge and the requirements of Judaism in this area.

We are thus led to conclude that H_1 is not acceptable, at least as a general description of how Jewish theology was done in the past. As a proposal for doing Jewish theology in the future, it appears unnecessarily limiting. However, in light of the Rav's own philosophic achievements in certain areas of the Halakha, the following proposition may be posited:

H_2 The Halakha is a source of authentic Jewish theology.[22]

Let us return to a consideration of H_1 as a conclusion which the Rav derives from the elaborate theory of religion which he develops in that essay. According to the Rav, the God-man relation expresses itself on three levels of human experience:

1. The subjective consciousness with its various contradictory tensions, such as "wrath and love, remoteness and immanence, repulsion and fascination, tremor and serenity, depression and rapture."
2. The objective theoretical level of logico-cognitive judgments and ethical-religious norms, such as "God exists, He is omniscient, moral, the creator, you shall love God, fear Him, love your fellow man."
3. Concrete deeds, psycho-physical acts, prayer, worship, rituals, cult.[23]

The Rav asserts that religious experiences on both the subjective and objective levels are authentic and veridical and "lie within the ontic zone."[24] That is to say, the Divine manifests itself both "in the [subjective] realm of time and consciousness and in the [objective] realm of time and space."[25] It is already in this initial presentation that we grasp the unique nature of the Rav's philosophy of religion and his overall strategy. Contrary to conventional wisdom,[26] the Rav insists on the cognitive and veridical nature of the "objectified" elements in religion, which in Judaism are constituted by the Torah and include halakhic as well as non-halakhic elements.

What is quite innovative in the context of Jewish theology is the Rav's acknowledgment of the ontic and spiritually significant nature of the subjective religious consciousness This is the belief that Divinity manifests itself in human consciousness not only in the rare and dramatic invasion of certain human beings by the prophetic spirit, but also in the tensions and conflicts, antinomies and polarities that are part of the general human condition. In so doing, the Rav is acknowledging the presuppositions of the phenomenological and existential approaches to philosophy which he presents, at least in this essay, as a given with no indication that it is derived from anything in the Halakha.[27]

However, the Rav goes on to state that because of the obvious difficulties of reporting and analyzing what goes on in the subjective realm, it can be reliably grasped only by reconstructing it from the two objectified levels by a method of "descriptive hermeneutics."[28] The Rav justifies such a reconstruction by positing a correlation between the subjective and objective levels so that any set of beliefs and rituals on the objectified level can be traced to and correlated with the subjective sphere.[29] What remains unclear is the precise relationship between these three levels of the religious act. The Rav uses language such as level 1 is "reflected" in levels 2 and 3, levels 2 and 3 are "evolved in the objectification process," level 1 finds its "concrete expression" in levels 2 and 3.[30] One has the impression that there is some natural process whereby the original "spirit" experienced on level 1 is then embodied, in some sense, in the objectified material on levels 2 and 3. If this is what happens, then indeed one is justified in reconstructing level 1 out of levels 2 and 3, because, in a sense, its very ability to appear on levels 2 and 3 constitutes a test of its strength, durability, and therefore authenticity. Thus, if certain sentiments about God appear in man's consciousness and are found reflected in related Halakha, then the latter can justifiably be used to reconstruct the true nature and import of the former. According to this theory, the ritual and the cult are to be regarded as the most fully evolved, concretized, and therefore "highest" expression of religion and the divine spirit. The ritual thus becomes the only reliable key to unlock the vital secrets of our religious consciousness.

In applying this general theory to Judaism, we must ask whether its underlying assumptions can be accepted. Can we say that religious subjectivity has this tendency to flow in the direction of objectification and that there is always some sort of correlation between the subjective and objective levels?[31] In Judaism the ethical norms, cognitive-logical propositions, and halakhic rituals are believed to have been revealed to man by God and did not evolve by any natural process. We are under no necessity to assume that they are expressive of any antecedent subjective experience. However, in some cases, the rituals may very well be directed at certain recurring human experiences which are accompanied by typical subjective reactions. Thus, the Jewish rituals of mourning are obligatory after the death of close relatives. Here we can agree with the Rav that "the Halakha is the act of seizing the subjective flow (the grief, the sorrow, and the bewilderment) and converting it into enduring and tangible magnitudes"[32] (the different periods of mourning: *onan*, seven days of mourning, thirty days, twelve months in the case of parents). And sometimes, someone with the insight of the Rav can indeed start with the Halakha and "reconstruct" by a process of "descriptive hermeneutics" the emotional depths of the mourner. However, neither this sequence, nor the correlation, nor the possibility of reconstruction seem to hold in every area of Halakha. For example, in regard to the laws of prayer and the obligation to pray three fixed prayers at three fixed times of the day, the subjective-objective correlation may very well be reversed. That is, the Halakha in this situation, unlike the laws of mourning, may be *impressive* rather than *expressive*. The worshipper, in starting out, may lack any distinctive religious consciousness, but may under the impact of his prayers begin to feel the Presence of God and other emotions. Here the Halakha is not the means by which to reconstruct but the instrument that creates subjectivity and impresses upon it a certain character. Then, there are still other areas of the Halakha, such as the dietary laws, the divorce laws, and the laws of ritual cleanliness, where there seems to be no obvious antecedent inner correlation at all that is waiting to be "structured and ordered."[33]

However, the greatest difficulty in viewing H1 as the logical conclusion of the theory of religion developed by the Rav in *The Halakhic Mind* is the following. According to the Rav, the objectification of the religious consciousness takes place on two distinct levels that we have designated level 2 and level 3.[34] The Rav calls level 2 theoretical because it contains logico-cognitive and ethical-religious statements. But it is level 3, called concrete deeds, which the Rav identifies with the Halakha and which he sees as "the single source from which a Jewish philosophical *Weltanschauung* could emerge." However, the Rav's preference for level 3 over level 2 seems unjustified. The items on level 2 are clearly in the objective realm. Moreover, it is precisely the logico-cognitive and ethical-religious propositions that, in fact, served as the primary sources for Jewish theology in the past. And, as the Rav himself says: "The canonized Scripture serves as the most reliable standard of reference for objectivity."[35] Indeed, the richest lodes of implicit theology that can be mined for an understanding of Jewish philosophy are still the first eleven chapters of Genesis, the Song of Songs, the Books of Job and Ecclesiastes – and they are part of level 2. Why then does the Rav give preference to concrete deeds, the ritual, as the source for reconstruction? Why does the Rav bypass the ethical norms, although they, in a sense, also belong to the Halakha? If, like the Rav, one accepts the assumption that there is a "trend towards self-transcendence on the part of the spirit…that it strives to infiltrate the concrete world and that subjectivity rushes along a path that points towards externality, spatialization, and quantification," then it follows that "concrete realization in external and psycho-physical acts is the highest form of objectification,"[36] so that ritual or the Halakha is to be preferred for purposes of reconstruction. However, nowhere is this assumption provided with philosophical justification.

The Rav, however, presents an additional argument for his thesis. He maintains that "religion is typified and described not so much by its ethos as by its ritual and cult," and "the unique character of a particular religion appears only in the ritual," while "the existence of an ethical norm is a common denominator in all religious systems."[37] Yet there is good reason to believe that in Judaism it is the reverse. Ritual and cult have instrumental value, while what is unique in Judaism and of intrinsic value is precisely its understanding of the ethical, the relationship between God and moral values, and the nature of the human being.[38]

Thus, on the basis of the Rav's own designation that objective religious constructs are found in the "norms, dogmas, postulates of canonized Scripture," many of which are non-halakhic, and that from these objective expressions (level 2) the subjective levels can be reconstructed, H_1 cannot be allowed the way it stands.[39]

However, in view of the centrality of the Halakha in Judaism, it would seem reasonable to postulate H_3:

> H_3 Any philosophy of Judaism, to be considered adequate, must be consistent with principles logically inferable from the Halakha.

Let us proceed to examine some of the Rav's philosophic writing to determine whether he employs the Halakha as the sole source of his theorizing about Judaism.

In arguing the importance of H_1, Professor Marvin Fox focuses upon a particular teaching which he claims is paradigmatic of the Rav's practice of deriving theology from the Halakha.[40] In one of his most important essays, the Rav begins with a discussion of the theological problem of human suffering, which often cannot be explained on the basis of the principle of provident reward and punishment or in terms of ensuring beneficial consequences. Judaism, says the Rav, with its realistic approach, refuses to cover up or minimize the horror of evil in the world or to overlook the rend and conflict at the heart of existence.[41] There is blatant evil, pain, and suffering which cannot be overcome by speculative, philosophic thought. This is because the human perspective is never based on more than a fragmentary view of life and history, so that the full picture, accessible only to God Himself, remains unknown.[42] Judaism bids the individual to confront his situation honestly and realistically, and must ask: What must the sufferer do so that he can get on with his life? We are interested neither in the metaphysical cause of suffering nor in its purpose but rather in the question of how the individual is to respond to his suffering. How may he elevate his suffering and weave it into the pattern of his chosen destiny in life?

Before the Rav introduces any halakhic source for this teaching, he states that it is the view of Judaism that man is obligated to creatively transform his fate into destiny, so that when confronted by suffering, instead of idle speculation, he must perceive his situation as a challenge and seek to use it as a springboard for personal growth.[43] And for this the Rav provides proof-texts from the Bible, Deuteronomy 4:30 and Jeremiah 30:7, to show that crisis can lead to repentance and to personal salvation. The Rav then goes on to show how this "practical" approach to the experience of suffering is reflected in the Mishnah: "Man is obligated to bless God for the evil which befalls him just as he is obligated to bless Him for the good."[44] According to the Rav, blessing God means more than saying "thank you." Man is obligated to reevaluate his entire life in the light of his good fortune. So too the experience of suffering obliges the individual to step out beyond the experience and consider new, creative initiatives how to integrate his suffering into a religious blessing for himself and for others.

According to Professor Fox,

> We have here one of the most clear and explicit cases in which important religious doctrine emerges from a proper understanding of the Halakha.[45]
> ...Halakhic norms generate theological principles.[46]

...It is the Halakha, not abstract theological speculation, that teaches us that we must use our pain as an occasion for self-refinement and moral growth.[47]

Fox seems to be making two different claims:

(1) In *Kol Dodi Dofek* (pp. 65–74) the Rav presents us with a clear and explicit case in which "important religious doctrine" emerges from a proper understanding of the Halakha (Mishnah Berachot); (2) In *Kol Dodi Dofek* (pp. 65–74) the Rav is saying that it is from the Halakha that we learn that we must use suffering as an occasion for self-refinement and moral growth.

I wish to argue that neither of these propositions are correct; i.e., the views attributed to the Rav are not found in this article.

First, the "important religious doctrine" Fox is referring to can only be the teaching that "we must use our pain. " But this is a normative statement prescribing a certain attitude and mode of response, and hardly an example of the philosophical world-view which analysis of Halakha is supposed to generate. Even if the Rav does derive the teaching "that we use our pain" from the Halakha, it hardly is the "clear and explicit case" that could exemplify the general principle. Moreover, even if the blessing prescribed by the Mishnah is understood in the full sense of the Rav's interpretation, it implies nothing as to whether, after having made the blessing, one may pursue the philosophical question as to the meaning and significance of human suffering and whether it is reconcilable with God's moral character. From the fact that the Halakha as Halakha addresses itself to the practical question of how one should existentially respond to suffering, one cannot infer anything as to the attitude of Judaism regarding the philosophical problem of theodicy. In fact, the Rav seems to base his assertion that according to Judaism seeking a purely philosophic-speculative solution to the problem of human suffering is futile upon the arguments (1) that no adequate solution has to date been offered, and (2) that the perspective of the human being is too limited to enable him to understand.

Even the lesser claim (2) does not seem to be borne out by the text. True, the Halakha in the cited mishnah in Berachot as interpreted by the Rav seems to reflect the teaching that "we must use our pain as an occasion for self-refinement and moral growth," but it is not at all clear that the Rav presents this as his source. Indeed, there seem to be better reasons for considering the biblical texts cited by the Rav as his source: Deuteronomy 4:30, Jeremiah 30:7, and the Book of Job.

Fox makes the following statement: "Rav Soloveitchik replies to these questions [human suffering] with what he specifically labels a Halakhic answer."[48] The passage that I believe Fox is referring to is the following:

> The halakhic answer to this question is very simple. Suffering comes to elevate the person, to purify his spirit and to sanctify him, to cleanse his thought and to purify it from all the dross, superficiality, and vulgarity and to broaden his horizons.[49]

A glance at the sentences immediately preceding this paragraph reveals that the question referred to is "How shall a man behave in a time of trouble? What shall a man do so as not to be destroyed by his suffering?" In short, the "halakhic answer" refers to the practical question of how a man should react to suffering and not to the broader philosophical question of how to reconcile human suffering with God's morality. But surely this is not only the halakhic answer to this question but also the answer of the Aggada. "Should a man see suffering come upon him, let him scrutinize his actions.... if he does not discover the cause, let him attribute it to neglect of Torah.... if he still finds no justification, it is certain that his chastenings are chastenings of love."[50] This aggadic answer is even more explicit than the mishnaic statement that in terms of personal reaction, suffering comes to elevate the person, purify his spirit, and sanctify him. We have argued that no theological principle can be deduced from this mishnah and that the Rav makes no claim to do so.

In further pursuit of the question as to how the Rav treats the Halakha in developing his philosophical insights, let us examine the opening sections of what may be the Rav's most philosophical essay, *Uvikashtem misham*.[51] Here the Rav paints on a very broad canvas indeed. He attempts to depict the complex, conflicted, and tension-filled relationship between man and God over the vast range of human thought. He notes the areas wherein man has sought to catch a glimpse of a reflection of his Creator: in the drama of the cosmos, in the dark recesses of his own consciousness, in the moral will, and in the voice of conscience. Ranging over the entire history of religious philosophy, the Rav shows how man's search for God has been disappointing and frustrating. While doing natural theology he believes he has discovered God at the end of a rational argument, as a deduction from categorical principles, only to learn in a later period that the entire enterprise was misconceived inasmuch as the finite mind using empirical categories cannot infer anything about the transcendent and the eternal. Then man begins to look elsewhere in the presuppositions of his own consciousness, in his sense of ontological awareness, in his nameless yearning for something that nothing in this entire world can seem to assuage. Sometimes he does catch a glimpse of something sacred, of some transcendent meaning – but in a flash the perception is gone and one is not sure whom or what one has glimpsed. From the other direction, as God turns to man, the results are equally equivocal and disappointing. Often man does not recognize the Presence of God in his crisis-filled situation. Often, man flees from His demand in fear of the responsibilities involved.

For the Rav, the dialectical character of the history of the relationship between man and God is also reflected in the religious consciousness of the individual. Contrary to those who present religion as "a realm of simplicity, wholeness, and tranquility" for "embittered souls and troubled spirits," the Rav insists that the religious consciousness, at its profoundest, "is exceptionally complex, rigorous and tortuous, antinomic and antithetic from beginning to end."

> It is in a condition of spiritual crisis, of psychic ascent and descent, of contradiction arising from affirmation and negation, self-abnegation and self-appreciation. The ideas of temporality and eternity, knowledge and choice (necessity and freedom), love and fear (the yearning for God and the flight from His glorious splendor), incredible and overbold daring and an extreme sense of humility, transcendence and God's closeness, the profane and the holy, etc., etc., struggle within his religious consciousness...it is a raging, clamorous torrent of man's consciousness with all its crises, pangs, and torments.[52]

According to the Rav, these conflicting thoughts and feelings are not the result of confused thinking or psychological pathology, but part of what it is to be man.

> This antinomy is an integral part of man's creative consciousness, the source of most of the antinomies and contradictions in man's outlook.[53]
>
> *Homo Religiosus* is suspended between two great magnets, between love and fear, between desire and dread, between longing and anxiety.
>
> He is caught between two opposing forces – the right hand of existence embraces him, the left thrusts him aside.[54]

From whence does the Rav derive this depth of insight into the complexities of the God-man relationship? In the opening section of the essay, the Rav poetically portrays the dialectical relationship between the two lovers in the Song of Songs and presents this as the grand metaphor for the relationship between man and God:

the going forward and the backing off, the tension between love and fear, searching and not finding, hesitation to respond when the beloved knocks. The following emotionally evocative passages are seen by the Rav as expressions of the conflicted character of the God-man relationship both in history and in the individual consciousness:

> Draw me, we will run after thee (1:4).
> Rise up my love, my fair one and come away (2:10).
> I sought him but I found him not (3.1).
> I will seek him whom my soul loveth (3:2).
> I sleep but my heart waketh, / Hark my beloved knocketh (5.2).
> I have put off my coat. / How shall I put it on? (5:3).
> I opened to my beloved, / But my beloved had turned away
> and was gone; /I called him but he gave me no answer (5:6).
> Whither is thy beloved gone? (6:1).
> I am my beloved, and his desire is towards me. (7:11).

The Rav writes:

> When man begins to draw close to God because he hears the voice of God traveling through the world, God distances himself from him. The Infinite and man the finite seek but do not find each other. This dialectical drama reveals itself in its full strength and loftiness. Man remains alone. Who can save and redeem him from his loneliness if not the God who hides Himself from him.[55]

The analogy fits perfectly. But in what sense can the Song of Songs be said to be the source of the Rav's teaching that the God-man relationship is of this conflicted, tortuous character? After all, it is not literally found in the text. Once again it is the Rav's descriptive hermeneutics that makes the connection.

In what appears to be an attempt to justify his interpretation, the Rav points out that it is the Halakha which is the basis for the judgment that "if all songs are holy, the Song of Songs is the Holy of Holies," meaning that it is to be interpreted figuratively and never literally as a mere love song.[56] Are we therefore to infer from this that the Rav derived this most innovative teaching from the Halakha? But all that the Halakha establishes is that the Song of Songs is to be considered Holy Writ and not to be interpreted as a secular love song. However, precisely which interpretation should be given remains in the realm of Aggada. Thus if the Rav decides to give the text a metaphysical-universal interpretation rather than the metaphysical-historical interpretation of Rashi and the tradition, the teaching acquires a midrashic warrant from the text but hardly from the Halakha![57]

A quick survey of the entire essay reveals that in referring to the religion whose doctrines he is analyzing, the Rav uses the term "Judaism" at least sixteen times, the term "Halakha" some twelve times, and "Kabbala" three times. In none of the contexts in which the term "Halakha" is used is it suggested that a particular item of theology is being *derived* from the Halakha. The Halakha seems always to be presented in a supporting role to Judaism. Once a theological teaching has been declared integral to Judaism by virtue of some biblical text or aggadic teaching, it is shown to be reflected in the Halakha (p. 16) or supported by the Halakha (pp. 9, 24, 42, 61) or "then comes Judaism headed by the Halakha" (p. 39). Sometimes, of course, the Rav makes philosophical observations about the Halakha itself (pp. 49, 55, 62). Of special interest is the Rav's use of the term "Halakhic Judaism," which occurs in connection with three different theological teachings. Upon consideration it might be suggested that the Rav uses this term when he wishes to imply that Judaism, in the absence of the corrective influence of the Halakha might have veered in a different direction: radical detachment from the material world (p. 59), concentration on either love or fear of God (p. 35), to seek complete mystical union with God (p. 33). For the Rav, therefore, Halakhic Judaism is not a Judaism that is derived solely from the

Halakha, but a Judaism in which the role of the Halakha is both practical and philosophical.

Thus, in spite of the many references to the Halakha in this major philosophical essay, the theological themes that are developed and presented by the Rav do not appear to be derived from the Halakha.[58]

It was stated earlier that somehow systematic exploration of the philosophy of the Halakha had been neglected. Yet the basic elements of such a philosophy can be found in rabbinic sources and in the writings of recent Jewish thinkers, so that the main outlines of such a philosophy can be described. Here in sketchy form is what might be called a prolegomenon to a minimalist view, a theory that will describe the place and role of Halakha within Judaism, and that will do so by making only those assertions which are logically necessary to sustain the enterprise called Halakha. The adequacy of this theory is to be judged by whether it accounts for the central importance attached to the study and practice of the Halakha by the tradition.

METHODOLOGICAL PRESUPPOSITIONS

The three central presupposition are set out below:

(1) The answer to the question "What is the purpose of Halakha?" which is a second-order question, cannot come from the Halakha itself for the same reason that the answer to the question "What is the purpose of playing chess?" cannot come from a study of the rules of chess.

(2) The answer, however, must come from *within Judaism* and not from cultural values outside of Judaism regardless of how universal or self-evident they may appear. This was stressed by the Rav: "It is impossible to reconstruct a unique Jewish world perspective out of alien material,"[59] and, before him, by Samson R. Hirsch, "We must take up our position within Judaism, to seek to comprehend Judaism from itself, as it represents itself to be."[60] This applies to efforts to discover the reasons for the individual

commandments as well as to the philosophy of the Halakha as a whole.

(3) Halakha is neither theology nor anthropology but is based on both.[61] From the Bible and rabbinic midrash-aggada comes a doctrine of God and a theory of man which are the preconditions of Halakha and within which Halakha as a whole is to be understood.

On the basis of the above, we may conclude that the Halakha, being essentially a collection of prescriptions and norms directed to man, constitutes the instrumentality by which God, the Giver of the Halakha, brings about the ends He intends for man, His creature. This view locates the purpose of the Halakha in man and not in God or in the world. Thus, the rabbis noted that the commandments were given "solely to purify" Israel and "make them worthy of life in the world-to-come."[62] The decision to live by the Halakha, behaving in accordance with the Halakha, and studying the Halakha all have crucial effects upon man's consciousness, his personality, and moral make-up. Unlike some of the medieval Jewish thinkers who saw only a social benefit in the practice of the Halakha,[63] we are stressing that the study and practice of the Halakha can bring about the spiritual and moral transformation of man which constitutes his salvation as intended by God. Unlike the mystical tradition, our "minimal" theory limits the consequences of halakhic practice to man rather than extend it to the cosmos.[64]

The Rav properly expresses the ultimate goal of Judaism in terms of the category of holiness (*kedusha*). Judaism believes that the Divine Presence must be brought down into our concrete world so that the Transcendent can be experienced in our everyday lives. "Holiness is created by man, by flesh and blood."[65]

Says the Rav:

An individual does not become holy through mystical adhesion to the absolute nor through mystic union with the infinite nor through a boundless, all-embracing ecstasy, but rather through his whole biological life, through his animal actions and through actualizing the Halakha in the empirical world.... Holiness consists of a life ordered and fixed in accordance with Halakha and finds its fulfillment in the observance of laws regulating human biological existence such as the laws concerning forbidden sexual relations, forbidden foods, and similar precepts.[66]

A similar thought is found in Samson Raphael Hirsch:

Law purifies and sanctifies even our lower impulses and desires by applying them with wise limitations to the purposes designed by the Creator.... Righteousness is the Law's typical end and aim.[67]

And so also Abraham J. Heschel:

The deed is the source of Holiness. To the Jew the mitzvoth are the instruments by which the Holy is performed. If man were only mind, worship in thought would be the form in which to commune with God. But man is body and soul and his goal is to live so that both "his heart and his flesh shall sing to the living God."[68]

The two divisions of the Halakha, the positive and the negative, the "dos" and the "don'ts" are thus accounted for by David Shapiro:

The positive in Halakha reflects on a human level the creative activity of God. The negative bespeaks the finite and unredeemed character of the universe wherein the evil derived from man's freedom is countered by means of man's withdrawal from contact with it.[69]

One should add here the observation of Nachmanides that refraining from the negative commands responds to fear of God," while observing the positive commands responds to love of God.[70]

This would bring into the very dynamics of the Halakha the dialectical polarities of the religious consciousness which the Rav sees reflected in the commands to love and fear God and in the divine attributes of *din* and *rachamim*.[71] The importance of this approach lies in its focus on the category of the holy, which is a uniquely religious category and one central to Judaism.

But the ideal of becoming holy by means of the Halakha is given deeper meaning by the Rav by being placed within the broader framework of *imitatio Dei*. The imperative to be holy in the Bible is couched in terms of *imitatio Dei*: "You shall be holy, for I the Lord your God am holy."[72]

By exercising his freedom to choose the good and the true, man is fulfilling part of the divine image within him. By acting in accordance with the Halakha, man rises above being "a mere random example of his species" and acquires an "I" identity and becomes a possession of individual existence and even individual immortality.[73] By being creative in the Halakha man imitates God, who is the supreme Creator – "maker of heaven and earth."

However, the ultimate instantiation of man as creator in terms of *imitatio Dei* could hardly be one who intellectually creates abstract conceptual worlds in the Halakha. For as the Rav states: "The peak of religious ethical perfection to which Judaism aspires is man as creator."[74] It is called "religious ethical perfection" because "the most fundamental principle of all is that man must create himself."[75] And self-creation makes sense only in religious *ethical* terms. Man, utilizing his divine trait of freedom and perceiving God as his model, remakes his personality to become truly merciful, kind, just, and righteous. So that from a being born in the image of God (i.e., with potentialities), man becomes in the likeness of God in reality. As the Rav acknowledges: "The whole process of self-creation all proceeds in an ethical direction."[76] Therefore an alternative way of expressing the purpose of the Halakha might be: "The Halakha is the medium for the implementation of *imitatio Dei*,"[77] with the latter understood primarily in ethical terms.

If this sketchy outline of a minimalist philosophy of the

Halakha be deemed adequate, how shall we judge the view of the
Rav which stresses the theoretical and cognitive importance of
the study of the Halakha?[78]

The Rav states:

> The Halakha is not a random collection of laws but a method,
> an approach which creates a noetic unity.[79]
>
> The essence of the Halakha which was received from
> God consists in creating an ideal world and cognizing the
> relationship between that ideal world and our concrete en-
> vironment in all its visible manifestation and underlying
> structure.[80]
>
> Halakhic man orients himself to the entire cosmos and
> tries to understand it by utilizing an ideal world which he
> bears in his Halakhic consciousness.[81]
>
> The foundations of foundations and the pillar of Hal-
> akhic thought is not the practical ruling but the determina-
> tion of the theoretical Halakha.[82]

We would seem to have here, first, an assertion as to what the
Halakha essentially is, namely a conceptual theoretical system
which is directed at our cognition, and second, a value judgment.
This latter refers to the classic issue of which in Halakha is greater,
study or deed?[83] And the Rav seems to be saying that intellectual
creativity in the study of the Halakha is greater and is of value
even in the absence of implementation. Let us first examine this
value judgment.

What is the religious significance of discovering systematic
connections between abstract concepts of the Halakha? In the
words of the Rav: "Halakhic cognition unites the finite with the
infinite."[84] In explanation he cites the views of both R. Shneur
Zalman of Lyady and R. Chaim Volozhiner:[85]

> When a person understands and grasps any Halakha in the
> Mishnah or Gemara fully and clearly, that, for example, it is

His will that in case Reuben pleads thus and Simon thus, the decision shall be thus, therefore when a person knows and grasps with his intellect this decision...he thereby comprehends, grasps, and encompasses with his intellect the will and wisdom of the Holy One.[86]

Through studying Talmud and commentaries and all the *pilpulim*, everything is made to cling to the Holy One, blessed be He.... Since, He, His will, and His word are one, by cleaving to the Torah it is as if one is cleaving to Him.[87]

As shown with incisive clarity and scholarship by Aviezer Ravitsky, the Rav bases his theory of human knowledge on the Aristotelian-Maimonidean principle of the unity of the intellect, the intellectually cognizing subject, and the intellectually cognized object.[88] Thus, if the thought content of the Halakha is the revealed thought of God, then he who intellectually grasps the Halakha unites in some sense with God.

What is problematic about this theory, however, is as follows:

(1) It does not appear that Judaism is congenial to the proposition that the intellect is to be viewed as the main link between man and God. The views of Yehuda Halevi and Chasdai Crescas have generally been seen to be more Jewish on this subject than those of Maimonides, in spite of the Rav's efforts to temper the strict intellectualism of Maimonides.[89]

(2) While the Halakha as a whole reflects the will of God for man, the content of the different parts of the Halakha might affect its ontological status. Thus, those portions of the Halakha which deal with moral norms, with the demands of the moral values of justice, righteousness, and loving-kindness, can more easily be understood as part of reality and in some sense part of God Himself: "The Lord, the Lord God, merciful and gracious long suffering and abundant in goodness and truth."[90] Thus creative intellectual involvement in the moral commandments of the Halakha could be defended as constituting communion with God.

However, this would not be the case were we to focus on ritual aspects of the Halakha, such as the theoretical concepts behind the dietary laws, which appear to be of instrumental value only. We saw earlier that the Rav maintains that the study of the Halakha is a cognitive process which somehow is related to understanding the entire cosmos. This is underscored by his statement in *The Halakhic Mind* that "the cognition of the world is of the innermost essence of the religious experience."[91]

What is the relationship between knowing the theoretical Halakha and knowledge of the real world? Certainly the Halakha itself was given to be known. These rules obviously cannot be obeyed unless they are understood in terms of recognizing both (1) the situation in which they become applicable, and (2) what one is called upon to do. On the theoretical level the Halakha has constantly undergone a vast development in which the principles behind the practical observances were identified so that further extensions and distinctions could be made in the law. The master of Halakha in both its theoretical and practical aspects could be said to have amassed a great deal of knowledge. But knowledge of what? Essentially about the Halakha, which is in some respects an autonomous system.[92] But can it be said that the Halakha provides us with a knowledge of the cosmos, of the phenomenological reality? Only perhaps as an indirect byproduct of our efforts to properly describe those aspects of reality which we must compare to the theoretical model in order to arrive at a halakhic ruling in an actual case.

On the highest level of halakhic scholarship there is, of course, a process that might be called "creating an ideal world," which is the development of abstract concepts of great generality that range over diverse halakhic fields that are useful in resolving contradictions and solving other related problems *within* the Halakha. However, the more abstract the concept, the more tenuous its link with phenomenal reality, the less justification there is for calling it knowledge.[93]

Thus the sort of understanding of the cosmos that one could

achieve by orienting oneself to it by halakhic concepts would appear to be extremely selective, fragmentary, and one-dimensional. One would end up knowing a great number of disconnected particular things about a wide variety of phenomena significant only in terms of the Halakha.

The Rav asserts, "Halakhic man's ideal is to subject reality to the yoke of the Halakha."[94] This suggests that the religious Jew somehow wishes to transform reality or perceives reality in some radically different way. Actually, the only way the halakhic master could make a proper ruling is to perceive reality just the way it is in all its brute facticity. And the ontological status of the chicken that is consumed after the halakhic ruling that it is kosher is the same and as "real" as before. The only reality that Judaism would like to submit to the yoke of the Halakha is the will and deeds of man.

It appears, therefore, that the effort to endow creative study of the theoretical Halakha, as such, with the ability to provide cognitive insight into the cosmos or mystical communion with the Revealer of the Halakha is open to serious objections. Moreover, it does not appear necessary for a minimal philosophy of Halakha which can otherwise meet reasonable conditions of adequacy.

The Halakha was given by God to His people to be developed creatively, so that it can be applied humanely and observed diligently to bring about ends that are for the ultimate edification of man and society: as a medium for the implementation of *imitatio Dei*. Thus the real significance of the Halakha, as such, is instrumental rather than intrinsic, "To bring down the Divine Presence into the concrete world," to inject holiness into all aspects of life. Holiness is created by man through actualizing the Halakha in the empirical world.[95]

ENDNOTES

1.   Etymologically the term halakha derives from the Hebrew verb *haloch*, "to walk" or "to go," and as a noun refers to that portion of biblical and rabbinic lore which takes the form of laws and practices obligatory upon the Jew. In talmudic literature halakha is used in opposition to the

term aggada, from the verb *le-hagid*, "to relate," which refers to types of material not encompassed by the Halakha, such as history, poetry, narratives, prayers, theology. It is important to note that moral teachings are to be found both in the Halakha and the Aggada.

2. See Ephraim E. Urbach, *Ha-Halakha* (Israel: Yad la-Talmud, 1984), pp. 3–4.
3. See Harry J. Leon, The Jews of Ancient Rome (Philadelphia: Jewish Publication Society, 1960).
4. Kiddushin 40b.
5. Avot 3:2.
6. Yoma 67b on Leviticus 18:4.
7. Avot 2:1, Sifra 45.
8. In the talmudic period both were treated with equal seriousness. Certain rabbis were known as specialists in the Halakha, others in the Aggada. There are no sages known as masters of the Halakha who did not also expound the Aggada. However, there are teachers of the Aggada in whose name no halakhot have been recorded. There is no halakhic work from the talmudic period in which aggadic teachings are not found. However, there are works of Aggada in which no Halakha is found. What must be stressed is the interdependence of Halakha and Aggada as indispensable constituents of Judaism and at the same time their distinctive characteristics. Thus Kariv: "The Halakha is the rigid skeleton of the life of Israel; the Aggada is its soul and spirit." For example, the Halakha of Shabbat treats the thirty-nine categories of work forbidden on the Sabbath, while the Aggada speaks of the Shabbat Queen, the Sabbath as wedded to Israel, and the special over-soul acquired by the Jew on Shabbat. Heschel put it this way: "Halakha without Aggada is dead; Aggada without Halakha is wild." Contemporary yeshiva heads prefer the expression: "Halakha represents the bread and meat of Judaism; Aggada contributes the seasoning."

It is difficult to formulate the defining characteristics (necessary and sufficient) of Halakha in a way that would precisely separate out all that is considered Halakha from all that is considered Aggada. For example, if we define Halakha as including all the rules in Judaism that involve "doing," then we exclude what have been called "duties of the heart," which include the important mitzvot of love of God and fear of God and others. Alternatively, the term Halakha can be given to any rule which carries an authoritative, prescriptive character. In this view, anything in Judaism which the individual is *obligated* to do or to say or to think or any attitude he is commanded to adopt is part of the Halakha. This would leave to the Aggada descriptive propositions referring to history or to the human being or to the actions of God in the world as well as rules whose observance is optional.

Maimonides, in his halakhic work, *Mishneh Torah*, apparently uses a very broad definition of the term, as he includes material that is clearly of a philosophical, cosmological, and psychological nature. Thus a moral theory based on Aristotelian ethics and psychology is included in the section called Hilchot Deot (Laws of Moral Character). Another well-known section is called Hilchot Teshuva (Laws of Repentance). But what part of the *teshuva* process is technically halakhic? Maimonides's own formulation seems to suggest that the mitzvah (obligation) focuses only on the recitation of the confessional (*vidui*). Are we to conclude that the entire subject of *teshuva* in Judaism, with its profound philosophical, moral, and psychological implications, is all a matter of the Halakha?

See Abraham Kariv, "Tefisat ha-Halakha ba-Aggada," in *Hagut ve-Halakha*, ed. Y. Eisner (*Misrad ha-Chinukh ve-ha-Tarbut*, 1972).

9. With the important exception, of course, of Rabbi Samson R. Hirsch (1808–1888), whose contribution to this subject is of historic importance and whose views we shall cite later in this article.

10. Gershom G. Scholem, *Major Trends in Jewish Mysticism* (New York: Schocken Books, 1941), p. 28.

11. *Halakhic Man*, p. 137.

12. David Singer and Moshe Sokol, "Joseph Soloveitchik: 'Lonely Man of Faith,'" *Modern Judaism* 2, no. 3, p. 232.

13. *Halakhic Mind*, p. 101.

14. Ibid., p. 102.

15. Marvin Fox, "The Unity and Structure of Rabbi Joseph B. Soloveitchik's Thought," *Tradition* 24, no. 2, p. 49.

16. Aviezer Ravitsky, "Rabbi J.B. Soloveitchik on Human Knowledge," *Modern Judaism* 6, no. 2 (May 1986): 181, n. 12.

17. Reported by Rabbi Jonathan Sacks, Chief Rabbi of England, of a conversation he had with the Rav in the summer of 1967, *Jewish Action* 53, no. 3, p. 30.

18. Rambam, Hilchot Teshuva 3:8.

19. S. Weisblat, "Pesukei Tanakh u-Maamarei Chazal ke-Asmakhtot le-De'ot Philosophiyyot," *Bet Mikra* 34.

20. Sifre, Parshat Aikev; see Avraham Kariv, *Mi-Sod Chakhamim* (Jerusalem: Mosad Harav Kook, 1976), p. 22.

21. Deuteronomy 4:39.

22. The Rav applies the term "descriptive hermeneutics" to the method by which the theology is generated from the Halakha. *Halakhic Mind*, p. 98.

23. Ibid., pp. 68–69.

24. Ibid., p. 75.

25. Ibid., p. 66.

26. Berlin in the 1930s.

27. In his essay "U-bekashtem Misham," which we shall deal with later, the Rav associates the dialectic in the religious consciousness with the dialectic in the Song of Songs and the divine attributes of *din* and *rachamim*.
28. *Halakhic Mind*, p. 67.
29. Ibid., p. 62.
30. Ibid., p. 67.
31. Ibid., p. 85.
32. Ibid.
33. Ibid., p. 59.
34. See p. xx above.
35. *Halakhic Mind*, p. 81.
36. Ibid., pp. 67–68.
37. Ibid., pp. 69–70.
38. See Shubert Spero, *Morality, Halakha and the Jewish Tradition* (New York: Yeshiva University Press, 1983).
39. What is rather curious is that when Fox cites what he terms "the unifying principle in all of the Rav's work" (p. 49), namely, "the Halakha is the objectification and crystallization of all true Jewish doctrine," he gives no written source for this quotation other than to say: "As he [the Rav] has often expressed it." However, if there is no other written source for H1 than these two sentences which I have cited from the very end of *The Halakhic Mind* (pp. 101–102), then perhaps they should be understood strictly within the context of that essay, which, after all, was written in 1944 and published without revision. Perhaps the Rav never meant H1 as a sweeping generalization covering all Jewish theology.

    Let us again examine the first crucial sentence of H_1 (p. 101): "To this end [the end of discovering what is singular and unique in a philosophy] there is only a single source from which a Jewish philosophical *Weltanschauung* could emerge: the objective order – the Halakha. The Rav seems to be using the term Halakha here as synonymous with "the objective order," although we pointed out earlier that the Rav explicitly states that the objective order includes norms, beliefs, articles of faith, religious texts (p. 99) which are not part of the Halakha. But perhaps this can be justified in view of the Rav's stated conviction that the Halakha is the "culmination of the entire process of objectification."

    Consider the second sentence of H_1: "Out of the sources of Halakha a new world-view awaits formulation" (p. 102). Here it is possible that world-view is meant in the narrow sense of developing a uniquely Jewish vision of such abstract metaphysical concepts as time, space, and causality toward which an analysis of certain aspects of the Halakha can be of crucial help (see pp. 48 and 101). Furthermore, this sentence with which the essay comes to a close may have the literary function of dramatizing what the Rav saw as the important implication of his theory, finding a central if not exclusive role for Halakha in the development of Jewish theology. The need for this can be better appreciated if we realize that in the essay entitled *The Halakhic Mind*, which ends on p. 102, the Rav does not deal with Judaism and Halakha until page 91!

40. Fox, "Unity and Structure."

41. *Kol Dodi Dofek* (Hebrew version), p. 67.

42. The fact is that in rabbinic literature this question is repeatedly treated philosophically, as it was by medieval Jewish thinkers, although we do have a point of view among the rabbis that in principle this question does not allow for rational explanation. See Avot 4:19.

43. *Kol Dodi Dofek*, last two lines on p. 67.

44. Berachot 48b.

45. Fox, "Unity and Structure," p. 52.

46. Ibid., p. 49.

47. Ibid., p. 54.

48. Ibid., p. 51.

49. *Kol Dodi Dofek*, p. 68.

50. Berachot 5a.

51. "U-bekashtem Misham."

52. *Halakhic Man*, pp. 141–142, n. 14.

53. Ibid., p. 68.

54. Ibid., p. 67.

55. "U-bekashtem Misham," p. 13.

56. Ibid. See n. 1 on p. 67.

57. In n. 1 the Rav claims that Bachya and Rambam adopt the metaphysical-universal interpretation. The Rav's claim that in essence both interpretations are one is not convincing.

58. Fox makes the added claim: "Careful study of the *Lonely Man of Faith* will show that its conclusions derive from the Halakha" (p. 54). Yet the Rav states explicitly in that essay: "My interpretive gesture is completely subjective and lays no claim to representing a definitive Halakhic philosophy" (p. 10).

59. *Halakhic Mind*, p. 100.

60. Samson Raphael Hirsch, *The Nineteen Letters of Ben Uziel*, trans. Bernard Drachman (New York; Bloch, 1942), p. 14.

61. See David S. Shapiro, "The Ideological Foundations of the Halakha," *Tradition* 9, nos. 1–2 (Spring–Summer 1967). See also Shubert Spero, "Is There an Indigenous Jewish Theology?" in the same issue of *Tradition* and in this volume, above, p. XX.

62. Genesis Rabba 44:1, Makkot 23b.

63. See Maimonides, *Guide for the Perplexed* 3:27.

64. See Hirsch, *Ben Uziel*, pp. 100, 138, 143.

65. *Halakhic Man*, p. 47. See also David S. Shapiro, "The Meaning of Holiness in Judaism," *Tradition* 7, no.1, who claims that *kedusha* is basically an ethical value.

66. *Halakhic Man*, pp. 46, 108, 109. In a beautiful interpretation of Isaiah 6:3 and its Targum, the Rav comments: "The beginnings of holiness are rooted in 'the highest heavens' and its end is embedded in the eschatological vision of the 'end of days'—holy forever and to all eternity. But the link that joins together these two perspectives is the halakhic conception: 'Holy upon the earth, the work of His might'— the holiness of the concrete."

67. Hirsch, *Ben Uziel*, pp. 100, 138.

68. Abraham J. Heschel, *Man's Quest for God* (New York: Charles Scribner's Sons, 1954).

69. Shapiro, *Ideology of the Halakha*, p. 106.

70. See Nachmanides on Exodus 20:8.

71. "U-bekashtem Misham," pp. 22–26.

72. Leviticus 19:2.

73. *Halakhic Man*, p. 125.

74. Ibid., p. 101.

75. Ibid., p. 109.

76. Ibid., p. 137.

77. Shapiro, *Ideology of the Halakha*, p. 114.

78. There is always the nagging question whether the Rav intended the view of the Halakha he presents in *Halakhic Man* to reflect the view of normative Judaism or perhaps only as a philosophic rationale for the manner of talmudic study found in the Lithuanian rabbinic scholarly tradition?

79. "Mah Dodeikh mi-Dod," p. 81.

80. *Halakhic Man*, p. 19.

81. Ibid., p. 23.

82. Ibid., p. 24.

83. Kiddushin 40b.

84. "U-bekashtem Misham," p. 204.

85. *Halakhic Man*, p. 148.

86. R. Shneur Zalman of Lyady, *Likkutei Amarim*, pt. I, chap. 5.

87. R. Chaim Volozhiner, *Nefesh ha-Chayim* IV:8, IV:10.

88. Ravitsky, "Soloveitchik on Human Knowledge," p. 162.

89. "U-bekashtem Misham," p. 68, n. 2. See discussion in Julius Guttmann, *On the Philosophy of Religion* (Jerusalem: Magnes Press, 1976) p. 89.

    For the views of Crescas and Albo, see HaRav S. B. Orbakh, "Ha-Halakha bi-Tefisatam shel R"H Crescas ve R"I Albo," in *Hagut ve-Halakha*, 12, ed. Dr. Yitzhak Eisner (Jerusalem: Misrad ha-Chinukh ve–ha-Tarbut), p. 43.

90. Exodus 34:6.

91. *Halakhic Mind*, p. 46.

92. It has been shown that the language of Halakha is not a purely artificial language like mathematics, in which all of its terms bear symbolic meanings given to them by the system. Halakhic propositions are often formulated in terms of the natural language, which means that some Halakhic concepts are not *a priori*. See the excellent article by Tsevi Zohar: "Al ha-Yachas ben Sefat ha-Halakha le-ben ha-Safa ha-Tivit," in *Sefer ha-Yovel le-ha-Gaon Y.D. Soloveitchik* (Jerusalem: Mosad Harav Kook, 1984), vol. 1, pp. 59–72.

93. The analogy drawn by the Rav between halakhic concepts and the mathematical equations of physicists in regard to their relationship to reality has been subjected to criticism. See Rachel Shihor, "On the Problem of Halakha's Status in Judaism, *Forum*, Spring–Summer 1978, pp. 146–153; Lawrence Kaplan, "The Religious Philosophy of Rabbi Joseph Soloveitchik," *Tradition* 14, no. 2 (Fall 1973): 51–52; Singer and Sokol, "Joseph Soloveitchik," p. 236.

94. *Halakhic Man*, p. 29.

95. Ibid., pp. 44–45.

CHAPTER 5

Descriptive Hermeneutics in the Rav's Thought

The philosophic essay entitled *The Halakhic Mind* (written in 1944 and first published unchanged in 1986) is unique among the published works of Rabbi Joseph Dov Soloveitchik. In this work, unlike his other writings, which focus on the Halakha and the philosophy of Judaism, the Rav attempts an excursus into general philosophy with the presentation of a general theory of religion. He concludes his essay by arguing that Rabbinic Judaism with its developed Halakha is most fruitfully understood when viewed as an exemplification of this general theory.[1] Since the Rav makes no claim to have derived this theory from Jewish sources, the sole criterion for its acceptance by Jewish theology remains a pragmatic one: Does it indeed facilitate better understanding of aspects of Judaism? I have argued elsewhere that it does not.[2] However, in this paper I wish to consider an important corollary of this theory, namely, a special methodology which the Rav calls descriptive

This article originally appeared, in slightly different form, in *BDD: Journal of Torah and Scholarship* 18 (April 2007).

reconstruction and sometimes descriptive hermeneutics, which, according to the theory, plays a crucial role in the development of every theology and particularly that of Judaism.[3]

According to the theory, the God-man relationship expresses itself first and foremost in the subjective consciousness of the human being, descriptions of which fill the pages of the literature on religious experience. It has, however, a self-transcending tendency to evolve or flow into objective realms, such as ethical norms (theoretical) and rituals and acts of worship (practical). In Judaism, these would be found in the Torah, the theoretical in cognitive judgments and ethical norms, such as God exists, He is merciful, you should love your fellow man, and in the practical aspects such as ritual commandments and the Halakha. How is one to gain knowledge of the subjective order, which is in constant flux? Fortunately, so the theory goes, subjectivity and objectivity have a correlative nature, so that, given the right methodologies, we are able to reconstruct, from items on the objective concrete level, its subjective correlate.[4] Thus, the key to gaining access to the religious consciousness is the proper methodology, which the Rav calls descriptive reconstruction or, more generally, descriptive hermeneutics. By employing the word "descriptive," the Rav wishes to suggest that when seeking the meaning of a particular rule of the Halakha, one must not look to its antecedent conditions or to its consequences, but rather one must examine the Halakha itself. The Rav contrasts descriptive hermeneutics with the standard causal or genetic explanation, which is to focus on what went before. This the Rav associates with the "why" and "how" questions, whereas the method of descriptive hermeneutics asks the "what" question:[5] What is the religious act? What is its structure, context, and meaning?

I wish to suggest that what the Rav in this essay calls descriptive hermeneutics designates a general approach to the explication of the Halakha that the Rav had been following from the very beginning, independent of any commitment to a general theory.[6] That is to say, it simply constitutes a method of interpretation in which one attempts to relate the objective (Halakha) with the subjective (inner thoughts and feelings of the observer) in all sorts of interesting ways. This is sufficient to commend the approach. The term "reconstruction" is used by the Rav in this essay in order to show its significance in terms of the general theory. However, I shall argue that to see this approach as reconstruction rather than just hermeneutics or even as constituting a special methodology is to needlessly complicate matters.

To illustrate my point, consider the Rav's well-known analysis of the laws of mourning (*hilkhot aveilut*), which is typical of the Rav's approach.[7] The two initial phases of mourning according to the Halakha are *aninut*, which begins at death and ends with the burial, and *aveilut* (*shiva*), which commences after burial and continues for seven days. During the *aninut* period, the mourner may not pray or put on tefillin and is exempt from any positive halakhic obligations. In the *aveilut* phase, the mourner resumes his mitzvah obligations but does not go to work or leave the house and is forbidden to wash, wear shoes, or engage in sexual relations. The Rav then shows how these different practices, stipulated by the Halakha for each phase, correspond precisely to the deepest emotions and thoughts stirring in the religious consciousness during such an experience. Under the shock of the death of a loved one, man begins to doubt his own humanity. Frightened and confused, the mourner is thrown into despair and skepticism, feeling shorn of his dignity. Responding to the reality of human nature, the Halakha steps back and exempts the mourner from making benedictions and proclaiming the Shema, realizing that at such a moment he is not to be burdened with commandments and obligations.

The laws of *aveilut*, on the other hand, reflect Judaism's belief that man has control over his emotions and therefore commands him to say the *Kaddish*, through which "despair is turned into intelligent sadness and self-negation into self-affirmation." In it the mourner pledges to "carry on the work of our ancestors until salvation is achieved."[8] During the *shiva* the mourner receives condolences and words of comfort, and begins "to pick up the debris of his shattered personality." The Rav points out that the experiential substance of *aveilut* is actually repentance – *teshuva:* "a contrite heart, an atoning heart," and in many cases a feeling of guilt brought on by regret: Did we really appreciate our beloved departed while alive?"

At first glance this appears to be a good example of the Rav's method of descriptive hermeneutics. The first step is indeed descriptive rather than genetic and asks the "what" question: What do we notice about the structure and context of the laws of mourning with its different rules for the *aninut* and *aveilut* phases? Having registered the differences, we then delve into the human psyche at the moment of the death of a loved one to see if there is anything that in some sense can be related to the Halakha's exemption from mitzvot? At this point, it should be noted, there is nothing in the method itself which informs us what it feels like to be an *onen* or how the experience is related to the Halakha. Ultimately it really depends upon the introspective and analytic abilities of the inquirer and his powers of articulation. Having noticed the correspondence here between the objective (Halakha) and the subjective (the raw emotions and fragments of consciousness), how do we explain it? The Rav at one point says: "*Aninut* represents the spontaneous human reaction to death,"[9] which implies a sort of recognition and appreciation by the Halakha of man's condition. At another point the Rav asks "What is the *reason* behind the Halakha exempting the mourner,"[10] implying that somehow behind the formal dynamics of the Halakha there is a deliberate *intention* to address the mourner's psychological state, which seems to be a teleological explanation.

Yet another question arises: In regard to the *aninut* phase it is possible to say that the Halakha expresses or represents the subjective experience. However, in regard to the relation between the subjective and the objective in the *aveilut* phase, the Halakha does not simply express but rather assumes a normative role: "The Halakha *commands* the mourner…"; "Halakha *tells* man…"; "the

Halakha *warns* the mourner."[11] Here the relationship between objective and subjective seems more *impressive* than *expressive*. The Halakha is prescriptive, instructing the mourner how to handle his emotions and how to work through his grief. Here the objective seems primary, and the movement is from objective to subjective. There seems no desire here to reconstruct the *original* experience but rather to reform and redirect, functioning as a sort of valve.

Another illustration of the Rav's use of descriptive hermeneutics is his treatment of the laws of *tefilla* (prayer). The starting point once again is a halakhic ruling, this time of Maimonides, who, disagreeing with other decisors, rules that the mitzvah to pray every day is a positive command whose source is biblical rather than rabbinic. His source is the verse "And you shall serve Him with all of your heart" (Deuteronomy 11:13), to which the rabbis ask: "And what is that service which is of the heart? It is prayer" (Ta'anit 2:a). In explaining the importance of Maimonides's ruling, the Rav makes two points.[12]

First, by identifying the service of the heart as prayer and as the *service* of God par excellence, he explains, the rabbis are saying in effect that authentic worship of God is unthinkable as silent devotion without words expressing our thoughts and emotions of love and reverence for God. Second, it is inconceivable that God should wish to be worshipped by words alone. The Torah wishes to expose the experiential inner world of man's religious consciousness, the "heart," by having these embodied in the poetry and music of liturgy. By identifying prayer as the service of the heart, Judaism teaches that "words without thoughts never to heaven go."

Thus, prayer is a vital necessity for the individual as the way to make contact with God. However, the Rav goes further and identifies prayer with the essential human condition, which is one of insecurity and a sense of finitude.[13] Prayer thrice daily, whether of biblical or rabbinic origin, bears witness to one unalterable fact, which is that man is always in need. The act of prayer is the religious response to this need, to the human experience of distress, of "existential straits and narrowness." It was, of course, always understood that a person prayed regularly for his basic needs and also during those special times when he found himself in trouble – *et tzara*. But it was the Rav who pointed out that man was in a constant state of *et tzara*, experiencing existential loneliness, and that the initial "answer" provided by prayer was first and foremost fellowship with God.

In this case as well, we have the Rav making a brilliant connection between the objective and the subjective, between the Halakha and some of the most basic inner human experiences. But was this the result of the use of a particular method? True, it is only by asking the "what" question of a particular Halakha and by examining its context and source that the Rav is led to make the connection. Yet it is only the Rav's profound insight into the conflicted nature of the human condition which creates the possibility of a connection. And this revolutionary insight is unrelated to any method of exegesis. Once again, therefore, while connecting the objective to the subjective in this case deepens our understanding of the Halakha, it was not for the purpose of reconstruction.

Toward the end of the essay, the Rav sets out to demonstrate the importance of the method of descriptive hermeneutics in the field of Jewish philosophy by considering the problem of *ta'amei hamitzvot*, the rationalization of the commandments.[14] He claims that the method used by most of the medieval Jewish philosophers, and particularly by Maimonides in his *Guide*, is one that seeks causes and asks the "why" and "how" questions. This approach, says the Rav, is fundamentally flawed and is actually detrimental to religious thought,[15] whereas the method of descriptive hermeneutics, which asks the "what" question, is a more retrospective procedure, enabling one to describe the religious act and thus get to "excavate hidden strata" of the religious consciousness. According to the Rav, "Instead of describing, Maimonides explained; instead of reconstructing, he constructed."[16] Let us consider the distinction between these two approaches.

The Rav claims that in using causal explanation we must have recourse to an "alien factor, be it within or without the system."[17] But why, if it is within the system, is it an alien factor? If, for example, I ask a scientific question, "Why did the volcano erupt?", and I give the causes in terms of the antecedent conditions, in what sense could this be termed alien to science? We are asked to consider the following example: The question is asked: "Why did God forbid perjury?" and the answer given is "Because it is contrary to the norms of truth." The Rav argues that in giving the above causal answer, we have gone outside the domain of religion to the domain of ethics to find an answer. However, this follows only because the Rav chooses to define religion in the narrow terms of his theory, which is the subjective religious consciousness. Surely, however, in the case of Judaism, moral values, principles, and norms are an integral part of religion and part of the "system." Actually, therefore, the causal answer given above has considerable explanatory power, subsuming a moral norm under a moral principle and revealing precisely that God is concerned with morality.

The general approach of the medieval Jewish philosophers to the question of *ta'amei hamitzvot* was influenced by the assumption that God, irrespective of what else He may or may not be, is a rational being, which is to say that He acts purposively. Thus, in examining the commandments of the Torah, we naturally ask not for its causes but for its purposes. I submit that this assumption is still valid. Therefore, we ask first what *reason* God had for giving the Torah to Israel. And then we ask for the *purpose* of each individual commandment. These are not only appropriate questions, given God's rationality, but also necessary ones. For, says Maimonides, "There is a reason for every precept, although there are commandments the reason of which is unknown to us."[18] On this basis, Maimonides declares, "The general object of the Torah is twofold, the well-being of the soul and the well-being of the body."[19] What seems beyond dispute, for it is supported by Scripture itself, is that the general purpose of the Torah is in some sense for the good of man.[20]

Then, in a most unusual turn, the Rav asserts that while Maimonides in his *Guide*, as we have seen, employs the causal approach to the question of *ta'amei hamitzvot*, in his *Code* there is evidence that Maimonides "attempts to reconstruct the subjective correlative of the commandments," that is, he switches to the method of descriptive hermeneutics. As evidence of this surprising observation, the Rav proceeds to give three examples which we will now consider.

(1) The first example is what Maimonides says about the mitzvah of shofar in the *Code*:

> Although the blowing of the shofar on Rosh Hashana is a decree of Holy Writ, nevertheless there is a *remez* [hint] to it, as if saying: "Ye that sleep, bestir yourselves from your sleep, and ye that slumber, emerge from your slumber. Examine your conduct, return in repentance and remember your Creator."[21]

According to the Rav, the fact that Maimonides mentions that the shofar is a decree of Holy Writ indicates that he wishes to exclude any causal interpretation. Whereas his use of the term *remez* indicates that we are to examine the mitzvah itself for hints and allusions which may point towards subjectivity.[22] Thus, Maimonides "ignores any historical motives and interprets the shofar purely from a symbolic aspect"; namely, "that the shofar *alludes* to repentance and self-examination."[23]

Can all of this reasoning be attributed to Maimonides on the basis of his choice of words ("Holy Writ," *remez*)? A much simpler interpretation commends itself. Although, says Maimonides, contrary to other mitzvot, such as Shabbat, tefillin, and *sukkah*, where Scripture itself provides a reason for the practice,[24] the mitzvah of shofar on Rosh Hashana not only is not given a reason, it is not even clear that it is a shofar that is to be sounded on that day.[25] Yet we can find a hint (*remez*) in the mitzvah that it is a call to repentance. What is the nature of the hint that takes

Maimonides from the sound of the shofar to a call for repentance? In the words of the Rav, the shofar symbolizes or alludes to self-examination. But we are not told how, nor is there any magic formula to be found in the words descriptive hermeneutics which tell us how it is to be done.

There are different ways in which A can be said to symbolize B. Sometimes it can be simply a matter of stipulation and convention, like the arithmetic signs for addition and subtraction. Other times there may be something in the symbol which reminds us of the symbolizandum, like the cross for Christianity or the number of stars in the flag of the United States. Sometimes the two can be identical objects like the shofar of Rosh Hashana, which is said to symbolize the shofar of the ram of the *akeda*. In our case, however, the blowing of a horn is universally regarded as a signal and by its very nature is a wake-up call. It does not require much imagination to view the practice of sounding a shofar in an assembly in the synagogue on Rosh Hashana, the Day of Judgment, as a call to repentance. All of this is perfectly understandable without relating it to the subjective-objective dichotomy or to a process of reconstruction or to a special method.

Moreover, consider the way Maimonides himself explains the mitzvah of shofar in the *Guide*. "Rosh Hashana is a day of repentance in which we are stirred up from our forgetfulness. For this reason the shofar is blown on this day as we have shown in *Mishneh Torah* [the Code]." [26]

Contrary to what we would expect, Maimonides does not give us a causal or "how" approach to shofar but simply refers us to the explanation he gave in the *Code*. However, he does not say that the shofar symbolizes a call for repentance or alludes to self-examination but simply that the sounding of the shofar is a wake-up call and is the reason why God commanded that it be done on Rosh Hashana, a day of self-examination. Therefore, we have here a case where Maimonides, in treating the same mitzvah in the *Guide* and in the *Code*, gives the same explanation. In fact, what he does is to place what he said in the *Code* within the philosophic context of the *Guide*, as a commandment given by a purposeful and rational God, which converts his *remez* into a teleological explanation.

(2) For his second example, the Rav cites the last sentences in Maimonides's *Hilkhot Mikvaoth* (11:12).

> It is apparent that contamination and purification (*tuma ve-tahara*) are among the nonrational statutes (*chukim*).... Nevertheless a hint (*remez*) is contained in this. Just as he who directs his heart to become pure, once he immerses himself in the water he becomes pure, although no actual physical change took place, so he who directs his heart to purify his soul from sinful thoughts and even character traits, once he has made a firm decision to depart from such evil, [and] immerses himself in waters of knowledge, he becomes pure.

Here Maimonides finds in the purifying act of immersion (*tevila bemikva*) for ritual contamination a *remez*, something analogous, to purification from moral sin. Just as the *intent* to be purified is a necessary condition for purification, so too in the area of repentance, what is essential is a sincere resolve to change. For the Rav this is another example of how the method of reconstruction leads Maimonides to the subjective realm.[27]

However, the concept of reconstruction here appears to be utterly irrelevant. Is one to infer that there is something in the religious consciousness which is the original source of the laws of *tuma* and *tahara* or can in any way offer an explanation for the halakhic rules of *mikveh*? There seems to be a great difference between Maimonides's *remez* of the shofar and that of the *mikveh*. The sounding of the shofar on Rosh Hashana is in fact a call which awakens, and a call to repentance may indeed have been its intended purpose or at least a possible consequence. However, learning from the halakha of immersion for purification from *tuma* that sincere resolve can bring about repentance from sin (a teaching well known from other sources), is hardly the "essential significance" of the halakha of *mikveh*.

Again, there is nothing remarkable about Maimonides's finding in one of the most nonrational complexes of mitzvot an analogy to a basic principle in the dynamics of repentance. After all, the purifying role of water in human life is universally recognized.

(3) The Rav's third example deals with the Sabbath. He begins by citing Maimonides's treatment in the *Guide* (III:43).

> We know that Sabbath means rest. Hence one-seventh of man's life is spent in comfort, in rest, free from the worries and cares to which both great and small are subject. The Sabbath also perpetuates and forever confirms the very sublime idea, namely, faith in the divine act of creation.

I find this third example most problematic. The announced purpose of the three examples was to illustrate the methodological difference between the *Guide* and the *Code*, that in the *Guide* Maimonides chooses the causal method, while in the *Code* he employs the method of descriptive hermeneutics. Yet here the citation given by the Rav, which gives both types of explanations, is from the *Guide*. Furthermore, the reference to the *Code*, where we are supposed to find the retrospective explanation that the Sabbath symbolizes the act of creation,[28] yields only the following: "The Sabbath is the sign between the Holy One, blessed be He, and us, forever."[29] It is clear from the context in the *Code* why Maimonides mentions only the relational aspect of the Sabbath ("sign between...") and does not state of what the Sabbath is a sign, namely creation. For there he wishes to explain why desecrating the Sabbath is as grave as the sin of idolatry. His answer is that both precepts reflect the unique relationship between God and Israel. It is that rather than any adherence to a particular method that explains Maimonides's reference to the Sabbath merely as a sign between God and Israel in Hilchot Shabbat.

The Rav goes on to state that of the two ideas for the Sabbath given by Maimonides in the *Guide*, only the one that sees that precept as the incarnation of the mystery of creation is of symbolic strain[30] and illustrates the method of descriptive hermeneutics. Whereas the idea of the Sabbath as rest, according to the Rav, yields a purely pragmatic interpretation. This distinction seems to me entirely arbitrary. Both explanations can be seen as legitimate responses to the "what" question, as emanating from an objective study of the structure, the context, and the meaning of the mitzvah itself. The Sabbath means, and its *halakhot* prescribe, a day of rest not only in the physical sense but in the profoundest psychological sense of freedom from anxiety. This flows from the scriptural assertion that God rested on the seventh day, which implies a cessation of activity because the project had been completed. Thus, added to the passive sense of tranquility on the Sabbath is the fulfilling sense of achievement. Surely it is precisely the idea of the Sabbath as rest that puts us in touch with the subjective religious consciousness. Both explanations are appropriately given by Maimonides in the *Guide* because both are consistent with his stated understanding of the general object of the Torah as twofold: the well-being of the soul and the well-being of the body.[31] Both explanations can be interpreted as reasons why God commanded Israel to observe the Shabbat.

While in the text the Rav confines himself to the three aforementioned examples of the difference between the *Guide* and the *Code* in terms of Maimonides's choice of method in explicating the rationalization of the commandments, in one of his last endnotes he offers a most intriguing explanation of the famous controversy between Maimonides and Nachmanides over the interpretation of animal sacrifices in Judaism. Maimonides, using the causal method, sees in sacrifices a "concession in order to elevate the Jew from such forms of worship," while Nachmanides, using the retrospective reconstruction method, claims that animal sacrifice symbolizes the internal act of self-negation. As to be expected, the Rav judges the explanation of Nachmanides to be far superior philosophically.

I find it extremely difficulty to accept the explanation that this most radical view of Maimonides is just another instance of his application of his causalistic method. There is an unspoken premise which informs Maimonides's entire approach to this question. There are many indications in the Torah itself which led him to believe that animal sacrifices could not be the preferred mode of divine worship.[32] His starting question therefore was not: What is the reason behind animal sacrifices? but rather, Why did the moral Creator, God, in spite of its inappropriateness, command Israel to bring sacrifices? Maimonides's explanation that it was a concession follows quite reasonably and helps to explain those laws in the Torah that seem to circumscribe the practice in terms of place, time, and type of animals. Were it not for his consequential premise, Maimonides might well have adopted the explanation of Nachmanides in the form of a *remez*. However, having decided that the reason for animal sacrifices was merely therapeutic, there would be no point in showing that its practice might have some symbolic significance.

CONCLUSION

It would appear from our analysis that what has been called descriptive hermeneutics cannot be seen as a logically distinct method of interpreting the mitzvot of the Torah. The attempt to distinguish it from what is called the causal or genetic approach by associating each with a particular question – the causal approach asking the "why" or "how" question, descriptive hermeneutics asking the "what" question – does not work. To a certain extent, language usage does ascribe fairly distinct functions to these expressions of interrogation. To ask "why" of an act performed by an intelligent being is to ask for the reason or purpose. To ask "why" of a natural event or of something mechanical is to ask for its cause. The answer to the latter question will come in the form of something antecedent to the act or event in question, whereas the answer to a question of purpose or use will come in the form of consequences. "How" is not the same as "why" and focuses more on "in what way" or "by what means." Thus, after one receives an answer to his "why" question in terms of purpose, one can proceed to ask the "how" question.

It is misleading to argue, as does the Rav, that the reason for the failure of Maimonides to have his rationalistic interpretation of the commandments "prevalent in our world perspective" is that he was entirely caught up with the causalistic problem, as if what hurt Maimonides was his method or approach.[33] As I indicated above, Maimonides indeed asked the "why" question, but it was in the sense of seeking God's *reason* or *purpose* in giving the precepts.[34] For he was convinced, and properly so, that every precept has a reason, although we may not always be able to discover it. His problem was not one of method but rather that some of the particular purposes he gives in the *Guide* for the precepts do not seem plausible.

The assertion that the method of descriptive hermeneutics asks the "what" question is not at all clear. By itself, the word "what" has no definitive meaning and depends on the context and the words that immediately follow.[35] Possibly what the Rav meant was simply that in the descriptive approach we must first focus not on what preceded it or followed it, but on the halakha or mitzvah itself, asking: "What is it?" That is to say, we must concentrate on its structure, context, and meaning.[36] Such an interpretation of the descriptive method could possibly account for Maimonides's *remez* in connection with the shofar or with the act of immersion. However, in the case of the third example, it is difficult to see how his use of the descriptive method brought Maimonides to view the Sabbath as a symbol of the divine act of creation rather than as a day of rest and spiritual regeneration.

We stated at the outset that while not calling it by this name, the Rav throughout his work seems to have been using an approach that has the main features of what he has called descriptive hermeneutics, with results that have brought him worldwide recognition. He starts by attending to the objective features of the

Halakha in question and goes on to link it up to certain aspects of the religious consciousness. It should be noted, however, that this can be done only with certain kinds of precepts, and even then there is no guarantee of meaningful results.[37]

I am afraid that the profound teachings of the Rav cannot be attributed to the use of some special method. If that were the case, he would long ago have had successful imitators. We can follow the moves of the Rav, understand what he is doing, and stand in awe before the finished product. Yet somehow the connections he makes, which appear so reasonable after we hear them, would never have occurred to us. The late Pinchas Hacohen Peli labored long and hard to find the words to describe the special character of the Rav's thought.[38] The best he could come up with was that it was a form of the historical process of midrash, which has been used throughout our history as the way to bring two distinct worlds, the contemporary world and the Torah world, together. If indeed, as he claims, the philosophic work of the Rav is to be seen as a form of *derush* which the Rav employs not only as a methodological tool but as a substantive component,[39] then it must be granted that never before has this mode of thought reached such profound depths or been expressed with such literary beauty. For, after all, what is *derush*? It is the encounter of a human mind with the word of God "as a hammer that breaks up the rock,"[40] and the sparks that fly are the product of both the hammer and the rock. Of course, the word of God remains what it always was, but the caliber of the sparks depends upon the caliber of the individual mind involved in the encounter. In the case of the Rav it has never been higher.

ENDNOTES

1. Ibid., pp. 99–102.
2. Shubert Spero, "Rabbi Joseph B. Soloveitchik and the Philosophy of Halakha," in *Exploring the Thought of Rabbi Joseph B. Soloveitchik* (Hoboken, N.J.: Ktav, 1997).

3. *Halakhic Mind*, p. 98.
4. Ibid., p. 42.
5. Ibid., p. 86.
6. To the best of my knowledge, the Rav does not employ this term elsewhere in his writing.
7. *Out of the Whirlwind*, pp. 46–85.
8. Ibid., p. 5.
9. Ibid., p. 1.
10. Ibid., p. 3.
11. Ibid., p. 4.
12. pp. 84–86 "רעיינות על התפילה."
13. Purim Lecture of the Rav, pp. 138–139.
14. *Halakhic Mind*, p. 91.
15. Ibid., pp. 98–99.
16. Ibid. p. 92.
17. Ibid., p. 93.
18. Maimonides, *Guide for the Perplexed*, Friedlander trans. (New York: Dutton, 1942), p. 310.
19. Ibid, p. 312.
20. Deuteronomy 6:24, 10:12–13.
21. Hilchot Teshuva 3:4. Interesting that this observation of Maimonides appears in Hilchot Teshuva rather than in Hilchot Shofar.
22. *Halakhic Mind*, pp. 94–95.
23. The Rav seems to be suggesting that if we see the mitzvah as a symbol, it no longer carries the taint of being a causal explanation. This explains why in n. 103 the Rav tempers his strictures against Saadia's reasons for the shofar (p. 95), admitting "of course we may always interpret Saadia's ten reasons for the sounding of the shofar in a purely symbolic sense." Thus the distinction between the "why" and "what" questions does not seem to be that hard-and-fast.
24. *Shabbat:* "Remember the Sabbath day to keep it holy…for in six days the Lord made heaven and earth…and rested on the seventh day" (Exodus 20:8–11). *Sukkah:* "You shall dwell in booths seven days…that your generations may know that I made the children of Israel to dwell in booths when I brought them out of the land of Egypt" (Leviticus 3:42–43). *Tefillin:* "And you shall bind them for a sign upon thy hand" (Deuteronomy 6:8).
25. See Leviticus 23:23, where all it says is *zichron terua*.
26. *Guide*, p. 353. See also Zev Harvey, "Haarot al Harav Soloveitchik ve-ha-Pilosophiya ha-Rambanit," in *Emuna Bizmanim Mishtanim*, ed. Avi Sagi (Jerusalem; Merkaz Harav Herzog, 1996), pp. 103–104.
27. *Halakhic Mind*, p. 96.

28. Ibid., p. 97.
29. Hilchot Shabbat 30:15.
30. *Halakhic Mind*, p. 97.
31. *Guide*, p. 310.
32. There are many hints in the Torah which give the impression that animal sacrifices are not the most preferred form of divine worship: (1) Originally it was not considered moral for man to kill animals even for food (see Rashi on Genesis 9:3). Why then should a merciful God require the death of animals as a form of divine worship? (2) The anthropomorphic language used in connection with sacrifices, such as "And the Lord smelled the sweet savor" (Genesis 8:21) and "For he [the priest] offers the bread of your God" (Leviticus 21:8) is unusually gross and may create the impression that the offerings are God's food and that He is nourished by the sacrifices. (3) In the story of the *akeda* (the binding of Isaac) the ram replaces Isaac as the burnt offering on the altar (Genesis 22:13). While the human sacrifice is rejected and the animal sacrifice accepted, the dramatic juxtaposition of the two raises the question that just as God does not seek the death of His human creatures, so He should not seek the gratuitous death of his animal creatures. Is it not written: "and His tender mercies cover *all* of His creatures" (Psalm 145:9). (4) The fact that the major prophets condemn the bringing of sacrifices when not accompanied by a contrite heart and thoroughgoing repentance would indicate that sacrifices are of instrumental value only. (5) Israel is forbidden not only to serve other gods but to employ the *means* by which the pagan nations worship their gods (see Exodus 134:13, 17; Leviticus 20:23; Exodus 20:20). Since the pagan world used animal sacrifices, should not the Torah have ordained for Israel a more spiritual form of worship? (6) Israel has survived for centuries now without animal sacrifices and seemingly without spiritual diminution. Does this not suggest that prayer has successfully replaced animal sacrifices?
33. *Halakhic Mind*, pp. 92–93.
34. In one paragraph in the *Guide* (iii:26, Friedlander trans., p. 310) Maimonides employs the following different terms to say the same thing: "There is a *reason* for every commandment...serve a certain *aim*...there is a *cause*...serve a *purpose*...serve a *useful* object." I do not know if there are corresponding variations in the original Arabic.
35. A vulgar use of the single word "what" would be as a short version of "what did you say?" or "what is it?" or "what do you want?"
36. *Halakhic Mind*, p. 86.
37. For example, how would the method of descriptive hermeneutics be used to explain the laws pertaining to forbidden foods?

38. Pinchas Hacohen Peli, "Hermeneutics in the Thought of Rabbi Joseph B. Soloveitchik," in *Exploring the Thought of Rabbi Joseph B. Soloveitchik* (Hoboken, N.J.: Ktav, 1997), pp. 57–88. Pinchas Peli is the editor of the Rav's work *Al ha-Teshuva*.

39. Ibid., p. 72.

40. Jeremiah 23:29.

CHAPTER 6

▌▌▌ Belief in God

During the last three-quarters of the twentieth century, those engaged in theology and the philosophy of religion were divided into two main camps over the question of what constitutes the epistemological basis for belief in God.[1] Some continued in the tradition of the medieval Scholastics, placing primary emphasis on a rational demonstration and justification of religious faith. They ranged from latter-day Thomists, who continued to defend the classical proofs for the existence of God, to others who saw fit to augment the original proofs with new arguments gleaned from moral experience, psychology, and aesthetics. In this camp could be found those who, acknowledging the refutations of Hume and Kant, scaled down their claims from having proofs which yielded *certainty* to the cumulative weight of converging lines of evidence yielding a high degree of *probability*.[2] However, the element common to these approaches was the conclusion that belief in the existence of God has the character of inferred or discursive knowledge.

This article originally appeared, in slightly different form, in *Modern Judaism* 19 (1999).

That is to say, the belief is accepted by the mind as true after it is derived or deduced from particular facts of the empirical world.

The other camp, although it too could point to early and even biblical forerunners, was much later in articulating its position. Its adherents claimed that holding God to be an inferred entity was not only invalid but inappropriate and unnecessary. It was invalid because the proofs in their classical form had already been indisputably refuted by Hume and others. It was inappropriate because logical *certainty*, even if it could be achieved, was intellectually coercive and, as such, not compatible with the voluntary commitment to God demanded by religion. It was unnecessary because if those involved with this question properly analyzed their consciousness, they would find that they already believed in God! Instead, maintained those in the second camp, God in the first instance is not a cognitive abstraction that comes as the conclusion of a syllogism but is a living reality that is immediately encountered or experienced by the total person. While this position had always been implicitly held by mystics, saints, and prophets, it was now argued that the omnipresence of God implies an immanentism such that unmediated religious experience is open "to all who call upon Him in truth."[3] This encounter with the divine was not to be identified solely with the extraordinary but could be sensed "in, through, and under" some of the familiar aspects of our world.[4] Once encountered in personal experience, the existence of God becomes self-evident and no longer waits upon proofs, evidence, or arguments.

This new emphasis on consciousness or awareness was rooted in the post-Kantian understanding that there was a basic obstacle in the way of human cognition. "It seems that we experience consciousness only as consciousness of something and we encounter reality only as a reality of which we are conscious. This means that we cannot know reality independently of consciousness and we cannot know consciousness independent of reality."[5] It would seem, therefore, that in dealing with problems of human cognition we have no alternative but to start with that which is given, i.e., from the data given in consciousness.[6] It was hoped that an analysis or description of the contents of consciousness could answer the ontological question, i.e., the very meaning of being itself and, in connection with religion, the reality of that of which we are aware.

This very exciting and welcome development in philosophy of religion, which was encouraged and fructified by the existential and analytic schools, took place primarily among Christian theologians and among philosophers who chose to discuss Christianity as representative of religion in general.[7] While certain prominent Jewish thinkers, such as Martin Buber and Franz Rosenzweig, were influenced by and contributed to this development, their views on the question of the epistemological basis for belief in God were not explicitly given but only hinted it and had to be drawn from their general teachings.[8] Among the very few traditional thinkers thoroughly acquainted with this theological ferment and with its general philosophical presuppositions, one who perceived its relevance for Judaism and used its vocabulary to explicate his world-view was Rabbi Joseph Dov Soloveitchik.[9]

The Rav's position on the important question of the epistemological basis for belief in God is quite clear:

> The problem of evidence in religion will never be solved. The believer does not miss philosophic legitimization; the skeptic will never be satisfied with any cognitive demonstration.... in some cases homo religiosus is so overwhelmed by the import of his experience that he very distinctly perceives the reality of his object. He is fully conscious of the existence of the transcendental order.[10]

This statement appears as part of a pair of notes in an early work, and the problem is further alluded to in the notes of later works. In general, the Rav treats this issue only in passing and never at any length. He assumes it to be a given and goes on to develop his own program, which is to describe in great depth the subjective consciousness of man in his relationship to God by means of finely drawn ideal types. The Rav's style is essentially midrashic; he applies psychological insights and philosophical distinctions to the interpretation of biblical and rabbinic texts. Except for this early work, *The Halakhic Mind*, in which he eschews the midrashic style and in a very straightforward analytic manner traces out a position for halakhic Judaism based on epistemological pluralism, the Rav does not do philosophy systematically. Nevertheless, much of the material treated by the Rav is related to the philosophical question of evidence for belief in God in such a way as to make possible the presentation of a more fully drawn picture.

In this article, I wish to argue the following points:

(1) From the published work of the Rav there can be drawn a philosophically defensible position as to the epistemological basis of an individual's belief in Judaism.

(2) The Rav has recourse to a form of argumentation which, while not a proof, is an attempt to show the *reasonableness* of religious faith. This can be useful to those whose religious experience may not possess the clarity and intensity that make them self-evident manifestations of God.

(3) A description of the phenomenology of certain key religious experiences as are uniquely found in the writing of the Rav can be helpful to the many who earnestly seek God but do not know where to find Him.

*   *   *

We cited earlier the Rav's view that the religious person may have a direct perception of the reality of the transcendent order. Elsewhere the Rav repeats approvingly the question asked sarcastically by Kierkegaard when told that Anselm spent days in prayer so that he might be successful in finding a rational proof for the existence of God:

> Does the loving bride in the embrace of her beloved ask for proof that he is alive and well? Must the prayerful soul

144

clinging in passionate love and ecstasy to her Beloved demonstrate that He exists?"[11]

According to the Rav, what is fundamental is man's primordial yearning and seeking after God, which in certain periods of history took the form of reasoned expression, i.e., "proofs." The fallacy was to believe that out of our finite, time-bound existence we could build categories that could establish the truth of some infinite supersensible reality; that a road of some kind leads by means of logically ordered steps from features within the world to that which transcends it.[12] Whereas, in actuality, man perceives the Presence of God in an unmediated manner. Eternity is accessible to immediate experience and intuitive apprehension even as is the sensible.

A cause for confusion has been the fact that the same areas of experience have been hailed by thinkers in both camps as providing support for their respective positions. Thus three of Aquinas's Five Ways are forms of the cosmological proof, which starts with the brute fact of there being something rather than nothing, and that something is in the process of constant change. "From that point, one proceeds by means of certain assumptions and arguments to arrive at a conclusion that there must be some first cause, itself uncaused, some unmoved mover, and that is what everyone understands by God."[13] Yet contemplation of the same cosmos in all its incalculable vastness, overwhelming power, and qualitative color and variety, "in the flowering of the plant and the rushing of the tide," constitutes an experience in which "man gets a glimpse of the Truly Real hiding behind the magnificent cosmic facade."[14] The Rav claims that the rationalist philosophers abstracted certain features of these key living experiences – the cosmic experience, the ontic experience, and the experience of a loving, benign Providence – and transformed them into the cosmological proof, the ontological proof, and the teleological proof, respectively. Says the Rav: "When God is apprehended *in* reality, it is an experience. When God is comprehended *through* reality, it is just an intellectual performance."[15]

The Rav frequently relates the subjective consciousness of the Presence of God to what he calls "ontological awareness." In the classic philosophical tradition, this term refers to the self-evident proposition that there must be an existent whose existence is a consequence of its essence and therefore necessary and is wholly other. In terms of the individual religious consciousness, ontological awareness is an empirical sense by the individual of being a principal creation of God, permanently rooted in Him, grounded in Him. The individual has a definite consciousness of a relation: an experience of the self, his own mind, as the reflected splendor of the divine.

Says the Rav:

> If there is a world, if there is being at all...then there is a God who is the ground of existence and its source. If there is an "I," if man exists, then there is a living personal God who fills this self-awareness. It is impossible to think, to speak, and to deliberate about existence without living and feeling the source of existence.... the religious consciousness feels and lives God in the very midst of the ontological awareness. Without Him there is no existence, no reality.... The ontological awareness which evinces movement, direction, and volition is itself awareness of God. Man unites with God by seeking out the nature and quality of existence.[16]

Man's existential I-experience is interwoven with the awareness of communing with the Great Self whose footprints he discovers along the many tortuous paths of creation.[17]

The Rav identifies this ontological awareness with Maimonides's description of the commandment to know (rather than believe) that there is a primary existent (being) who brings into existence and is the ground of all other existents. "And all that is in heaven and earth and in-between do not exist except by the truth [the reality] of His existence...and the primary existent is God of the universe, master of all the earth."[18]

The Rav continues:

> Creation is the separation of something from the lap of the infinite. The ongoing existence of the world apart from God is impossible. The unmediated ontological awareness acknowledges there is no existence without God.
>
> Divinity is pure being who brings all into existence and encompasses all. God's relationship to the world is not summed up merely by the terms "cause and effect," but rather by a constant outpouring of being. The relative creature is hewn out of the Rock of the Absolute. There is no existence without God and no reality that is not grounded in God. Therefore, God draws after Himself the creature who feels the emptiness and dependence of his own finitude and yearns for an existence that is complete and whole.[19]

The Rav calls this the new doctrine that was revealed to Moshe in the disclosure *aheyeh asher aheyeh*, "I am that I am," which is interpreted by Maimonides to mean, "Behold, I am the necessary existant, and wherever you will find being, it is only a reflection of my infinite necessary existence."[20] This absolute Reality is God. While Maimonides calls this *"knowing God,"* the Rav points out that such apprehension "transcends the bounds of the abstract logos and passes over into the realm of the boundless, intimate, and impassioned experience where postulate and deduction, discursive knowledge and intuitive thinking, conception and perception, subject and object are one."[21]

It is important to probe further into the notion of ontological awareness and see how it relates to other aspects of the Rav's phenomenology of the religious consciousness. He says at one point:

> "To be" is not to be equated with "to work and produce goods..." "To be" is not identical with "to think..." "To be" does not exhaust itself either in suffering or in enjoying the

world of sense. "To be" is a unique in-depth experience and means to be the only one, singular and different, and consequently lonely.... The "I" is lonely, experiencing ontological incompleteness and casualness.[22]

Man experiences many kinds of situations that shake his sense of security and commensurability with the given world. He finds himself in predicaments that suddenly make him aware of his dependent, transient nature and the inadequacy of the empirical mode of being. We might call this a sense of "creature consciousness" in which the individual begins to estimate the self, the personal "I," as something not perfectly or essentially real, indeed a mere nullity.[23] In contrast, there is the sheer plenitude of being, that "awful majesty" and tremendum which he senses all around him as the "embracing, the enveloping, the encompassing," and identifies as the transcendent.[24]

The heart of the religious experience, then, would appear to be a series of discrete, antithetic, mutually interacting feeling-states, of which one successively becomes aware, but not necessarily in this order:

1. The plenitude of overwhelming power and beauty in the world in all of its complexity, vastness, lawlike uniformity, variety, novelty, and fecundity, of which I am an integral part.
2. I (and other human beings) am superior to much of all this by virtue of my being a "subject," conscious and appreciative of what I perceive, and for being able to communicate and relate to other human beings.
3. I am endowed with conscious freedom and the ability to adopt my own leading principles, organize my life around them, and transform given reality into something different. This ability generates within me an awesome sense of responsibility and great anxiety. "Judaism declares that man stands at the crossroads and wonders about the path he shall take. Before him is an awesome alternative – the image of

God or the beast of prey…and it is up to man to decide and choose."[25]

4. I am unique, alone, finite, and dependent. I know that I did not make myself or the world around me.[26] I am subject to a frightening "time-consciousness."

"I know of an endless past which rolled on without me and of an endless future which will rush on long after I am dead…. I began to exist at a certain point and my existence will end at another arbitrary point…. How accidental and insignificant am I!"[27]

5. I feel alienated and estranged and cut off from nature and society. I no longer experience a satisfying sense of belonging in the various collectives of which I am considered a member: family, nation, party, workforce, etc. I feel I am in exile.[28]

"I am a stranger on earth; hide not Thy commandments from me."[29]

6. I have a thirst for something but I know not what! "God reveals Himself to man in his very striving and yearning. Why does man not know tranquility? Why does he seek that which he cannot find in the world? It is God who is drawing man to Himself. Man is tired and exhausted. He is not satisfied with his life or his achievements. He is perplexed and gropes along the byways of his existence. That which he wants most he does not achieve. Yet failure in his search does not prevent him from continuing to seek. This 'thing' does not give him rest. It pushes him and pulls him with great force. What is the nature of this desire? This is nothing but a thirst for God, for communion with Him."

The ontological awareness becomes identical with the transcendental awareness.[30]

7. I am not my own but feel under some authority. I feel like one who owes something, like one who ought to be something which I am now not.[31]

"Know before Whom you will have to give account and reckoning."[32]

8. A consciousness of interacting and establishing relationship with a higher power that is experienced as objective and outside the self and endowed with volition, overwhelming power, majesty, holiness, and goodness. I sense this wholly other, in, through, and under things and events in my own life, in the history of Israel, and in the texts and observances of the Torah.[33]

Of these eight feeling-states, the first two seem fairly objective, familiar, and unexceptional reactions to man's place in the world he actually inhabits. Points 3 to 6 turn our attention to experiences that are completely subjective, that seem somewhat abnormal and rather unwarranted. It has been suggested that contemporary man's feelings of anxiety and alienation are the result of the dislocations, disorientations, and tensions of our modern age of bewildering scientific discoveries and transforming technologies.[34] The last two feeling-states (7, 8) are crucial in that, while also subjective, i.e., given to us in consciousness, they have a *dialogical* character. We have a distinct impression of being in contact with a reality that is not an extension of ourselves but "stands over against us." Much will depend upon the clarity and intensity of these two types of experiences. However, a crucial factor to be considered here is that in the relationship between man and God, as seen by the Rav, a distinction is to be noted between what happens when man takes the initiative and when God does.[35] In the former, man's efforts can take him only a part of the way. He may catch a glimpse of a transcendent power but will learn little of His nature or what He demands of man. But when man's experience goes beyond the consequences of his own efforts and he feels a Presence freely coming toward him, sometimes when he least expects or wants it, man is actually the recipient of a *self-disclosure,* a revelation of God.[36]

> The Revelation of God to man that occurred at Sinai and at different occasions to special individuals that were chosen by

Providence to be "good prophets" has, for all time to come, turned into a constant possibility, a part of Jewish consciousness. Man, throughout all generations, lives and feels revelation as he lives and experiences a natural turning to God.[37]

The logically restructured sequence of events is therefore to be seen as follows: Once a person has a sense of the Presence of the Absolutely Real as the Absolutely Holy and Supremely Good, there immediately follows a sense of the partial nothingness and impotence of all relative being. "Thou all – I nothing!" However, once man begins to reflect that he is still a positive entity, that "I am not utterly nothing, that I have been privileged to stand before God, to recognize Him and to be recognized by Him" – then he begins to experience his own *creatureliness*, i.e., "I am a part of and grounded in the Absolute Reality and the Supreme Goodness that makes possible my existence."[38] The paradox of my own existence becomes understandable – I am indeed far from home and on alien territory. Therefore do I experience these profound anxieties, nameless dread and threat of nonbeing. "Man in his chancing upon the contradictory and absurd in life apprehends the vision of a Hidden God."[39]

The response of the individual to his religious experience that takes the form of an all-embracing commitment is called by the Rav "the act of faith" and is described more in emotional and volitional than in cognitive terms.

> The *act* of faith is aboriginal, exploding with elemental force as an all-consuming and all pervading eudaemonic-passional *experience* in which our most secret urges, aspirations, fears, and passions, at times even unsuspected by us, manifest themselves. The *commitment* of the man of faith is thrown into the world of the in-depth personality and immediately accepted before the mind is given a chance to investigate the reasonableness of the unqualified commitment. The man of faith animated by his great experience is able to reach the

point at which not only his logic of the mind but even his logic of the heart and of the will, everything – even his own "I" awareness – has to give in to an "absurd" commitment. The man of faith is "insanely" committed to and "madly" in love with God.[40]

*   *   *

From a passage we partially quoted earlier it would appear that the Rav is employing the language of material implication, of the "if *p* then *q*" variety:

> (1) "*If* there is a world…and on this there is no one who has doubts…*then* there is a God who is the Rock and source of all being."
> (2) "*If* there is an I…and this too is known to man with certainty…*then* there is a living personal God who fills the "I"-awareness" (see n. 16).

In this type of conditional implication, one is saying that if the antecedent is true, then the conclusion must be true. Since we all agree that there *is* a world and that each of us possesses an "I" awareness, there must be a God! We shall soon examine whether this relationship does indeed hold between these two propositions. But does it not appear from this that the Rav, contrary to his stated position, is using arguments to demonstrate the existence of God; deriving the existence of God from the fact that there is a world!

What sort of argument do we have here? Statement (1) can be understood as a version of the cosmological argument: "If there is a world and that world is contingent, i.e., does not contain within itself any adequate explanation for its existence, then there must be a God who by definition is a necessary existant, and this explains the existence of the world." The validity of this argument has long been questioned because it rests on the principle of sufficient reason, which, according to Leibniz, applies to the metaphysical as well as to the empirical realm. But the Rav could hardly have had this in mind, because he rejects the very idea that belief in God rests upon inferential reasoning. Moreover, on this basis what possible interpretation could we give to statement (2), except perhaps to expand it into some form of the argument from moral experience.[41]

Perhaps the Rav's position can best be understood against the background of the teachings of Max Scheler, a thinker whom he cites favorably a number of times. While Scheler emphatically rejects the idea that there can be any proof for the existence of God, or for the existence of anything, for that matter, he acknowledges by inference from facts of the world that "every judgment requires justification."[42] However, "there are other kinds of justification which differ from proof."[43] This was precisely the new approach of phenomenology which rejected the premises of sensualist empiricism even with the modifications of Kant, and holds that not all knowledge and cognition is provable. As Scheler puts it, "while only the true is provable, it is not correct to say that only the provable is true."[44] On this view there is given to consciousness, true and genuine data which are asensual and are present to the mind before there is sensation. Among these are the following "data": space, time, quantity, value-qualities, unity of the self, and the unity of the world.[45] These last two concepts are significant for understanding the Rav's argument.

How to prove the existence of an external world, i.e., an environment existing independently of myself, of which I must take account, is, of course, an old and favorite philosophical conundrum. Descartes, with his methodological skepticism, was able to instill the doubt that perhaps we are all dreaming! Later Kant weakened our confidence that we even understand the terms "world" and "existence." Yet it is clear that no normal person, including the philosophers themselves, acts otherwise than on the assumption that there is "outside" a real, rugged, and intractable world! It is established for us by our experience, broadly conceived. But how do we justify this belief? Here is the conclusion of a philosopher, after carefully reviewing the entire history of the problem:

> If someone were to ask, "How do you know of the world's existence or that the statement 'the world exists' is true! Is it by sense experience or by conceptual analysis?" I should have to reply that it is neither. The knowledge of the existence of the world is nevertheless part of ordinary experience.... It is not the outcome of a process of reflection or inference.... We have no common name for it; we might call it "cosmic consciousness." It is primary and not reducible to any other type of experience.[46]

The problem of the self is an equally venerable and stubborn philosophical puzzle. What we start out with is again an undeniable part of human experience (if Descartes is to be believed, the *most* undeniable part). One becomes conscious of an "I" as pure subject that is most distinctively myself, seems to be an abiding center of consciousness experienced as agent, will, desire, and striving, and constitutes the seat of my identity, continuity, freedom, and responsibility. Yet, can we prove its existence? Recall the famous response of David Hume:

> There are some philosophers, who imagine we are every moment intimately conscious of what we call our Self; that we feel its existence and its continuance in existence; and are certain, beyond the evidence of a demonstration, both of its perfect identity and simplicity...nor is there any thing of which we can be certain if we doubt of this.... For my part, when I enter most intimately into what I call *myself*, I always stumble on some particular perception or other...I never can catch *myself* at any time without a perception, and never can observe any thing but the perception.[47]

Once again we are confronted by an important aspect of our regular experience which seems to be the manifestation of something real but whose existence we are unable to prove. How do we justify our ongoing belief in the self? Here is the conclusion of a modern theologian:

> The answer is that the self, far from being a mysterious reality behind the scenes, is in fact what we know best. But we know it in a *very special way*, in the very fact of *being it* and having the experiences we do have including the activities we ourselves initiate.... We are aware of ourselves in the radical sense which is involved in our *being* ourselves.[48]

What both of these men are saying is that in these two special cases we are unable to "prove" anything, nor do we have a need to do so. In both of these cases, we have direct knowledge, and they are given to our consciousness as primary data. What is the connection between these two classical epistemological problems and the question of the existence of God? Once again, Max Scheler:

> Just as the existence of an external world or the existence of a unitary self cannot be proven and are considered primary data albeit asensual and as present before the sensations transmitted via the senses of a living being – so too the sphere of the phenomena disclosed to the mind by the religious act. The sphere of the divinity and of the general reality it contains is a primary datum which it is impossible to derive from anything else.... Hence there can be no question of proving the existence of the entire religious sphere by inference from other facts of the world, as little question as there is of "proving" the existence of the external world, of the self or of one's fellow creatures. To insist on such proofs is to misconstrue in principle the limitations of proofs and the extent of their validity.[49]

Let us return to the statements of the Rav. It will be noticed that in statement (1) above he includes the parenthetic phrase, "and in this there is no one who has any doubts," and a similar phrase in statement (2). Why is it necessary to emphasize that, in connection with the unity of the world and the unity of the self, this reality is accepted by all? If the Rav intended here an inferential argument (if p then q; p is true, therefore q is true), then the fact that "no one has any doubts about p" is irrelevant. We suggest, therefore, that the Rav, like Scheler, is drawing an analogy between conditions of reasonableness considered acceptable in regard to the existence of an external world and a unitary self, on the one hand, and those which should obtain in regard to the existence of God, on the other. In regard to both of the former, we have no demonstrative proof and yet the belief in their existence is held with certainty. So too, then, in regard to the existence of God, the religious experience itself should be adequate.

But what are the features of sense experience of an outside world and of the "I" awareness, in virtue of which we are prepared to consider them real? A bit of reflection will suggest two considerations:[50]

1. The involuntary or compelling character of the experience. That is to say, try as we may to disbelieve, the sense data reporting an outside world constantly flood in upon us with great clarity and intensity. Similarly, in connection with "self-awareness," our sense of an abiding core of self-identity over the years is not something we choose but is prerequisite to being a person.
2. We can act successfully in terms of that belief. Our belief is not contradicted by further experience but is confirmed and strengthened.

Does religious experience of the type we are discussing exhibit these two characteristics? Certainly what the Bible tells us about some of its main figures fits the pattern. For Moshe, Amos, and Jeremiah, the call of God has a compelling quality.[51] "God is known as a dynamic will interacting with their own wills; a sheerly given personal reality."[52] In the words of Heschel: "Prophetic revelation was not merely an act of experience but an act of being an object of experience, of being exposed to, called upon, overwhelmed and taken over by Him who seeks out those whom He sends to mankind."[53]

Although the God-man relationship does not destroy man's freedom and the Sinai covenant was "the result of free negotiation," nevertheless, according to the Rav, the rabbis introduced an element of coercion because "covenantal man feels overpowered and defeated by God even when he appears to be a free agent of his own will."[54] In regard to the second feature, the careers of Abraham, Joseph, and David illustrate how, in the course of their long and eventful lives, their further experiences ultimately sustain and confirm their religious beliefs.

It follows, therefore, that for the individual today, the question of whether it is reasonable to believe that God exists and to act accordingly depends upon the extent to which the above two characteristics are part of his experience. So that this becomes a judgment which only the individual can make on the basis of his own experience and the experiences of his community. At this point we must distinguish between what the so-called argument from religious experience, in which God is inferred as the cause of the special experiences described by mystics all over the world, and the approach we have sketched above and which we attribute to the Rav. The entire question of the rationality of religious beliefs must be reformulated.[55]

Historically speaking, philosophic proofs of God did not come about in order to create belief but to support and confirm what the person already believed. For the question generally arises for someone who already has had religious experiences and participates in religious life. So that the question has to be judged separately in each case, for we are judging not the reasonableness of propositions but the reasonableness of people and their behavior. Therefore, the issue is whether this particular individual, given the distinctive religious experience he claims to have had, is entitled as a rational person to believe as he does, to trust his own experience and proceed to live on the basis of it. This is consistent with the Rav's view of the role of the intellect in the religious act: "The intellect does not chart the course of the man of faith: its role is an *a posteriori* one. It attempts ex post facto to retrace the footsteps of the man of faith."[56]

∗   ∗   ∗

In light of the above, discussions about belief in God, at least initially, should not focus on evidence or arguments but should employ the vocabulary of seeking and searching, discovery and finding. Indeed, prophets and psalmists frequently exhorted the people in these terms:

> But from there you will *seek* the Lord thy God, and thou shalt *find* Him if thou *search* after Him with all thy heart and with all thy soul.
>
> For thus saith the Lord to the House of Israel: *Seek* me and live.
>
> *Seek* the Lord while He may be found, call upon Him while He is near.
>
> Let the heart of them rejoice that *seek* the Lord; Seek ye the Lord and His strength, *seek* His face continually.[57]

It is precisely in this context that the teachings of the Rav have much to contribute. At first glance this statement would appear to be quite strange. After all, the bulk of the Rav's philosophical writings focus upon the dialectical intricacies of the religious consciousness of the halakhic man and the halakhic mind, the man of faith and the highest reaches of *devekut* – cleaving unto God, all matters that would appear to concern those who are already deeply immersed in religious life. Yet let us look back and reconsider the various elements that make up the ontological awareness. In particular, let us reexamine items (3) to (6). These are states of consciousness of whose significance the literary public (and later the philosophers) started to become aware in the early 1930s. This trend was accompanied by a new emphasis on subjectivity and the importance of the qualitative aspects of life. It was followed by a new understanding of man, his condition and destiny, and was associated with a philosophic approach loosely called existentialism. On this view some of man's most persistent dreads and anxieties, antinomies and polarities, heretofore perceived as consequences of radical social change or symptoms of psychic disorders, were now recognized as natural and inevitable features of man's unique dialectical existence. This new view of the human predicament received popular expression in literature and the arts, and seemed to reflect experiences that were widespread. Since at that time existentialism was not a body of doctrine but a way of doing philosophy, it developed into very diverse points of view. At one end of the spectrum existentialism was conjoined with atheism, and at the other it was adopted by a variety of Catholic and Protestant theologians.[58] While early accounts of existentialism were quick to point out the biblical affinities of the new approach, liberal Jewish thinkers largely rejected the new trend.[59] However, as far back as the early 1940s, the Rav had already demonstrated an incisive grasp of the underlying philosophical principles of the existentialist approach and was using it in his explication of various aspects of Judaism.[60]

According to the Rav the four core feeling-states we described above in statements (3) to (6) are part of the primary data of the human consciousness and, as such, are existential experiences in that they reflect the unique nature of man's existence. Furthermore, as components of man's ontological awareness they are, in one way or another, intimately bound up with a consciousness of the Presence of God as ultimate reality and ground of all being. The Rav stands alone among Jewish thinkers in his ability to describe these feeling-states with the vocabulary of a poet, the analytic skill of a psychologist, and the emotional fervor of personal experience.

I wish to suggest that the identification and in-depth analysis of these feeling-states can be helpful as part of a fully balanced program designed to assist people who are seeking God. There are many who at one or another point in their life may experience estrangement, time-consciousness, or nameless dread, and are disturbed by this. However, unable to find the cause, they succeed, for long periods of time, in repressing such feelings by getting more deeply involved in the myriad details of the many facets of modern everyday life. I imagine they would be relieved to learn of the existential significance of their disturbing experiences.[61] Even young people who at present find life quite satisfying and exciting, having learned of the possibility of estrangement and alienation through art and literature, are eager to talk about the nature of the "human predicament."

It might be asked: Do we have the right to dampen the happy enthusiasm of people who are looking forward to life as a "bowl of cherries"? Indeed, I would answer that we have an *obligation* to do so. As William James put it: "The evil facts of life may be the best key to life's significance and possibly the only openers of our eyes to the deepest level of truth."[62] The image of the individual perfectly at ease with himself and the world, well-adjusted and self-satisfied, is the image of one living a lie. Deep within biblical man is a certain uneasiness that pervades his entire being and emanates from his sense of finitude, feebleness, and imperfection in the Presence of God.[63] It has been suggested that "Man is the question to which God is the answer."[64] It follows, therefore, that to him for whom man does not pose a question, God may be a superfluity! Thus, along with participation in the positive activities of Judaism – prayer, study, mitzvah-observance in line with the dictum of "taste and see that the Lord is good" – we can help those who seek God by sharing with them the insights of the Rav (and other existentialists) so as to prepare them to understand and appreciate the nature and the role of these core-experiences which are keys to our identity as creatures of God.

For those who have never associated Judaism with feelings of estrangement and alienation, and resist incorporating into their religious consciousness any of the darker aspects of human experience, let me close this article by pointing to two rabbinic sources which seem to have anticipated the existential approach.

The first is an effort to deal with the unusual spirit of Koheleth, who poses a disturbing question: "What remains to a man from all his work which he toils under the sun…a generation comes and a generation goes but the world remains forever?"[65]

So alien does Koheleth seem to the general spirit of Judaism that there were thoughts to remove the book from general circulation.[66] The rabbis, however, in a striking midrashic comment, opened wide the possibility of a new understanding: "'Under the sun,' there is nothing that remains but 'above and beyond the sun,' there is surely that which remains."[67]

That is to say, Koheleth's description of the human condition as transitory, futile, unjust, and empty may very well be valid, taken as life lived "under the sun," i.e., in purely naturalistic terms, as if life in the here-and-now exhausts all possibilities. If one has not discovered the transcendent, senses nothing beyond the physical universe, nor perceives any metaphysical anchor for values, then indeed, "all is vanity." However, if one analyzes one's ontological awareness to its very depths – "beyond the sun" – then the same circumstance we call life "takes on a new meaning."[68] As one discovers God, says Koheleth at the very end, one realizes that "*this* is the whole man."[69] For the human being, self-fulfillment lies in self-transcendence.

In support of the idea that man has a persistent, indeterminate thirst which, upon analysis, turns out to be a thirst, a yearning for holiness, for true fellowship, for God, consider the following midrash in a verse in Koheleth:

All the labor of man is for his mouth and yet the soul is not filled.[70]

This may be compared to a provincial who married a princess. Were he to present her with the finest things in the world, it would not satisfy her. For she is the daughter of a king [and accustomed to the special quality of life at a royal court]. So it is with the soul of man. Even if all the delicacies in the world are brought before her, it is as nothing. This is because the soul originates in heaven.[71]

Here we have the suggestion that the reason for man's unease, his unsatisfied yearning and sense of being everywhere a stranger and an outsider, has something to do with his special origin, his unique nature as a human being created in the image of God, which may hint at a special destiny.

It is reasonable to assume that this midrash served as the basis for the following teaching of Saadia Gaon:

> I feel furthermore that none of God's creatures known to me feel secure and tranquil in this world, even when they have reached the most exalted ruling position and the highest station therein. Now this feeling is not something natural to the soul. It is due rather to the consciousness of the fact that there is reserved for it an abode that is superior to all the excellencies of its present dwelling. That is why it yearns for that abode and why it looks forward longingly to it. Were it not so, the soul would have felt secure and have been at rest.[72]

Note that Saadia does not offer his teaching as a commentary on a scriptural verse but as an empirical observation based on his own personal experience. Evidently he feels his sampling is representative enough to warrant a universal proposition: no matter how fulfilled in all other ways, the human being will not experience complete security and tranquility.

In a second step, Saadia offers an explanation for this empirical phenomenon: Deep in man's consciousness is an intuition that he is capable of altogether different sorts of experiences, and destined for some higher mode of existence. It is for this that he subconsciously yearns and longs, precluding any abiding sense of security and tranquility. Here Saadia lays the theological groundwork for a new appreciation of the content of man's consciousness in which we may find traces of man's mysterious origin as a creature formed in the image of God; an appreciation which would first find its fullest expression in our own day in the works of the Rav.

ENDNOTES

1. See John Baillie, *Our Knowledge of God* (New York: Oxford University Press, 1939); Jerry H. Gill (ed.), *Philosophy and Religion* (Minneapolis: Prometheus Books, 1968), pts. 1 and 5; Donald A. Wells, *God, Man and the Thinker* (New York: Random House, 1962) chaps. 6 and 9.

2. David E. Trueblood, *Philosophy of Religion* (New York: 1957), pp. 59–78.

3. Psalm 145:18.

4. Baillie, *Knowledge of God*, p. 178.

5. Quentin Lauer, *The Triumph of Subjectivity* (New York: Fordham University Press, 1958). pp. 6–7. See also F.H. Heinemann, *Existentialism and the Modern Predicament* (New York: Harper, 1958), pp. 53–54.

6. This approach, associated with phenomenology, holds that consciousness is a kind of being which an object of knowledge has in its being known.

7. See John Macquarrie, *Twentieth-Century Religious Thought* (London: SCM Press, 1963), chaps. 19 and 22; David E. Roberts, *Existentialism and Religious Belief* (New York: Oxford University Press, 1957).

8. Regarding Franz Rosenzweig, the following may be taken as authoritative: "According to the structure of *The Star of Redemption*, it seems as if the existence of God—that is, of the personal God—is a self-evident fact that needs no proofs…. But he still does not give us the experience, on the basis of which we cognize the existence of God and his personal character." Julius Guttmann, *Philosophies of Judaism* (Philadelphia: Jewish Publication Society, 1964), p. 376.

   "The central fact around which the current of Rosenzweig's thought winds in ever-widening circles is the one of Divine revelation. That God speaks to man on occasion, he asserts, is a fact which cannot be evaded or explained away…. Yet it is true that Rosenzweig never gives a detailed account of the experience of revelation as he had known it." Jacob Agus, *Modern Philosophies of Judaism* (New York: Behrman House, 1941), p. 158.

   Martin Buber had a large non-Jewish readership and is influential among Christian theologians. He too believed that the basis of religion is in actual experience, a psychic event. Man encounters reality only when he adopts an "I-Thou" attitude to the world, to others, and ultimately with the Eternal-Thou that is God. The reality is to be found in *relation*; in the "between." Buber's argument is based primarily on his own metaphysical intuition. His position has been called "a mild form of mysticism" (Agus, p. 267). Like Rosenzweig, Buber speaks much of revelation, which he describes as "neither experience nor knowledge, comes not with a specific content but as the self-communication of 'Presence as power' and the inexpressible confirmation of meaning. In every sphere in its own way, through each process of becoming that is present to us we look out towards the fringe of the eternal *Thou*, in each we are aware of a breath from the eternal *Thou*; in each we address the eternal *Thou*." Martin Buber, *I and Thou*, trans. Ronald Gregor Smith, 2nd ed. (New York: Scribner's, 1958), p. 6.

While in a sense the philosophies of Buber and Rosenzweig uphold the Jewish view of God, neither presents a philosophy of Judaism. Unlike the approach of the Rav, the Jewish religion did not serve as the presupposition for Rosenzweig's or Buber's thought. In both cases their philosophies emerged out of their own experience which they believed found expression in Judaism (Cf. Guttmann, *Philosophies of Judaism*, p. 372.)

9. Two other traditional Jewish thinkers who incorporated this new approach into their presentation of Judaism were Eliezer Berkovits, in his *God, Man and History* (New York: Jonathan David, 1959) and Abraham Joshua Heschel, in his *Man Is Not Alone* (New York: Farrar, Straus & Giroux, 1951) and *God in Search of Man* (New York: Farrar, Straus & Giroux, 1955). See the interesting article by B. Ish-Shalom (in Hebrew) on the Rav as a postmodernist in comparison to R. Samson R. Hirsch and Rav Kook, in "Rabbi J.D. Soloveitchik and Neo-Orthodoxy," in *Faith in Changing Times*, ed, Avi Sagi (Jerusalem, 1996).

10. *The Halakhic Mind*, p. 118, n. 58. It is interesting to note that Heschel held the same view: Thus, "the certainty of the realness of God does not come about as a corollary of logical premises, as a leap from the realm of logic to the realm of ontology, from an assumption to a fact. It is, on the contrary, a transition from an immediate apprehension to a thought . . . from being overwhelmed by the presence of God to an awareness of His existence" (*God in Search of Man*, p. 120). "There is a certainty without knowledge in the depth of our being that accounts for our asking the ultimate question" (*God in Search of Man*, pp. 121–22).

11. "The Lonely Man of Faith," p. 32; "From Thence Ye Will Seek," p. 8 (Hebrew).

12. "From Thence Ye Will Seek," p. 69, n. 3.

13. See Rem B. Edwards, *Reason and Religion* (University Press of America, 1972), pp. 254–271.

14. Ibid., pp. 30–31.

15. Ibid., p. 32 n.
16. "From Thence Ye Will Seek," pp. 6, 7, 9.
17. "Lonely Man of Faith," p. 18.
18. Hilchot Yesodei ha-Torah 1:1–6.
19. "From Thence Ye Will Seek," pp. 29, 69 n. 4.
20. Exodus 3:14.
21. "Lonely Man of Faith," pp. 32–33 n.
22. Ibid., p. 27.
23. *Halakhic Man*, p. 68. See also Rudolf Otto, *The Idea of the Holy* (New York: Oxford University Press, 1958), p. 21.
24. James Collins, *The Existentialists* (Chicago: Regnery, 1952), p. 111.
25. Soloveitchik, *Halakhic Man*, p. 109.
26. Psalm 100:3.
27. "Lonely Man of Faith," pp. 45–46. In *Halakhic Man* the Rav speaks of another "collective consciousness of time" possessed by the Jewish people (p. 117).
28. "Lonely Man of Faith," p. 25. Joseph D. Soloveitchik, "The Synagogue as Institution and Idea," in *Thoughts and Appreciation* (Jerusalem, 1981), pp. 102–103 (Hebrew).
29. Psalm 119:19.
30. "From Thence Ye Will Seek," p. 8.
31. Baillie, *Knowledge of God*, p. 182.
32. Avot 3:1.
33. William James, *The Varieties of Religious Experience* (New York, 1925), p. 465. Otto, *Idea of the Holy*, pp. 10–11. See also Rivka Horvitz, "Rabbi Soloveitchik and Religious Experience," in *Faith in Changing Times*, pp. 45–75 (Hebrew).
34. See Heinemann, *Existentialism and the Modern Predicament*, pp. 14–29.
35. "From Thence Ye Will Seek," pp. 14–15.
36. In the words of Max Scheler, in *On the Eternal in Man*, trans. Bernard Noble (London: SCM Press, 1960), p. 250, "all knowledge *of* God is knowledge *from* God."
37. "From Thence Ye Will Seek," p. 18. Once again Scheler's terminology is helpful in explicating the teachings of the Rav: "Revelation as such is simply the manner in which a reality of the Divine character is given to human consciousness. There is a difference between natural and positive revelation. The former is general, symbolically mediated through things, events and orders of the natural reality. In positive revelation, the Divine announces Itself through the medium of the *word* and through persons" (*On the Eternal*, pp. 161, 254).
38. See Scheler, *On the Eternal in Man*, pp. 161, 167.
39. Soloveitchik, *Halakhic Mind*, p. 3.

40. "Lonely Man of Faith," pp. 60–61.
41. See John Hick, *Arguments for the Existence of God* (New York, 1971), chap. 4. See also Trueblood, *Philosophy of Religion*, pp. 106–118.
42. Scheler, *On the Eternal in Man*, pp. 256, 258.
43. As Scheler points out, it was Aristotle who already said in his *Ethics* that we could only demand the kind of justification that the situation allows.
44. Scheler, *On the Eternal in Man*, p. 258.
45. Ibid., p. 257.
46. Milton K. Munitz, *The Mystery of Existence* (New York: Appleton-Century-Crofts, 1965), pp. 78–79.
47. David Hume, *A Treatise of Human Nature*, bk. 1, pt. IV, sec. VI. See discussion in Alburey Castell, *The Self in Philosophy* (New York: Macmillan, 1965).
48. Hywel D. Lewis, *The Self and Immortality* (New York: Macmillan, 1973), p. 43.
49. Scheler, *On the Eternal in Man*, pp. 257, 258.
50. See Hick, *Arguments for the Existence of God*, p. 110.
51. Amos 3:8, Jeremiah 20:9.
52. Hick, *Arguments for the Existence of God*, p. 112.
53. Heschel, *God in Search of Man*, p. 419.
54. "Lonely Man of Faith," p. 29 n.; also pp. 60–61 n.
55. Hick, *Arguments for the Existence of God*, pp. 109–110.
56. "Lonely Man of Faith," p. 60. This would seem to be in line with the following statement of Cook Wilson, as quoted by Baillie (*Knowledge of God*, p. 240): "The true business of philosophy seems to be to bring the belief to a consciousness of itself."
57. Deuteronomy 4:29, Amos 5:5, Isaiah 55:6, 1 Chronicles 16:10.
58. See Macquarrie, *Twentieth-Century Religious Thought*, p. 351.
59. See Eugene Borowitz, "Existentialism's Meaning for Judaism," *Commentary*, November 1959, pp. 414–420.
60. See Shubert Spero, "The Meaning of Existentialism for Orthodoxy," *Perspective* 1, no. 2 (Winter 1959–60): 25–33; idem, "Is Judaism an Optimistic Religion?" *Tradition* 4, no. 1 (Fall 1961) and in chap. 2 of this volume. Also, Zvi Kolitz, *Confrontation* (Hoboken, N.J.: Ktav, 1993).
61. Two popular books in the 1950s which traced the broader cultural background of existentialism were *The Outsider* (Boston: Houghton Mifflin, 1956) by Colin Wilson and *Irrational Man* (New York: Doubleday, 1958) by William Barrett.
62. James, *Varieties of Religious Experience*, p. 163.
63. See Barrett, *Irrational Man*, p. 63.
64. Frederick E. Greenspahn (ed.), *The Human Condition in the Jewish and Christian Traditions* (Hoboken, N.J.: Ktav, 1986), pp. 26–30.

65. Eccles. 1:3–4.
66. Shabbat 30.
67. Midrash Koheleth Rabbati 1:4.
68. "When we study the process of religious regeneration, we see that one frequent change for the subject is a transfiguration in his eyes of the face of nature. A new heaven seems to shine upon a new earth. In melancholiacs there is usually a similar change in the reverse direction. The world now looks remote, strange, sinister, uncanny. For some this experience results in profound astonishment! This strangeness cannot be! What then is real? Where do I really belong? 'An urgent wondering and questioning is set up' – to which a religious solution may be found" (James, *Varieties of Religious Experience*, p. 151).
69. Ecclesiastes 12:13.
70. Ecclesiastes 6:7.
71. Midrash Koheleth Rabbati 6:7; see different version in Yalkut Shimoni.
72. Saadia Gaon, *The Book of Beliefs and Opinions* (New Haven: Yale University Press, 1948), pp. 324–325.

CHAPTER 7

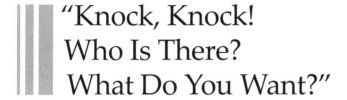

"Knock, Knock!
Who Is There?
What Do You Want?"

*K*ol *Dodi Dofek* is a unitary composition in terms of the Rav's
style of *darshanut* and his particular purpose at the time. Included
therein, however, are independent treatments by the Rav of three
basic subjects of Jewish theology: theodicy, the nature of God's
covenant with the people of Israel, and the meaning of history.
What follows will focus on the last subject.

It is generally agreed that the biblical God manifests Himself
in history and that the divine plan for man plays itself out within
that framework. However, as generally conceived by the sages, the
main components of God's plan had already come to pass by the
time of the destruction of the Second Temple. The exilic condition had consigned the Jewish people to a sort of limbo in which
its full-time task was struggling to maintain its physical survival
and Jewish identity. Thus, up to the beginning of the nineteenth

---

This article originally appeared, in slightly different form, in *Tradition* 39
(2006).

century, conventional rabbinic wisdom held that nothing of significance was to be expected in history before the occurrence of the radical and clearly recognizable eschatological events associated with the redemption, with all its restorative and utopian elements.

In later writings (e.g., *Chamesh Derashot*) the Rav described the personal and often painful spiritual journey that brought him into the ranks of organized religious Zionism. It was, he said, based upon his belief in two principles: (1) that the successful establishment of the State of Israel was a wondrous act of God expressing His *chesed* toward His people; and (2) that the Torah is demanding and capable of application not only in the area of the family but in the wider communal and national arena that a sovereign Jewish state would make possible. It is important to note that what impelled the Rav in 1956 to look back over the previous eight years, and to restate in the dramatic form made possible by his *darshanut* the religious significance of the establishment of the Jewish state and the response it should have evoked, was the mortal danger that the *yishuv* faced at that time. It was clear to the Rav that the Arab enemy had not given up and was intent upon the total destruction of the Jewish state. Had American Jewry, and among them the Orthodox, utilized the previous eight years to populate the Negev and the Galilee with educated, religious families, the state would have been much more secure and its ties to tradition so much stronger. In this essay, the Rav adds a dynamic temporal element to the Zionist equation: The window of opportunity presented by the state for *yishuv* and *binyan haaretz* may not remain open for long! Furthermore, our moral responsibility for our people in the *yishuv* is absolute. We who did not do enough for our people during the Holocaust must now do everything in our power to aid our brethren in *Eretz Yisrael*.

What shall we say to this, fifty years later?

The declaration by the Rav that the establishment of the State of Israel was "God's creation" and a "miraculous act of *chesed*" was an insightful and courageous reversion to the biblical view that

God remains active in history. But in this view the Rav had been preceded by R. Tzevi Hirsh Kalischer (1795–1874) who – writing in 1862[1] and using the same metaphor – declared that the emancipation, the rise of nationalism in Eastern Europe, and changes in the political situation in Palestine constituted "the knocking of the Beloved" on the doors of Jews everywhere. This "knocking" signified that the time had come to take a proactive role in settling Eretz Yisrael. Kalischer argued that it was God acting in history who had created the conditions that made it possible for Jews to return. Therefore, Jews were now obligated to leave the Exile and return home.[2]

Both Kalischer and the Rav saw the hand of God in the natural events of their own day, but they differed as to which element within those events implied divine agency. For the Rav it was the improbable victory of the outnumbered Israelis in the War of Independence and the improbable immediate recognition of Jewish statehood by the United Nations ("knocks" 1 and 2), plus the beneficial consequences of a Jewish state for the Jewish people at that time ("knocks" 4, 5, and 6). However, for Kalischer it was, first and foremost, the fulfillment of biblical prophecy.

The prophets had foretold that one day the exiles would be gathered and returned to their land, which would once again flower. And, Kalischer argued, Ramban and Radak had stated that the promised ingathering and return could take the form of a great political power granting permission for the return, as had occurred with the return from the Babylonian exile. Clearly, that time was now upon us. Because of this emphasis, Kalischer cites the following words of the Beloved: "The winter is over, the rain is past...the time of singing has come" (Song of Songs 2:11–12). The "knocking" signifies that changing world conditions have made possible the renewal of settlement in Eretz Yisrael. The Rav, however, cites the Beloved as simply saying: "Open for me, my sister, my love" (Song of Songs 5:2), leaving its message rather vague in terms of contemporary application.

The difference between the two is significant and rather

puzzling. Is the Rav's omission from *Kol Dodi Dofek* of any reference to the fulfillment of biblical prophecy principled or inadvertent? I put the question in terms of the fulfillment of prophecy rather than *athalta de-ge'ula* (a term Kalischer uses) because it is the former which is logically prior and lends itself to a more objective determination.

Both the sources and human experience suggest that the final redemption will be a *process*, the precise order of whose components was not fixed by tradition. Central to that process, however, was return to Eretz Yisrael. Thus, the miraculous salvation of an important Jewish community or even a Jewish state elsewhere in the world might merit public thanksgiving prayers or even a semi-holiday, but would not be associated with the prophetic eschatological promise. These three elements are linked. Only if an event can be identified even partially as a fulfillment of prophecy can it be seen as part of the redemptive process, in which case the appropriate response is *aliya*. However, if Kalischer in 1862 could see the emancipation as a fulfillment of prophecy, how could any traditional Jew not see it in a sovereign Jewish state within the boundaries of historic *Eretz Yisrael*?

The omission of fulfillment of prophecy seriously weakens the Rav's thesis. If the only evidence for the establishment of the State of Israel as the *chesed* of God is the improbability of its happening, then a jarring dissonance is created between the reality and its analogue in the knocking of the Beloved in *Shir ha-Shirim*. The text leaves no doubt whatsoever as to the answer to the three questions that are always asked in such a situation: "Is that a knocking at the door? Who is there? What do you want?" The refusal of the Beloved to respond in this case is tragic. However, in the case of the knocking in 1956, the answer to none of these questions was unambiguous. Therefore, it is understandable that the response was so weak.

Moreover, by not referring to fulfillment of prophecy, the Rav weakens his argument that the establishment of the State of Israel must be seen as the hand of God. Logically speaking, an event, no matter how extraordinary or seemingly supernatural, does not by itself constitute conclusive evidence of divine agency. If the event was predicted in the name of God and fits into some preannounced plan, however, then one can reasonably claim it to be the work of God.

I am inclined to believe that the Rav's omission of references to fulfillment of prophecy or redemption in 1956 was not principled. At the time, few of us from the yeshiva world thought of the Zionist enterprise in those terms. Jewish statehood appeared too little, too late, and seemed to be an impetuous step fraught with peril. Only after eight years of tenuous survival and the realization that its existence constituted a benefit was the Rav ready to pronounce it a creation of God. The question that remains, however, is why, in the years after the Six-Day War, with an undivided Jerusalem, the proven military might of the state, and the acceleration of the ingathering, did the Rav not update his thesis and take note of the increase in the intensity of the knocking?[3] The answer may be found in some remarks by the Rav in which he explains his dislike of the term "messianism."[4] It would appear that based upon his reading of Rambam, the Rav believed the central component of the eschatological process to be the appearance of the *melech hamashiach* personality whom he saw not merely as the instrument to bring about the other components, but as the ultimate expression of the spiritual heights latent in the human being created in the divine image. Lacking that, the Rav was not willing to describe anything, even involving the State of Israel, as messianic or part of the final redemption.

ENDNOTES

1. *Derishat Tziyyon* (Jerusalem: Mosad Harav Kook, 1964), p. 107.
2. In the period between R. Kalischer and the Rav we have, of course, R. Avraham Yitzhak ha-Kohen Kook, who also resorted to the metaphor of *kol dodi dofek* and the term *athalta de-ge'ula* to describe the special events of his time. What impressed R. Kook was the Balfour Declaration, the devotion to the land shown by the *chalutzim,* and the fact of successful Jewish agricultural settlement in Israel. See Tzevi Yaron, *Mishnato shel*

ha-Rav Kook (Jerusalem: Joint Authority for Jewish Zionist Education, Department for Torah and Culture in the Diaspora, 1974), pp. 263, 270, 272. However, preceding all of them in invoking the *kol dodi dofek* metaphor was Yehuda Halevi, who in *Kuzari* 2:24, acknowledging the blindness of the majority of Jews in Babylon because they chose to remain in exile, gives the following interpretation to verses 5:2–4 of *Shir ha-Shirim*, which he applied to the Cyrus proclamation permitting Israelites to return to rebuild the Temple: "*Kol dodi dofek* means God's call to return. *Dodi shalah yado min ha-hor* [My beloved put in his hand by the latchet of the door] may be interpreted as the urgent call of Ezra, Nehemiah, and the prophets." The point is that for Yehuda Halevi, Kalischer, and Kook, regardless of which events they saw as emanating the knocking, the clear message was nothing less than to return physically to the land!

3. The Rav makes an intriguing aside in one of the *teshuva derashot* he delivered between the years 1962 and 1974. The text will be found in R. Joseph B. Soloveitchik, *On Repentance*, trans. Pinchas H. Peli (Jerusalem: Orot Publishing House, 1980), p. 330. In it he refers to the eschatological concept of *kibbutz galuyot*: "[T]o some extent, we see it happening now in our day, not exactly as prophesied, but there has occurred a beginning of the ingathering of Jews from all the remotest corners."

4. R. Joseph B. Soloveitchik, *Divrei Hashkafa*, p. 242.

CHAPTER 8

 The Tale Told by
the Heavens

One of the more popular of the David Psalms, the Nineteenth, opens with the much-quoted words:

> The heavens declare the glory of God and the firmament, His handiwork.... There is no speech nor language, their voice cannot be heard (Psalm 19:2–3).

The general meaning of these verses would seem to be quite straightforward and reflects one of man's earliest and most moving religious experiences, the awe and wonder with which he contemplates the starry skies, its vast distances and mysterious celestial bodies. It was not only primitive man who was filled with reverence but philosophers as well. Consider the oft-cited statement of Immanuel Kant: "Two things fill the mind with ever new and increasing admiration and awe, the more often and the

---

This chapter originally appeared, in slightly different form, in *Tradition* 41 (2008).

more steadily we reflect on them: the starry heavens above and the moral law within.”[1]

But lest anyone miss the connection between the drama of the heavens and God, the prophet was on hand to help. “Lift up your eyes on high and see – who has created these? (Isaiah 40:26). The sheer magnitude, regularity, and beauty of the heavens, its contents and processes, pointed to some intelligent supernatural source. Indeed, medieval philosophers devised what they took to be logical proofs for the existence of God based upon the very existence of the cosmos and the features of design that they believed it to exhibit. While the idea of proving the existence of God is no longer considered feasible, these verses from the psalm continue to fascinate, reverberate, and raise questions: precisely *how* do the heavens do their “declaring,” especially since there is “no speech nor language”?

The reason for the sustained interest in these verses is probably to be found in the fact that while apparently dealing with the theologically significant relationship between nature and God, the use of poetic-metaphoric language lends itself to broader homiletic treatment. I have found it of particular interest to note that Rav Yosef Dov Soloveitchik employs the verse in at least three different contexts, each time giving it a different interpretation.

*   *   *

In *Halakhic Man*, the Rav, in describing Halakhic Man’s relationship to existence, says, “It is not only ontological but normative.”[2] While he desires to know the world, he does so for the purpose of determining the ideal norm and then prescribing the actions by which one may implement or apply the halakhic norm. And then, in a sudden poetic leap, the Rav reverses the logical sequence, which until now has it that the Halakhic Man introduces the normative elements to his involvement with the concrete world, and asserts:

> Homo Religiosus hears the echo of the norm forthcoming from every aspect of creation: “The heavens declare the glory of God and the firmament reciteth His handiwork” (Psalm

19:2). But what is the tale of the heavens if not the declaration of the commandments? All of existence declares the glory of God – man's obligation to order his life according to the will of the Almighty.[3]

There is no way in which one may read into this verse the view that "glory of God" entails a norm for man stating that he is to live by the commandments. This could hardly be what the heavens are declaring or the firmament reciting! We are compelled to say that we have here a flight of the homiletic imagination in which the Rav, in his idealization of the Halakhic Man's deep involvement in the intricacies of the Halakha and its application to the concrete world, portrays him as hearing echoes of the norm emanating from all aspects of creation. Indeed, the Rav himself will interpret this verse quite differently elsewhere.

* * *

In the *Lonely Man of Faith*, the Rav points out that while the man of faith is inquisitive about the cosmos, it is only the covenantal confrontation that can provide him with answers to his questions. On the one hand, man's cosmic experience is, in a sense, revelatory, in that "man beholds God in every nook and corner of creation, in the flowering of the plant, in the rushing of the tide, and in the movement of his own muscle, as if God were at hand." And yet the very moment man turns his face to God, he finds Him remote, unapproachable, enveloped in transcendence and mystery. According to the Rav, the cosmic experience for man is "antithetic and paradoxical." While God is experienced as "the cosmic ruler reigning supreme in boundless majesty, His will crystallized in natural law, His very exaltedness and remoteness render the personal relationship with God difficult."

Says the Rav:

Of course God speaks through His works: "The heavens declare the Glory of God and the firmament shows His handiwork." Yet let me ask, what kind of a tale do the heavens tell? Is it a personal tale addressed to someone or is it a tale which is not intended for any [particular] audience? Do the heavens sing the Glory of the Creator without troubling themselves to find out whether or not someone is listening to this great song or are they really interested in man the listener? (pp. 30–31).[4]

This is a brilliant and most dramatic extension of the psalmist's metaphor. Instead of simply saying that the message of the cosmos, whatever it might be, is not personal and does not invite relationship, the Rav picks up the metaphor, seeing the heavens as a speaker, and asks: "Is it a personal tale addressed to someone" or is it "to whom it may concern"?

Here, the Rav again cites Psalm 19:2 in order to contrast the cosmic experience with the living encounter experienced by the patriarchs and by Moshe and the nation as a whole at Sinai. There the individual is addressed by name. It is personal, it obligates and it makes demands. The Rav concludes: "The message of the heavens is at best an equivocal one," and hence the need for God to seek out man via a covenantal encounter.

The Rav's reference to Psalm 19:2 in this work is intended to point out the shortcomings of all natural theology. In searching for God in the cosmos, man can never be sure it is God whom he has briefly met, and even if it is, he doesn't know what it is that God wants from him.

* * *

A recent publication of the Rav's teaching on prayer contains another rather surprising reference to Psalm 19:2. It appears as part of an unusually extensive treatment of the aesthetic, which the Rav defines as "an immediate constant contact with reality at the qualitative sensible level."[5]

Elsewhere, the Rav has repeatedly pointed out that the success of modern science is based upon its ability to discover repeatable relations between different aspects of our world expressible in quantifiable-mathematical terms. Thus the knowledge of the world that science gives us is not of reality itself but rather of a parallel universe composed of abstract concepts which in some mysterious fashion fit the conclusions of human reason. Therefore, the Rav maintained, the ordinary experiences of the individual with the qualitative aspects of the world through direct sense perception has a better claim to knowledge of reality than the theories of science. In terms of religious significance, the aesthetic, seen simply as the immediate experience of qualitative sense of perceptions, was already pronounced by the Rav as "equivocal and paradoxical."

However, in moving from a consideration of the aesthetic as simply immediate sense perception to an analysis of aesthetic man à la Kierkegaard, the term "aesthetic" for the Rav takes on the connotation of the artistic with its emphasis upon the hedonic and apprehension of the beautiful. Unfortunately, the Rav does not analyze the concept of the beautiful to any extent, other than to say that "Beauty is apprehended in the colors and forms conveyed by the senses, not comprehended."[6] Harmonious form is perceived, not conceived. We are also introduced to the concept of the sublime, or "exaltedness," which according to the Rav is a "primary feeling" that is "connected to witnessing the beautiful" and reveals itself in beauty. But as to the phenomenology of the sublime, all that the Rav tells us is that "exaltedness [the sublime]... suggests to man the vision of something unique and great."[7]

And then the Rav goes on to say:

> In the light of this thesis we may state that God for Judaism is not only the source and root of truth and light, of fact and values constituting the foundations of our theoretical and ethico-practical world but also that He is the origin of beauty, of the delightful and the pleasant. God is not only omniscient (infinitely wise), not only full of grace, kindness and morality (infinitely good) but also sweet and lovely, fair and pleasant.

179

> God not only addresses Himself to man through the logos, by emanating wisdom and knowledge to the finite mind, not only through the ethos, revealing to natural man, driven by insensate desires and impulses, a great order of absolute values and ideals – but also through aesthetics – the immediate sensible apprehension of reality which is beautiful and grandiose "The heavens tell the glory of God" (Psalms 19:2). In this enthusiastic explanation, David does not refer to the mathematical precision of the movement of the planets and the propagation of light but to the grandeur and splendor of the skies, to the innumerable natural phenomena whose charm and loveliness are beyond human imagination reaching and saturating every fiber in creation"[8]

The interpretation that the Rav gives here to Psalms 19:2 is probably closest to the plain, intended meaning of the text. Indeed, what must have impressed the psalmist most about the heavens were the vast stretches of space and distance, as well as the sheer plenitude of the celestial bodies. In short, an experience of the sublime in the Kantian sense of the term.

However, what is most surprising and rather puzzling is the heightened significance that the Rav accords here to the aesthetic, placing it on the same level as the cognitive and the ethical, and even, as we shall see, claiming it to be exclusively constitutive of the religious experience.

In the passage cited above the Rav equates the beautiful (aesthetic), the rational (cognitive), and the good (moral-ethical) in terms of their relation to God on three levels:

1. As God is the "*source and root*" of the cognitive and the ethical, so is He the "origin" of the aesthetic.
2. As God "addresses Himself to man" through the cognitive and the moral, so does He through the aesthetic.
3. As God is *Himself* infinitely wise and infinitely good, so is He "sweet, lovely, fair, and pleasant."

Let us examine these bold equations.

1. God is indeed the "source and root" of the cognitive in that He has endowed man with a mind that can reason, formulate the laws of logic, and invent the computer. He is the "origin" of the ethical in that He has endowed man with a moral sense and revealed moral teachings to him. Thus, there is no problem in asserting that God is the origin of the aesthetic in the sense that the world He has created exhibits qualities which, when perceived by man, evoke a special pleasure we call the aesthetic.

2. While God may "address" man through all three types of experience, the clarity of the call will vary. In all three media God only affords a glimpse of Himself and what is heard, seen, or inferred is always equivocal. The preferred area for man's search for God is subject to the vagaries of philosophical fashion. First it was characterized by the vigor of deductive proofs, and then it was the "sheer grandeur of the moral ought," and more recently the personal religious encounter as immediate experience.

3. The third equation, however, seems rather strange. For while God's wisdom is certainly quite different from man's wisdom, both qualitatively and quantitatively, it is nevertheless meaningful to use the term ("God has knowledge") because its core meaning is known to us from our own experience, where it entails a positive, substantive, and measurable attribute. Similarly, moral value is experienced by us as an intrinsic good, and while within God it surely takes on a different form, there is no difficulty in saying that God is good according to the same essential criteria He has held out for man. However, what can we possibly mean when we say "God is sweet and lovely, fair and pleasant," particularly as there is general agreement as to the essentially subjective nature of aesthetic judgment? God may indeed appear at times as lovely and pleasant, but at other times as severe

and angry. Surely, then, all such terms, if seen as substantive descriptions of God, must be rejected, particularly as they are not even taken seriously even when applied to man!

However, our puzzlement only grows as we read on a bit further:

> Only the aesthetic experience, if linked with the exalted, may bring man directly into contact with God, loving, personal and intimate. Only through coming into contact with the beautiful and exalted may we apprehend God instead of comprehending Him, feel the embrace of the Creator and the warm breath of infinity hovering over a finite creation. The reason for the immediacy and impact implicit in the aesthetic experience is its sensuous character.
>
> The direct revelation of the Creator has always been explained by Judaism as a revelation of *kevod Elokim* (*majestas Dei*). This conveys the thought that *absolute beauty* rests in God and that only He is the *fountainhead* out of which pulchritude, grace and loveliness flow into the world. The latter abounds in magnificent forms, in harmony, style and charm because it was created in the likeness of its Master whose majesty and transcendent grace penetrate into every ramification of reality to the point of saturation. God sanctions not only the true and the good but also the beautiful.[9]

Among the statements cited above, I find the following most radical:

> Only the aesthetic experience (if linked with the exalted) may bring man directly into contact with God, living, personal and intimate.

Let us for the time being consider this assertion without the conditional:

> Only the aesthetic experience may bring man directly into
> contact with God, living, personal and intimate.

As it stands, this statement is a truism, if, as it seems, the Rav
holds that man can have direct contact with God only through
the media of sense perception. For that is precisely what the "aesthetic" means! But why *should* we think that direct contact with
God can come only through the senses? But let us go along with
this, for the moment.

Now, what is the nature of this condition, "if linked with the
exalted"? Here the Rav is stipulating that the aesthetic experience
he is referring to is not mere sense perception but must include
the quality of the sublime which he sees as connected to the beautiful. Can such a view be sustained: that only through this kind
of a sensual immediate experience (sublime–beautiful) can man
have direct contact with God?

Had the Rav written that the aesthetic experience is *one of the
avenues* by which man may meet God, it would have been considered a major breakthrough in Jewish theology. The assertion by a
leading Jewish thinker that "absolute beauty rests in God and that
only He is the fountainhead out of which pulchritude, grace and
loveliness flow into the world" has been a long time in coming. As
I pointed out in a 1964 article, there is much in biblical and rabbinic sources to support such a view.[10] However, early connections
between idolatry and the plastic arts, and the perceived difficulty
of maintaining a disinterested appreciation of the beauty of the
human body, discouraged serious Jewish philosophical inquiry
into the domain of the aesthetic.

But what could have brought the Rav to (suddenly) elevate
the realm of the aesthetic (the sublime, the beautiful) to being
the *only*, the *exclusive* kind of experience through which man has
direct contact with the living God?

Perhaps what brought the Rav to this conclusion is his overly
Kantian view of the ethical. He explicitly equates the ethical with
the cognitive in that in both "one approaches God by the process

of deduction."[11] According to the Rav, the ethical experience is primarily an awareness of a moral norm whose legitimacy, "long and careful study" may bring us to realize, requires that we relate it to an absolute good which is God. This is a process of inferential reasoning. Thus, here, as in the cognitive experience, "there is no direct apprehension of the Creator," "no actual meeting."[12] This is why he says, "One neither essentially admires goodness nor adores intellectual greatness."

Actually, however, the moral experience need not be seen as primarily deontological, with emphasis on the moral *law* or *norm* or on the *right*, but rather as the apprehension of the *good*, the *benevolent*, which is outgoing and full of love and compassion. So that a glimpse of the Absolute Good may arouse in man a passionate love for the source of that good which can reach ecstatic intensity. After all, the Rav states, the emotional approach "is to be considered a direct beholding of Him," particularly so when it is generated by a moral experience which gives a glimpse of the Absolute Good. In certain places the Rav seems to be edging toward the realization that the good may indeed be more than a general abstract norm. Thus he says: "In thanksgiving God is proclaimed primarily as Good, arousing a feeling of gratitude and indebtedness.... Good becomes an aesthetic value, it turns into beauty," and "God is good and therefore beautiful." But is this not to confuse basic categories? Goodness as benevolence is an intrinsic value with sufficient attraction to arouse love and passion to qualify as a religious experience with God perceived as the Absolute Good without recourse to the beautiful. Why, therefore, does the Rav insist that "only beauty can be desired passionately, only loveliness can arouse enthusiasm and frenzy?"

Let us return to the Rav's earlier assertion that only through aesthetic experience via the senses can man achieve a direct immediate experience of God. It is extremely difficult to reconcile this position with much of the Rav's writing elsewhere.

In an earlier article I examined the Rav's view of the epistemological basis for our belief in God and showed that according to the Rav, man is able, in his own existence and personal experience, to apprehend a transcendent reality. The Rav states that man's ontological awareness can become identical with the transcendental awareness. However, all of these feeling-states, apprehensions, awareness, appear to be "asensual and are given directly to our consciousness." Thus while, as I said, it is groundbreaking to have the Rav add the aesthetic (sublime – beautiful) to the class of experiences in which one can experience the transcendent, it is extremely problematic to see it as the exclusive venue to encounter the divine. Indeed, the Rav later in this work makes it rather clear that his use of these terms is quite equivocal. Thus he says:

> When we speak of religious sensuousness we must note carefully that there are many senses to this term…. religious sensibility may manifest itself not in bold pictorial representation but in experiential immediacy. Contact is established with the Almighty in the abyss of a warm heart, in a lovesick soul…. However devoid of sensuous material this feeling is, it is still an immediate reality whose impact upon the religious person is enormous.

But if the phenomenon we are discussing is not sensuous in the ordinary meaning, why use the term "aesthetic"? The expression "experiential immediacy" seems quite adequate. Furthermore, in applying the concept of the beautiful to the religious sphere, the Rav makes a number of extravagant claims:

> In beautiful things, the transcendent hint to the something beyond is inherent.
> The craving for beauty is nothing but the eternal longing for eternal noumenal Being.
> God is extolled and adored because He is beautiful.

And, as we sit and wonder what this could possibly mean, the Rav says: "The beauty of God is expressed in holiness."

Earlier, we quoted the Rav as saying that in the divine alchemy, God's goodness can turn into beauty, which we are now told in God is really holiness. But if so, why not dispense altogether with the terms "beautiful" and "aesthetic" when speaking of God, and get back to the traditional concepts of goodness and holiness, which have long been considered quite adequate and integrally connected?[13]

However, if the words of the Rav on the aesthetic and the beautiful as we found them in *Worship of the Heart* represent his considered and final views, then indeed the tale told by the heavens and the cosmos as a whole takes on a significance that even David could not have imagined.[14]

ENDNOTES

1. *Critique of Practical Reason*, Abbott trans. (London, 1889), p. 260.
2. *Halakhic Man*, p. 63.
3. Ibid., p. 64.
4. "The Lonely Man of Faith," pp. 30–31.
5. *Worship of the Heart*, p. 51.
6. Ibid., p. 42.
7. Ibid., p. 55.
8. The concept of the sublime as an identifiable element of the aesthetic experience has a long history. From Longinus (1st cent. c.e.) through Edmund Burke (1729–1797) to Immanuel Kant (1724–1804), there has been the recognition that there are aspects of nature, such as "clouds piled up in the sky moving with lightning flashes and thunder peals, volcanoes in all their violence, hurricanes, the boundless ocean in a state of tumult" (Kant) that are so vast and overwhelming, immense and mighty, that they arouse in man unique feelings of grandeur, wonder, and amazement. These may be called experiences of the sublime when they are not mixed with feelings of personal fear or terror. As early as Longinus this concept was recognized as a biblical quality, as expressed in such praise as "How *great* are thy works, O Lord" (Psalms 92:6), "how *manifold* are thy works, O Lord" (Psalms 104:24), "Say unto God, how *awesome* is thy work" (Psalms 66:3), and, in the words of Job 37:14–22. The feeling of the sublime is explained as follows: "A sensible object of great magnitude strains our imagination till it fails." There takes place a failure of human sensibility in the presence of the size, the might and multiplicity of nature. The stars of the heavens or the sands of the seashore in their infinity

overwhelm the mind's ability to form a simple, articulate impression of the number of extent. Kant saw the experience of the sublime, while part of the aesthetic, as quite distinct from the perception of the beautiful. See Katherine Everett Gilbert and Helmut Kuhn, *A History of Esthetics* (Bloomington: Indiana University Press, 1954), pp. 321–344. Kant then added an interesting twist. The overwhelmed imagination, in its effort to widen itself, falls back on itself and realizes the dignity and value of its own subjectivity as a creator of consciousness which alone can be aware of and can appreciate nature's grandeur.

The concept of the sublime is extensively developed by Abraham Joshua Heschel in *God in Search of Man* (New York: Farrar, Straus & Cudahy, '955), chaps. 2–5. He sees it as "the silent allusion of things to a meaning greater than themselves" (p. 49). Compare the Rav, "In beautiful things, the transcendental hint to the something beyond is inherent" (*Worship of the Heart*, p. 60). Heschel applies the terms "wonder" and "radical amazement" to man's response to the sublime, and sees it as the beginning of all philosophy and religion. "Radical amazement leads to a feeling of the hidden love and wisdom in all things."

9. Shubert Spero, "Towards a Torah Esthetic," *Tradition* 6, no. 2 (Spring-Summer 1964): 53–66.
10. See my article "Rabbi Joseph Dov Soloveitchik and the Role of the Ethical," *Modern Judaism* 23 (2003), p. 58.
11. See my article "Rabbi Joseph Dov Soloveitchik and Belief in God," *Modern Judaism* 19, no. 1 (February 1999): 59.
12. See David S. Shapiro, "The Meaning of Holiness in Judaism," *Tradition* 7, no. 1 (Winter 1964–65): 48.
13. In light of the difficulties inherent in the Rav's treatment of the aesthetic in this work, I am inclined to question the propriety of publishing material found in "notebooks" and presenting it as part of his philosophical canon (as is the case of the material found in chaps. 1–5, which we are told was composed by the Rav in 1956–57 as the basis of a course at Yeshiva University; see the Introduction, p. xxviii). To my knowledge, the Rav did not deal with the aesthetic in any other of his published works to the extent that he does here.

CHAPTER 9

▌▌▌ The Aesthetic in Jewish Theology

This chapter explores the relationship of Judaism to that aspect of human experience called the aesthetic.[1] The choice of the term "aesthetic" to designate our subject matter instead of the usual "art" or "the beautiful" signals that we will be taking a different and broader approach than is generally employed.

Historically, the use of the term "aesthetic" in this context was first introduced in the eighteenth century.[2] Its advantage was to provide a new and much broader framework in which to consider the philosophic problems usually treated under this heading. From Plato onwards, philosophers had concentrated on what have been termed theories of art which focused upon the *process*, i.e., the techniques, the skills by which certain objects or activities considered particularly pleasing/beautiful are produced. In this approach, it is the artist and his creation which are the primary objects of scrutiny. Other theories were built on the concept of beauty, but never got much beyond the issue of whether beauty was an objective property of things or only something in the eyes of the beholder. With the introduction of the term "aesthetic," the primary focus of interest was no longer the creative act but rather the experience itself during which the object is seen or the sound heard and contemplated. This enables us to extend the area of the aesthetic to include aspects of nature as well as human artifacts. Now the primary subject matter becomes the faculties and experiences of all those exposed to art, which must be carefully analyzed.

One of the assumptions of aesthetic theory is that the characteristic experiences which arise out of exposure to any and all of the fine arts, while distinct from other kinds of experiences, are similar in significant respects to each other. It also assumes that all objects and activities which are regarded as works of art possess certain special properties. What these are and whether they are to be deemed necessary conditions are questions still under discussion.

For our purposes and for the time being, it may be sufficient to give the following preliminary description of the aesthetic experience: It is sensuous (perceived by the senses), provides a particular kind of disinterested pleasure which arises from the surface qualities of what is being sensed, i.e., the sight, the sounds, the fragrance, the texture, and perhaps the taste. One's interest is concentrated on appearance only: how the object looks, how it sounds, how it feels. One is not focused inwards to try to understand the underlying forces which give rise to the appearance. One is not forward looking, wondering what use I can make of the object or what future event I can predict from this appearance. Nor is one's interest outward, how does this object relate to its surroundings?

> Aesthetics is not physics nor psychology or yet physiology. Its direct object is presented conscious content objectively discernable, sensuous presentations.[3]

Since man has learned to his great advantage that what is important usually lies *below* the surface of things, aesthetic elements, which, as we have said, concentrate on surface qualities, have generally been seen as mere *secondary* features of reality. Today we are conditioned to take notice of aesthetic values only when attending a clearly marked art event or when totally relaxed, as when all other basic needs and obligations have been met. Even then, a person must free himself from the ingrained way of looking at things before an aesthetic experience can occur.

Once we have the sketch of a theory, we can roughly reconstruct the stages in the development of the aesthetic. In the beginning man experienced a certain pleasure in seeing colors and forms in nature, in hearing certain modulations in the human voice, in the fragrance of flowers. While pleasant enough, this in itself did not arouse any special interest because it did not assuage any felt need. In the next stage, man fashioned instruments by which he could produce sound and rhythms and which even surpassed the pleasures of the human voice.[4] Then man learned to draw the likeness of animal and human forms, catching the gracefulness of their movements. While originally the motive for doing this may have been utilitarian for purposes of magic, the visual pleasure it gave soon became apparent. After a while these were considered valuable additions to human culture for their own sake. This explains why the first attempt to theorize about art focused upon the artist and his work.[5] However, with the advent of modern aesthetic theory, each of the three different participants in the process – the artist, the object, and the spectator – was fitted into its proper niche, although each related to the aesthetic experience in a somewhat different way. The artist, upon completing his work, is the first spectator and in contemplating it, experiences the aesthetic. The work itself, having been endowed with certain properties, is able to evoke the aesthetic experience in those who contemplate it. With this broad concept of the aesthetic in hand, which plainly encompasses much more than the visual, let us trace its role in the early development of the people of Israel.

* * *

Tradition locates the formative events of the Jewish people, starting with the biblical patriarchs, as occurring in the Fertile Crescent at a time when the river civilizations in Egypt and Mesopotamia had already reached impressive heights. Although originally a nomadic tribal society based upon herding and subsistence agriculture, the Jews were from the very beginning a people aware of and exposed to the highly developed material culture of their neighbors.[6] In these cultures, the ruling and priestly classes, who are everywhere the sponsors and main consumers of the arts, enjoyed life-styles enriched by the beauty of architecture and painting, music and dance, sculpture and poetry, only aspects of which trickled down into the lives of ordinary people. While the latter could only be occasional spectators of royal parades and dramatic religious rituals, in their individual lives they had ample opportunities to cultivate the aesthetic in their personal jewelry, colorful woven clothing, listening to and composing epic narratives and music, participating in folk dancing. We have every reason to believe that in this respect the lives of the ordinary folk in Israel, during the first six hundred years or so of their existence in the land, followed this course.[7]

With the establishment of the United Monarchy under David and Solomon, the people acquired further opportunities for aesthetic appreciation from the appearance on the scene of grand public buildings in the form of royal palaces and a central Temple where the God of Israel could be worshipped. It is precisely here, in the scripturally mandated construction of a House of God, Judaism's holiest institution, from its inception as a portable wilderness Tabernacle to the Temple of Solomon in Jerusalem and on to its Herodian expansion, that we have the best evidence that the second of the Ten Commandments did not smother the natural and widespread tendency of religion in general to make aesthetic experience part of the divine service. In all of these structures, the specific prohibition to make any visual representation of Israel's God was scrupulously heeded. In regard to Solomon's Temple we are told that in the Holy of Holies, where in pagan temples there usually stood a statue of the god, "there was nothing in the Ark save the two tablets of stone which Moses put there at Horeb when the Lord made a covenant with the children of Israel" (1 Kings 8:9). Yet, the second commandment notwithstanding, in all of these structures, the very materials used, the designs employed, and the interior furniture seem to have been chosen in large part in order to impart the maximum aesthetic effect.[8] Indeed, in the very Holy of Holies, from the Ark cover, which was made of pure beaten gold, there rose at each end in full relief the form of a cherub with outstretched wings.[9] The man chosen to head the construction of the wilderness Tabernacle had the following skills: "to devise skillful works, to work in gold, silver, and bronze, in cutting of stones for setting and in carving of wood" (Exodus 35:9). Other craftsmen and women were skilled in "weaving in colors, in blues, in purple and in scarlet and fine linen" (Exodus 35:35). The garments of the priests were designed for "splendor and for beauty" (Exodus 28:2) and included a breastplate encrusted with twelve different precious stones. Among the ritual furniture of the Tabernacle was the seven-branched candlestick (*menora*) made of pure beaten gold with each branch adorned with "cups, loops, and flowers," all part of the same seamless piece.

Solomon, who no longer had the architectural constraints that came with a portable Tabernacle, was able to give full expression to his aesthetic sensibilities. Thus, for example, we are told "that for the entrance to the sanctuary he made doors of olive wood, the door posts with the frame having five angles. As for the two doors of olive wood he carved upon them carvings of cherubim and palm trees and open flowers and overlaid them with gold" (1 Kings 6:32). Moreover, in order to make the Temple more impressive from the outside, Solomon added two elements which were marvels of bronze metallurgy at the time: on each side of the entrance to the Temple was placed a tall free-standing bronze pillar, named Yachin and Boaz respectively. Each was capped by an elaborate double capital reaching an overall height of over forty feet.[10] Since the text gives no hint of their religious significance, we can assume that the pillars was primarily for aesthetic purposes. Solomon also cast a great bronze basin known as the "sea" which rested on the backs of twelve bronze oxen and was placed inside the Temple courtyard.[11] While it was used, of course, for ritual purification, its size and composition aroused wonder. Ever since, rabbinic commentators have striven to find religious meaning for all the artistic detail. It should, however, be clear that regardless of whatever symbolic significance may be imputed to the particular form, size, materials, and colors of the Temple and its contents, clearly a major consideration in including them was their visual aesthetic value.

However, far more important than the visual was the development of a form of daily worship combining religious poetry, choral singing, and instrumental music composed and performed by succeeding generations of Levitical families. Unlike musical chants in other religions, which were usually formulistic, esoteric, and believed to have magical power, the institution of psalmody, as initiated by David long before there was a Temple, invited individual creativity and participation, and became a national resource accessible to the people as audience, composers, and performers.[12] During the monarchy we read of the Levitical choir and orchestra performing at military and civic events, while at the height of the Second Temple period, the singing of the Levites was the most impressive part of the Temple service.[13]

Nor must we overlook the fact that the epic stories and legal traditions that have come down to us in the form of the Five Books of Moses were also a source of aesthetic appreciation. Although primarily considered to be Holy Writ, they contain aesthetic elements. First, there is the high poetic quality of those portions formally labeled *shir* or *shira* (song). In addition, the sparse style of the many narratives that appear throughout the books of the Bible has been shown to exhibit compelling literary merit. All of the available evidence tends to show that during the millennial national existence of Israel in their land, the aesthetic dimension, in all of the forms generally cultivated by peoples at that time and in that part of the world, was an integral part of their regular lives. Indeed, in the particular areas of religious choral music, poetry, and literature, aesthetic development reached unusual heights of sensitivity and creativity.

Nevertheless, after archaeological discoveries and historical research revealed the magnificent architectural and artistic works of the ancient civilizations, particularly those of Egypt, Babylon, and Greece, the paucity of Israel's material culture, by contrast, soon became apparent. And even when circumstances in Israel permitted more grandiose public construction, as in the periods of Solomon and Herod, the style and techniques were deemed borrowed and imitative, and seen as reflecting a lack of artistic talent and interest on the part of the Jewish people. However, the actual causes of this should have been obvious. First, there is the fact of the late appearance of a Jewish political entity on the stage of history. There was, therefore, no need to reinvent skills and styles that were already available. Nor did the natural resources of the land invite innovation. Second, the cultural values of Israelite society, insofar as they were expressed in their literature, tended more to the spiritual. Finally, the ruling classes were never rich enough nor interested enough to embark upon monumental construction programs. After the destruction of the Second Temple and the end of an independent national existence, this entire area of material culture and artistic creativity was restricted to the domain of the individual, who now found himself living a marginal existence in a strange culture. Happy just to be alive and free to practice his religion, the Jew, in terms of material culture, had to make do with whatever he could get. He rarely had his own space long enough to decorate it.

Over the years, cultural historians devised elaborate theories about the Jews and the arts from which they drew far-reaching and rather fanciful conclusions regarding the character of Jewish culture and the talents of the people who had produced it. For example, it was maintained that the second of the Ten Commandments and other rabbinic restrictions on the making of images had a "negative impact on the artistic development of the Jewish people,"[14] that Jewish culture seeks to emphasize the auditory sense over the visual to the extent that this people thought of understanding as a kind of hearing, whereas the Greeks thought of it more as a kind of seeing, "that Jewish thought *zigs* towards the auditory, the verbal and the temporal because it *zags* away from the visual, the pictorial and the spatial," "that there is an inherent lack of visual talent among Jews." Thus, starting with the second commandment, which forbids the making of images *representing God*, we jump to general statements about Jewish thought which supposedly affects this people's very definition of "understanding," leading to the factual assertion that there is an "inherent lack of visual talent among Jews in general"! Kalman Brand, in his comprehensive study of the attitude of Jewish thought toward the visual in various periods, has conclusively demonstrated the unsupported nature of these generalizations.

Even if we factor in the additional rabbinic safeguards against image-making, it is simply not the case that the visual has been neglected or underestimated either in Jewish thought or Jewish life. However, even more misleading than the canard of Jewish undervaluation of the *visual* is the insinuation that this somehow implies a demeaning of the *artistic* in general, which in turn is wrongly equated with the area of the *aesthetic* as a whole. Indeed, it is this conceptual confusion that is at the root of the inconclusive nature of the perennial discussions of the question of whether there is a Jewish art where both terms usually remain undefined. However, as stated in at the beginning of this discussion, my purpose is not to trace the practical effects of the iconoclastic tradition in Judaism or to define Jewish art but rather to determine the place, if any, of the aesthetic in Jewish theology. Towards this end we shall now proceed.

* * *

To speak of *Jewish theology* might, of course, be almost as problematic as speaking about *Jewish art*. Nevertheless, while no such thing as a clearly marked theology is to be found either in the Written or the Oral Torah, there are several concepts that after careful explication can be incorporated into a coherent theology of Judaism.[15] Indeed, aspects of such a theology have been successfully developed by Jewish thinkers since the Middle Ages. Thus we have a highly developed theology about God (Maimonides), epistemology (Saadia), history (Yehuda Halevi), and the Halakha (Rav Soloveitchik). However, few if any have attempted a systematic treatment of the aesthetic in spite of the fact that the artist and his art had already been a subject of interest for classical Greek philosophy. This was probably because in the Middle Ages philosophy became the handmaiden of the major religions of the time, for which the arts, while highly regarded for their usefulness in enhancing religious services, were not considered worthy of further philosophic analysis. Let us see why this was so.

The words "true," "good," and "beautiful" are probably the most familiar, the most overworked, but certainly the most significant in our natural languages. These words and their equivalents are universally seen as terms of approval, while their opposites ("false," "evil," "ugly") indicate disapproval. They are used to make judgments, i.e., to distinguish between that which is important and valuable and that which is not. As with all linguistic entities, their use is regulated by rules of grammar and semantics. Thus, for example, good and beautiful can be a matter of degree, while true cannot.

After a while it became apparent that the true and the good invite philosophic exploration, which does not seem to be the case with the beautiful. The true and the good serve a variety of functions in ordinary discourse, but since the process of judgment requires some sort of objective criteria, they each ultimately point to a reality beyond the sphere of language. To say, for example, that a statement is true is usually to assert a certain relationship between the word and some object that is in some sense out in the real world. The verification process, i.e., the way we make sure that what is said about the object is indeed veridical, implies that the world around us is in some fashion accessible to human cognition. Philosophy would like to understand how and why this is so. Similarly, to say that something is good in a moral sense is ultimately to appeal to some abstract ideal or normative principle that again ostensibly takes us outside the realm of language and its uses. Thus, the areas of the true and the good compel us to deal with the enormously complex question of epistemology and ethics, which are of fundamental importance to philosophy in general. Analysis of the beautiful, however, reveals some interesting contrasts. More so than the true and the good, the experience of the beautiful is accompanied by a palpable pleasure and seems to arouse a desire to possess the object so designated. While the use of the subject-predicate form ("the *picture* is beautiful") seems to suggest that there are particular qualities in the object which deserve the adjective "beautiful," the most outstanding element in the experience is the subjective feeling of pleasure. Thus, the beautiful does not immediately point beyond itself or raise serious philosophical problems. The dominant religions in the Middle Ages, therefore, eagerly harnessed the aesthetic to serve their goals of religious inspiration: music, architecture, sculpture, drama, and poetry. However, they did not see the area of the aesthetic as offering great promise for further exploration of its metaphysic. The same can be said of Jewish theology. As early as the talmudic period the rabbis saw the psychological benefits of aesthetic experience. "There are three that broaden the mind of a person: a beautiful dwelling, a beautiful wife, and beautiful utensils."[16] Rabbi Samson R. Hirsch, one of the few traditional Jewish thinkers in modern times who was exposed to Western culture, found a place for aesthetics in his philosophy of history. He saw art as the meeting point of mind and sensuality, representing the middle stage in the spiritual development of mankind. Says Hirsch:

> And the Creator in His infinite Goodness had endowed the human soul with the kind of beauty which in itself is a first step towards higher perfection and only in an existence enriched by the sense of beauty can man find happiness and serene enjoyment of his life on earth.

Each time man experiences the grandeur of the star-studded firmament and the radiant diadem of the rising or setting sun, each time he enjoys the grace and beauty of a flower, he is elevated above the narrow range of mere materialistic usefulness and a note is struck in his heart which is very close to the even higher feeling for all that is *morally* beautiful and which carries him an important stage nearer to its understanding.[17]

This attitude toward the aesthetic remained constant throughout Jewish history. That is to say, at a very minimum, the aesthetic, in the forms made possible by the Jewish condition of the time (music, song, visual ornamentation of religious objects and the synagogue interior) was cultivated and valued for its role in enhancing the overall quality of man's life by sensitizing him to non-materialistic values.

Given the absence of philosophical challenges in the aesthetic, why should we even suppose that the theology of Judaism would be seriously interested in that particular aspect of human experience? The answer appears if we consider the conjunction of two basic assumptions, one empirical and the other theological. Beauty and the aesthetic are undeniably distinct qualities of our world as we experience it. Theology tells us that our world, its very existence and all of its qualities, is the work of God. It is therefore quite legitimate, if not required, that we ask whether the fact that man can experience and appreciate the aesthetic in nature and is endowed with the ability to create works that generate an aesthetic experience tell us anything significant about God or indeed about ourselves?

Let us start by examining the sources in Scripture that associate God with beauty (הוד והדר), such as "O Lord my God, You are very great. You are clothed with glory and beauty" (Psalm 104:2).

It is clear from the context that the psalmist is essentially extolling the beauties of nature and praising its Maker, who, as it were, "clothed Himself in light." If there is beauty in the world and it is considered a good, then indeed we ought to be grateful. So the psalmist concludes, "Bless the Lord O my soul," drawing the logical conclusions from the two assumptions mentioned above.

Of course, all along we have been dimly aware of the fact that we on planet Earth are fortunate to have an atmosphere with just the right amount of oxygen, water, a livable temperature, and to have been endowed with minds that can understand and therefore influence aspects of nature. Yet these obvious goods have not sent us into paroxysms of joyful thanksgiving. For these are such absolutely necessary conditions for human existence that God almost *had* to provide them, if He were to have us here at all! However the prevalence of beauty in the world seems to be a gratuitous plus. Science fiction has no difficulty portraying alternative worlds where you might have sunsets without color, flowers without fragrance, living forms without grace. Thus, the discovery of aesthetic pleasure in a world where it didn't have to be, is more prone to arouse sentiments of gratitude. We may therefore conclude that it is precisely the aesthetic experience more than any other, more than the realization of God's power, or of His wisdom, that is the proper source of gratitude and praise of the Creator.[18]

Consider the refrain of the psalmist: "Praise the Lord, for He is good (*tov*), for His kindness is forever" (Psalm 136). What is meant by the term "good"? Generally speaking, when it is used as an adjective, we are attributing to somebody or something qualities that are deemed right or desired, satisfactory or adequate. The term, of course, is most significant when used in a moral sense, as in the biblical tree of knowledge of good (*tov*) and evil (*ra*). However, a most interesting use of the word *tov* occurs in the first chapter of Genesis, where, as after most acts of creation (Genesis 1:10, 12, 18) we are told, "And God saw the light that it was good" (Genesis 1:4). Now *tov* here could not simply mean that what came into being was exactly as God had intended, because after other acts of creation we are just told, "And it was so…" (Genesis 1:7, 11, 15, 24, 30), which tells us precisely that what came into existence was exactly as God had intended. If so, what does the adjective "good" come to add? The problem is compounded when, at the end of the six days of creation, we are told: "And God *saw all* that He had made, and behold, it was *very* good" (*tov me'ode*) (Genesis 1:31). If aspects of the creation were already in themselves declared good, in what sense was the completed cosmos to be considered *very good*?

I would suggest that the phrase "saw that it was very good" in this context comes to denote *perception of value*, including aesthetic experience. God, as it were, must step out of Himself and contemplate His creation *as a whole* in order to appreciate its perceptible aesthetic qualities, resulting in the judgment "very good."

The text deliberately uses the general term "good" (*tov*) because it wishes to denote the concept of *value*, which can include both aesthetic and moral value. For the very act of creation coming from God *ex nihilo* may be seen as a moral gesture, gratuitously extending life and consciousness to others. God, according to Jewish theology, is good in a moral sense and, to be morally good, by definition, is to want to do good to others.[19] So that God is good in the sense that He is the source of value, both aesthetic and moral, which translate into important features of the human being. By creating man in His image, He has endowed man with a moral sense by which to recognize the good and with the freedom by which to choose the good and reject the evil. In terms of the aesthetic, God has clothed the world with natural beauty and has endowed man with the ability to recognize and appreciate beauty, and the capacity to create objects of beauty.[20]

Let us return to Psalm 136: "Praise the Lord, for He is good (*tov*), for His kindness (*chasdo*) is forever."

As we have shown, when used as an attribute of God, "good" means not only that God is morally good but that He is the *source of all value* – the true, the good, and the beautiful, in the sense that man is able to distinguish the true from the false, choose the good over the evil, and appreciate and generate the beautiful. However, in spite of its philosophical aridity, the aesthetic plays a unique role as a generator of love for God. This, as we know, is one of the fundamental and most difficult of the Torah commandments, constituting possibly the highest relationship to God attainable by man. "And you shall love the Lord your God with all your heart, and with all of your soul, and with all of your might" (Deuteronomy 6:5). How is man to love what he cannot see? How can man love with such intensity and exclusivity? These are questions which continue to concern the conscientious believer. The religious importance of a love for God is thus spelled out by Joseph Albo: "For love is the union and complete mental identification of lover and the loved."[21] Maimonides suggests that such a love might be generated if men would contemplate God's wondrous works and creations, for if they perceived His incomparable wisdom they would "straightaway love Him, praise Him, and glorify Him."[22] However, it is difficult to see how discovering someone's wisdom, no matter how great, will lead to love for him![23] But perhaps this is where the aesthetic enters the picture.

It should be remembered that one of the defining characteristics of aesthetic pleasure is that it is disinterested and intrinsic; that is to say, the pleasure arises solely and exclusively from contact with the object (seeing, hearing, or feeling) without thought of personal benefit or practical use. When we therefore discern and appreciate the aesthetic aspects of our world and realize that they are plus-values, unearned gifts from our Maker (which practical man could very well have done without), we will instantly feel not only gratitude but a rush of love for the sender of the gift. For what else could that sort of gift express if not a disinterested love on the part of the Donor? Thus, to the extent that man is sensitive to beauty in the world, he is detecting the handiwork of divinity, he is discovering traces of the divine love. Indeed, Plato already noted the relationship between love and beauty and saw the latter as the presiding genius of procreation. "Beauty stimulates our re-creation of ourselves in the image of divinity."[24] A Christian theologian expressed the relationship in a most pithy way. "His

[God's] love *causes* the beauty of what He loves, whereas our love *is caused* by the beauty that we love."[25]

Rav Soloveitchik is most emphatic in insisting that the Jewish view of God's love for Israel (man), which is to be reciprocated by Israel's love for God, differs completely from the Aristotelian view, which was one-directed only ("There could be no love on the part of the Prime Mover for the world"). Says the Rav:

> However, the Torah, which based entire Judaism upon the principle of creation and providence, on the one hand, and upon the principle of the election of Israel, on the other, introduced the concepts of kindness and love as reciprocal actions into the very navel (center) of our world. The creation of the world is the materialization of God's kindness. His Providential care of His creatures in general and His election of Israel in particular are expressions of His infinite love.[26]

While ample sources indicate that classical Judaism was fearful of the deleterious effects that indulgence in the aesthetic might have upon the human personality, from a theological point of view understanding and appreciating the aesthetic can uniquely lead to that most important religious emotion of love for God. This would be the natural response of the individual who sees, in the very possibility of the aesthetic experience and aesthetic creativity, the love of God for man.

Is there anything more substantive that the aesthetic experience can tell us about God? In a poetic flight of aggadic hyperbole, the rabbis compared the beauty of modern man to the beauty of the *Shechina*. "The comeliness of Rav Kahana was similar to that of the patriarch Ya'akov, which was similar to that of Adam, and the beauty of Adam was similar to that of the Divine Presence itself."[27]

Kalman Brand reports that the approach of medieval Jewish philosophers to the subject of beauty split along familiar lines.[28]

Upholders of the unknowability of God, led by Maimonides, were on one side, while the late medieval thinkers and followers of the Kabbala were on the other. Maimonides was well aware of the Muslim philosophers' equation of perfection and beauty, and therefore could speak of the "perfection of God's splendor which dazzles the eye." He cautioned that God's beauty/perfection was *sui generis*, and that the only thing it had in common with human experience was the name. In short, "beauty" was one of the many homonyms by which men may speak of God. On the other hand, mystical poets such as Ibn Gabirol (*The Royal Crown*), in groping for words by which to describe the bliss of the soul in the world-to-come, could write that "in the realm of the Divine Presence there is celestial light where goodness and beauty have no end."[29] Joseph Albo, a disciple of Chasdai Crescas, wrote:

> God rejoices with His own essence because He has beauty and majesty and perfection within Himself…and by comprehending the activities which flow from His loving-kindness (*chasdo*) people derive wonderful pleasure and satisfaction in the world of souls.[30]

Kabbalists, encouraged by the Zohar, believed that the cosmic beauty we experience originates within the mysterious depths of God's being.

In terms of the approach of modern Jewish philosophers to the aesthetic, it was to be expected that the Rav Joseph Dov Soloveitchik, with his emphasis on the qualitative sensuous aspects of human experience, which he believed would bring the individual closer to reality (which is ontologically anchored in God), would stress the importance of the aesthetic.[31] Furthermore, according to the Rav, man may experience the Presence of God by means of his ontological awareness, i.e., that God is the growth of all being, without Whom nothing exists.[32] Therefore every immediate apprehension of reality, and particularly those with distinctive and inspiring qualities, such as the aesthetic, creates a window to the divine. Nevertheless, early surveys of the thought of the Rav, based on his published works as of that time, concluded that as to his approach to the aesthetic, "the evidence is contradictory."[33]

The recent publication of the Rav's 1956–57 lecture notes on prayer, however, reveals much about his view of the role of the aesthetic in Jewish theology.[34] To begin with, the Rav explicitly affirms what our discussion in this paper indicates is the implication of Judaism's doctrine of creation; namely, that "God is the origin of beauty, of the delightful and the pleasant."[35] We said earlier that aesthetic experience, empirically speaking, is the result of a transaction between subject and object, between man's sense apparatus and the outside reality given to his senses. For the philosopher, that is an adequate explanation of the aesthetic. However, by saying that "God is the origin" we are saying more than that it is God who, after all, created man and his senses and the outside reality. We are asserting that God is responsible for the fact that the observed interaction between man and the surface qualities of reality results precisely in the uniquely pleasurable experience we call the aesthetic.

The Rav elaborates on this further by saying:

> Absolute beauty rests in God and that only He is the fountainhead out of which pulchritude, grace, and loveliness flow into the world. The latter abounds in magnificent forms, in harmony, style, and charm, because it was created in the likeness of its Master, whose majesty and transcendent grace penetrate into every ramification of reality to the point of saturation. God sanctions not only the true and the good but also the beautiful.[36]

Here the Rav seems to be going in the direction of the Kabbalists rather than of Maimonides. He is suggesting that God created not only man in His image but the entire cosmos, that the harmony, the charm, and the beauty we experience are material reflections of the grace and loveliness which "flow out of the divine fountainhead." Clearly we are not talking homonyms here!

At one point the Rav states:

> God not only addresses Himself to man through the logos,
> by emanating wisdom and knowledge to the finite mind, not
> only through the ethos revealing to natural man…a great
> order of absolute values and ideals but also through aesthet-
> ics, the immediate sensible apprehension of reality which is
> beautiful and grandiose.[37]

To address someone usually means to speak and to say something
substantive. If that is what the Rav intended in the preceding passage, then what God is saying to man through the logos and the
ethos is fairly clear. However, what God could be saying to man
via the aesthetic experience is not at all clear. But perhaps to address should be here interpreted as "to direct to." God is *directing*
the aesthetic, the experience thereof and the analysis of the conditions which make it possible, to the attention of man.

> Ponder this: the aesthetic in all of its many different forms,
> natural and artefactual, is a gratuitous plus in the universe
> which is an expression of the love of the Creator for His
> creatures, invoking reciprocal emotions on the part of man.[38]

Perhaps all of this is implicit in the passage from Psalms 136:

> "Praise the Lord for He is good" – the source of all value, the
> true, the moral and the aesthetic.
>   "For His loving kindness is forever" – and it is particu-
> larly from the aesthetic experience that we learn that, with
> great love have You loved us O Lord our God.[39]

CONCLUDING SUMMARY

This essay has been in turn historical and philosophical. In our
approach we have identified the *aesthetic* as encompassing all of
the branches of art and the *aesthetic experience* as common to

both creator and consumer. As such, we have shown that the role of the aesthetic in the public and private lives of the people of Israel during their formative period as a landed national entity was generally quite similar to what it was for the peoples around them. However, the evidence is quite clear that this people exhibited special creativity in the areas of music, vocal and instrumental, and in literature. The second commandment, forbidding the making and worshipping of any material representation of the deity, while generally observed in terms of its specific prohibition, does not seem to have inhibited the cultivation of the visual arts, which were amply on display in the furnishings and decorative detail of Israel's three Houses of God.

In terms of the question posed in the title, we have suggested that the aesthetic, although largely ignored by our medieval Jewish philosophers, may very well be considered the most impressive sign of God's love for man. Admittedly, manifestations of beauty are not as revelatory of the nature of the Creator as are the discovery of moral value and the extent of human cognition. That is to say, philosophic analysis of the aesthetic does not seem to yield any hints as to the substantive nature of the divinity. Yet, psalmist and prophet are eager to speak of God in aesthetic terms and to praise Him for the possibility of the aesthetic experience. We have noted that aesthetic pleasure is a disinterested pleasure, i.e., pure pleasure, from which all traces of the self have been eliminated, and perceived as the property of an object or activity. As such, the very possibility of the aesthetic as experience, and the natural structures of colors, sounds, and shapes that facilitate elaborate artistic creativity, stand out as a gratuitous plus signifying the love of a good God who brings into existence a cosmos that is "very good" in the hope that this may inspire man to do good and thus actualize the good that is implicit within him.

ENDNOTES

1. The lexical entry for "aesthetic" (alternative spelling: esthetic) as an adjective is "concern with the appreciation of beauty," and as a noun, "the philosophy of the beautiful in the arts."

2. It was Alexander Gottlieb Baumgarten (1714–1762) who gave the name "aesthetics" to these diverse activities. The term provided a new framework in which to view the intellectual problems of the arts, a framework which, while inclusive, was at the same time delimiting, implying that aesthetics was a distinct sphere. It was neither science nor philosophy. It was unique in terms of both the material involved and the type of judgment to be employed.

3. D.W. Prall, *Aesthetic Analysis* (New York: Crowell, 1967), p. 11.

4. See Genesis 4:21.

5. We are told that it was the Sophists in ancient Greece who were the first to raise productive activity to the plane of self-conscious reflection. "And in aesthetic the question 'What is beauty?' will always be accompanied by the other question: 'How are beautiful things created?' The Sophists were pioneers in seeking the solution of the second problem." Katherine Everett Gilbert and Helmut Kuhn, *A History of Esthetics* (Bloomington: Indiana University Press, 1954), p. 13.

6. Even during the patriarchal period visits were made to Egypt and beyond the Euphrates, and during their long stay in Egypt, the people had to have become aware of and somewhat acculturated to the material civilization of their hosts.

7. Here and there in the Bible we have incidental evidence of the use of jewelry by women (Genesis 24:22, Exodus 3:22), the practice of singing and dancing to the accompaniment of musical instruments (Exodus 15:20), and an objective recognition of beauty in women and men (Genesis 12:14, 29:17, 39:16 and other places).

8. See Rashi on Exodus 25:31.

9. According to the rabbis, the cherub had the face of a human child. See Rashi on Exodus 25:18.

10. The first capital was round in shape and surrounded by nets in which pomegranates were set. Above these there was another capital shaped like a lily.

11. In addition to the molten sea, there were ten smaller basins in two groups of five which were set on elaborately decorated wheeled stands (I Kings 7:15–39).

12. See I Chronicles 16:1–7.

13. See II Chronicles 20:19–22 and Sirach 47:8–10 (Ecclesiasticus).

14. The source for this citation and the three that follow may be found on pp. 2, 6, 15, and 7 respectively of Kalman P. Brand's masterly and compelling

study, *The Artless Jew* (Princeton, N.J.: Princeton University Press, 2000). I am beholden to him for much of the material in this section.

15. See my article "Is There an Indigenous Jewish Theology?" *Tradition* 9, nos. 1–2 (1967), and in Chapter 1 of this volume.

16. Berachot 57.

17. See his *Judaism Eternal* (London, 1959), p. 190.

18. There is a little-noticed fact about the conditions necessary for the flowering of the visual and auditory arts, such as painting and music, which when understood vastly increases our appreciation of the Creator. The question has been asked: "Why is it that art never developed in the areas of taste and smell despite the fact that these are qualities as subtle, specific, and characteristic as those of colors, shapes, and sounds? First, let us bypass the subjective-objective controversy by acknowledging that the aesthetic experience is a transaction between the surface of our world and the senses of the individual. What the artist does is to compose various unified structures by working with the sensuously qualitative materials he finds in nature – sounds, colors, shapes. So much is obvious. Now consider the fascinating observations of D.W. Prall (see above, n. 3), which I herewith summarize using his words. "In order to create objects of more than elementary aesthetic value, artists must work with materials that have relations, degrees of qualitative differences, established orders of variation, and structural principles of combination." Thus, the artist of music can order his materials in terms of tones, pitch, octave, timbre, and intensity. These serially ordered differences in sound are naturally given, making possible combinations of infinite variety. The same is true of color. In that medium, varieties of hue can be shown to be serially ordered along a continuous scale. In addition, there are varieties in degrees of intensity, light and darkness. "Every variety of color lies at a measurable distance from others along any single dimension chosen." There are also built-in ordering principles specific to shape and space relations. Lines, areas and volume have their own peculiar characteristics that make possible the perception of balance, symmetry, and proportion.

Another fundamental factor in the aesthetic experience of music, poetry, and dance that is intrinsic and natural, that is, it is just there, is the element of rhythm. According to Prall, rhythm can be evoked by almost any sensuous element that occurs in time. "Rhythm is always perceived through feeling, distinguished by feeling, and introduced by the body to the mind."

In short, the aesthetic experience as we know it in all of its forms "is possible, as far as the philosopher can see, only because of certain accidental, 'fortunate,' brute natural physical facts (including the physical and nervous system of the eyes).

(1) The surface qualities of our world (sight, sound, touch) when contemplated in an impartial manner, are a natural source of pleasure and delight.

(2) Sound, color, space, and shape relations occur in nature with their own intrinsic scales of order and structural principles of variation which can serve as compositional elements for artists. These do not exist in the senses of taste and smell.

So much for Prall. For a believer, of course, these natural facts are not accidental but striking signs of God's love of man, and justify evocations such as "How great are Thy works, O Lord, Thy thoughts are very deep" (Psalm 923:6),

"How manifold are Thy works, O Lord, in wisdom hast Thou made them all" (Psalm 104:24). Shubert Spero, "Judaism and the Aesthetic," *BDD: Journal of Torah and Scholarship* 1 (Summer 1995).

19. See Shubert Spero, "Rabbi Joseph Dov Soloveitchik and the Role of the Ethical," *Modern Judaism* 23 (2003): 12–31.
20. See Shubert Spero, "Towards a Torah Esthetic," *Tradition* 6, no. 2 (Spring–Summer 1964).
21. *Sefer ha-Ikarim* 3:36.
22. Hilchot Yesodai ha-Torah 21–22.
23. See Shubert Spero, "Maimonides and Our Love for God," *Judaism* 32, no. 3 (Summer 1983).
24. *Symposium* 206 a–b.
25. Jacques Maritain, *Art and Scholasticism* (New York: Sheed & Ward, 1943).
26. Joseph B. Soloveitchik, "U-bekashtem Misham," in *Galuy Venistar* (Jerusalem, 1979), pp. 182–183, n. 2.
27. Bava Batra 58a.
28. Brand, *The Artless Jew*, pp. 71–92.
29. Ibid., p. 101.
30. *Sefer ha-Ikarim* 2:15.
31. "U-bekashtem Misham," p. 129.
32. See Shubert Spero, "Rabbi Joseph Dov Soloveitchik and Belief in God," *Modern Judaism* 19 (1999): 4–6.
33. David Singer and Moshe Sokol, "Joseph Soloveitchik: Lonely Man of Faith," *Modern Judaism* 2, no. 3 (October 1982): 252.
34. *Worship of the Heart* (Ktav, 2003).
35. Ibid., p. 57.
36. Ibid., p. 59.
37. Ibid., p. 57.
38. Perhaps this is why God chooses, as the sign of His everlasting covenant with mankind never again to send a flood to destroy the earth, "*my*

rainbow in the cloud" (Genesis 9:13). For it is the rainbow, which is a dazzling display of the serially ordered colors of the spectrum built into the natural light, which, by affording man an aesthetic experience, assures man of God's love.

39. Prayer preceding the Shema in the daily *Shacharit* service.

Albo, Joseph (1380–1444) Philosopher, Jewish community leader, took prominent part in the Christian Jewish disputes in Tortosa and San Mateo (1413–1414), lived in Daroca, province of Saragossa, Spain, was a student of Hasdai Crescas and R. Nissim ben Reuben, author of *Sefer ha-Ikkarim* (*Book of Principles*), which achieved great popularity. He was a clear and systematic writer, knowledgeable in rabbinic literature and the works of Jewish philosophers before him, and felt free to weigh their views and present a coherent picture of Judaism.

Anselm, (1033–1109) Christian theologian, Archbishop of Canterbury, chiefly remembered for what he called the Ontological Proof for the existence of God.

Aquinas, Thomas, (1224–1274) most prominent medieval Christian theologian, lectured at the Universities of Paris, Naples and Rome. Known for composing a philosophic system which harmonized the teachings of Aristotle with Christian theology. Continues to exert influence on Catholic theology.

Aristotle (384 B.C.E.–322 B.C.E.) attended Plato's Academy as student and member. Later founded his own school called the Lyceum. His interest in empirical data led him to differ with

Plato on important questions and made him the trail-blazer in science as well as philosophy. Remembered for his theory of the Four Causes and in ethics for his formulation of the Golden Mean. Remained the dominant influence in philosophy and theology up to the Renaissance.

Axiological, pertaining to value in general, moral, aesthetic or other.

Berkovits, Eliezer (1908–1992) Rabbi, theologian born in Transylvania, ordained at the Hildesheimer Rabbinical seminary, served communities in Berlin, England, and Australia. In 1958 appointed professor of Jewish philosophy at the Hebrew Theological College of Chicago. In his writing Berkovits was an effective expositor and defender of Modern Orthodoxy. Important books: *God Man and History* (1954), *Jewish Critique of the Philosophy of Martin Buber* (1962).

Borowitz, Eugene (1924–2000) Educator, theologian, professor of education and Jewish thought, Hebrew Union College, national director of education, Union of American Hebrew Congregations, advocate of a holistic theology that would include as much as possible of traditional religious concepts and way of life based on a subjective commitment to Jewish peoplehood. His book *The Masks Jews Wear: The Self-Deception of American Jewry* contains an incisive analysis and critique of the culture of American liberal Jews and points a way toward "authenticity" and a clarification of values. He attempts to reinstate concepts of faith, covenant, and worship along subjective existential lines. For many years, Borowitz published and edited a small magazine called *She'ma* in which Jews of all ideological stripes discussed issues of Jewish concern reasonably and amiably.

Buber, Martin (1878–1965) Philosopher, theologian, Zionist, Jewish communal leader, born in Vienna, brought up by grandfather, rabbinic scholar Solomon Buber, in Lemberg, Poland (now Lviv, Ukraine), attended German universities, among them University of Berlin. As a Zionist favored Jewish cultural creativity and education over political activity. Impressed by the message of Hasidism, Buber at age twenty-six decided to tell their story to the world in a series of books. Worked on behalf of Jewish communities in Eastern Europe during World War I. Together with Franz Rosenzweig authored a new German translation of the Bible, which he claimed was not "a dead book but living speech in which the Eternal Thou becomes present to one who truly listens"; served as professor of religion at University of Frankfurt and head of the Juedisches Lehrhaus in that city. In 1938 appointed professor of social philosophy at Hebrew University of Jerusalem. Known for his philosophy of dialogue, that man must develop an I-Thou relationship with the world, which can lead to a relationship with the Eternal Thou that is God. Buber's teachings have been quite influential among Christian theologians.

Burke, Edmund (1729–1797) member of what is called the Eighteenth Century British School who wrote extensively on the nature of the aesthetic experience. Burke emphasized the role of passion in the aesthetic process and argued that the recognition of beauty is part of the social instinct of mankind.

Cohen, Hermann (1842–1918) received a traditional Jewish education, studied at Breslau Rabbinic seminary, interest turned to philosophy and became professor of Philosophy at Marburg, considered one of the founders of Neo-Kantianism. Followed the assimilationist tendencies of the Emancipation. Later in life grew more aware of the significance of Judaism in that the Jewish people represented an instantiation of a true religion of reason whose center is ethics. This is reflected in his book, *The Religion of Reason as Drawn from the Sources of Judaism*, which was published posthumously in 1919.

Cosmological proof, see Five Ways.

Descartes, (1596–1650) known as the "father of modern philosophy," lived at the time of important breakthroughs in the physical sciences: Copernicus, Kepler, Galileo William Harvey and did important work in mathematics. In his book, *Discourse on Method*, he developed what is called "methodological skepticism." Remembered for his: "I think therefore I am."

Empirical, pertaining to experience, information derived from sense-data rather than from speculative theories.

Epicureans, followers of the philosophy and way of life of Epicurus of Samos, (341–270 B.C.E.) The supreme value and goal of life is to attain a state of "happiness" which is "health to the body and repose to the soul." The Wise Man is he who is able to bring into balance positive pleasures and serenity of soul. Although egoistic and hedonic, this philosophy was quite refined and had many followers.

Epistemological pluralism, a philosophical position which claims that there is more than one valid method by which to gain knowledge of reality. Such a position is developed by the Rav in his *Halakhic Mind*.

Epistemology, that branch of philosophy that deals with the theory of knowledge, its methods and validation.

Eudemonia, pertaining to happiness, eudemonism, a system of ethics that defines moral good or right action as one that results in happiness.

Existentialism, See p. 24, note 11.

Five ways, the "five ways" by which Thomas Aquinas attempted to prove the existence of God. They are 1) Argument from motion: There has to be a Prime Mover (who is God) who started it all, if not you are reduced to infinite regress. 2) Argument from efficient cause. There has to be a First cause (who is God) who is himself uncaused. These two together are sometimes called the cosmological proof. 3) Argument from contingency (that everything in the world really did not have to be. There must be a necessary existent (that is God). 4) Argument from gradations. There must be an all perfect being (who is God).

5) Argument from teleology. Much in the natural world shows "purpose" or complex processes which work out for the benefit of man. Hence there must be a "designer" (who is God).

Fox, Marvin (1923–1996) Philosopher, educator, ordained as rabbi, Hebrew Theological College of Chicago, doctorate in philosophy from Ohio State University, where he started Jewish studies program; taught Jewish philosophy at Brandeis University. His published works focus on Maimonides and problems of ethics.

Fromm, Eric (1900–1980) Psychologist, psychoanalyst, came from an Orthodox Jewish home but left formal religion. Many of his insights reflect Biblical and Rabbinic teachings. See his *The Heart of Man* and *The Art of Loving*.

Halevi, Judah (1075–1141) Hebrew poet, philosopher, born in Toledo (or Tudela), Spain, to a wealthy and learned family, received comprehensive Jewish and Arabic education, initially lived in Cordoba and practiced medicine, traveled throughout Moslem Spain, befriended by Moses ibn Ezra and Abraham ibn Ezra, communicated with Jewish poets in main Jewish centers including North Africa. Some 800 of his poems, secular and religious, are known, among them several hundred liturgical poems (*piyutim*) as well as the often-recited *Shirei Ziyyon*. Halevi's poetry ranges over the full gamut of human emotions; expressed with great passion and intensity, reflecting personal religious experiences of all sorts, it has been called "among the greatest in Jewish religious poetry after the psalms." His philosophy is contained in his *Sefer ha-Kuzari*; written in Arabic; it is a polemical work directed against Aristotelian philosophy as well as against Christianity and Islam in the form of a dialogue between the king of the Khazars and a rabbi. At the end of the book, the rabbi agrees with the king that it is indeed shameful that the Jewish people pray daily for the restoration of Zion yet do nothing about it. Fitting deeds to words, Halevi in 1141 set out for the land of Israel, stopping off in Alexandria and Fostat. The rest is legend.

Hedonism, an ethical theory that asserts that pleasure is the highest good and the proper aim of mankind.

Heidegger, Martin, (1889–1976) Professor of philosophy at Universities of Marburg and Freiberg, author of *Being and Time,* deals with the usual existential themes of anxiety, death, repetition and history, claims a new approach to ontology. His use of German terms in new constructions makes for difficult reading. His support of the Nazi regime brought him in disfavor in some circles.

Hermeneutics – concerning interpretation of Scripture or any literary text.

Heschel, Abraham Joshua (1907–1972) Torah scholar, philosopher, descended on both sides from Hasidic masters, doctorate from University of Berlin in Jewish studies; in 1937 appointed by Martin Buber to succeed him as director of Lehrhaus in Frankfurt, deported by Nazis to Poland, emigrated to United States in 1940, professor of philosophy and rabbinics at Hebrew Union College, Cincinnati. In 1975 professor of Jewish ethics and mysticism, Jewish Theological Seminary. Played an active role in the civil rights movement and in Jewish-Christian relations: works that focus on the classical sources of Judaism include *The Prophets* and *Torah min ha-Shamayim* (2 vols.; Eng. trans. *Theology of Ancient Judaism* [1962]). Works such as *Man Is Not Alone* (1951) and *God in Search of Man* (1956) present Judaism as responsive to modern man's existential problems.

Hirsch, Samson Raphael (1808–1888) Rabbi, author, community leader foremost exponent of Orthodoxy in Germany at the time. Born in Hamburg, student of R. Jacob Etlinger and R. Isaac Barnays. Attended University of Bonn for a year. In 1839 appointed state Rabbi of Oldenburg, formed friendship with Abraham Geiger and Heinrich Graetz, 1846 moved to Nikolsburg as State rabbi of Moravia. In 1951 became Rabbi of an Orthodox congregation in Frankfurt on the Main where he built a complete community with its own institutions including an educational system that integrated Jewish religious and secular studies, considered , a model of a modern Orthodox congregation. Most influential works are "Nineteen Letters of Ben Uziel"(1836) Horeb (1961English) and his translation into German and commentary on the Pentateuch. He sought to show that enlightened traditional Judaism can be compatible with general culture. *Torah im derech eretz* achieved state's recognition of Orthodox congregation that had separated from Reform- controlled communal organization.

Homiletics, the art of preaching or moralizing using texts from Scripture.

Hume, David, (1711–1776) belonged to the British school of Empiricism, believing that all of our knowledge comes from experience and that human reason using the scientific method can discover the true nature of the universe. He demonstrated however, that if so, it is doubtful whether we can have any secure knowledge at all. Hume's skepticism set the stage for all subsequent philosophy.

Ibn Gabirol, Solomon (1021–1069) Poet, philosopher, born in Malaga, Spain, lived in Saragossa and Granada, a most gifted poet driven by a love of God and a passion for the Hebrew language of Scripture. At the age of nineteen wrote a poem of 400 verses on the rules of Hebrew grammar and put to verse the 613 commandments. His best-known religious poem is *Royal Crown* (*Keter Malchut*), in which he celebrates the greatness of God and how man through repentance can ascend to God. His philosophic work *Fons Vita* (Fountain of Life), which follows a Neoplatonic approach and mentions no biblical or rabbinic sources, was translated from the Arabic into Latin in 1150 and was studied by Christian theologians who thought it had been written by a Christian called Avicebron. Only in the nineteenth century was it discovered to be the work of Ibn Gabirol.

Immanentism The belief that God is (but not only) an indwelling

Presence that pervades the universe, *mello ha-aretz kevodo.* According to Judaism He is also transcendent, that is above and beyond the cosmos and our understanding.

Incorporeal, not composed of matter.

James, William, (1842–1910) Psychologist turned philosopher. One of the founders of the philosophic movement known as Pragmatism- that the meaning and worth of a concept is to be determined by the practical effects it may have. Works most relevant to philosophy of religion are *The Will to Believe* and *Varieties of Religious Experience.*

Jaspers, Karl, (1883–1969) Professor of philosophy at Heidelberg and Basel. Believed that all philosophy today must be "existential philosophy," that is, must arise out of a realization of the human condition. By focusing only upon objective data, science misses out on that which is the most important part of reality which is subjectivity, the unique inner experience of concrete individual human beings each one completely irreplaceable. Existential philosophy is a way of thought in which each person seeks out his genuine self in dialogue with others and this activates his own being. By diminishing his own finitude man becomes aware of the transcendent. Jasper's writing is considered more accessible to non-existentialists.

Kalischer, Zvi Hirsch (1795–1874) Rabbi, harbinger of modern Zionism, born in Lissa, Posen district (Leszno, Poland), studied under prominent rabbis Jacob of Lissa and Akiva Eger. In 1824 settled in Thorn (Torún), where he lived and served as rabbi. Published works in halakha and religious philosophy. Kalischer spent his life publicizing and trying to implement his idea that the time had come, with the rise of national movements in Europe, for the Jewish people to organize a return and resettle the land of Israel. Only after such a human initiative could one hope for a miraculous redemption. He expressed his views with great passion and learning in his influential *Derishat Ziyyon*

(1862). In the course of his practical efforts, he met with Amschel Rothschild in 1836, and was instrumental in the founding of the first school for agriculture in the Holy Land, Mikveh Israel, in 1870.

Kant, Immanuel, (1724–1804) born, lived and died in the town of Kongsberg in East Prussia. Appointed Professor of Philosophy at University of Konigsberg. In his attempt to reconcile the methods of science which assumes that all events are the products of necessity and our own experience of moral value based on freedom of will, Kant effectuated a revolution in philosophy. In his major work, *The Critique of Pure Reason*, Kant analyzes the limitations of human reason, producing a new understanding of the relations between the mind and its objects. His thought was considered congenial to Judaism by virtue of his positing of an unknowable transcendent and by providing a rational basis for morality by his categorical imperative.

Kierkegaard, Soren, (1813–1855) Christian theologian (Denmark) whose writing is characterized by great passion, analytic depth and psychological penetration, rebelled against the metaphysics of Hegel with its emphasis upon reason saying it ignored the "personal predicament of men existing before God." Considered the father of modern existentialism. Kierkegaard distinguished three spheres or stages of existence: the aesthetic, the ethical and the religious, and treated in great depth themes such as freedom, boredom, despair, dread and anxiety that will continue to occupy later existentialists. His little book, *Fear and Trembling*, on the sacrifice of Isaac, analyzes with unusual clarity the relationship between morality and religious faith.

Kimchi, David (1160–1235) Known as Radak, grammarian, biblical exegete, teacher from Narbonne (Provence), active in public affairs, composed important works in Hebrew philology, grammar, and the Masoretic text, had a profound influence on the Christian Hebraists of the Renaissance. In his biblical commentary Kimchi stresses philological analysis while often including rabbinic homiletical material (*drashot*). In his philosophy he generally followed Maimonides, whose views he defended in the Maimonist controversy.

Leibniz, William, (1646–1716) brilliant mathematician and philosopher, rejected the Cartesian assumption that all matter consists of a simple substance that has extension and instead proposed that reality consists of what he called monads which are like force or energy without shape or size rather like a mathematical point. The fact they all cooperate in harmony to give us our variegated world was to Leibniz the result of God's activity. Known for what he termed the Principle of Sufficient Reason which is merely a restatement of the argument from a First Cause and for his assertion that in view of God's omniscience and moral requirements we can affirm that "this is the best of all possible worlds."

Lieberman, Saul (1898–1983) Talmudic scholar, born in Belarussia (Belarus), studied at Yeshivot of Malch and Slobodka, attended University of Kiev; in 1928 settled in Jerusalem, where he studied talmudic philology and Greek language and literature at the Hebrew University. In 1940 joined faculty of Jewish Theological Seminary, New York, becoming rector of the rabbinical school in 1958. His books on Greek and Hellenism in Jewish Palestine remain valuable contributions to our knowledge of the period, as are his textual studies of the Jerusalem Talmud and his massive work on the *Tosefta.*

Longinus, (first century c.e.) author of a treatise called "On the Sublime," more of a literary critic than a philosopher. In the intellectual ferment of the Greco-Roman world he called the attention of the poets and orators away from "the outside" of the aesthetic object to the "inside" of the artist. He emphasized passion and "greatness of soul" over technical proficiency and pleasing exterior.

Maimonides, Moses (son of Maimon) (1135–1204) Known as Rambam, rabbi, philosopher, codifier, physician considered the most significant Jewish philosopher of the Middle Ages, born in Cordoba, Spain, to a learned family, forced to flee when city fell to the fanatical Almohads, settled in Fez, North Africa, in 1160; fearing persecution traveled to Acre, from there Maimonides visited Jerusalem and Hebron and in 1165 settled in Fostat (Old Cairo), became head of the community and one of the royal physicians to the vizier of Egypt; buried in Tiberias, Israel. His greatest works, which account for his incalculable influence on the development of Judaism, are: *Commentary on the Mishneh, Mishneh Torah,* and *Guide for the Perplexed. Mishneh Torah*: a systematic codification of the entire talmudic and post-talmudic halakhic literature in lucid Hebrew in fourteen books, each representing a distinct category of the Jewish legal system into which Maimonides incorporated many scientific and philosophic aspects. *Moreh Nevuchim (Guide for the Perplexed*): written for those who after studying philosophy were perplexed by the literal meaning of the biblical text, deals with such subjects as attributes of God, creation, prophecy, divine providence, nature of the commandments.

Marcel, Gabriel, (1889–1973) His literary output has been termed Christian Existentialism In reality his view of the human condition and understanding of Being is compatible with any revealed religion.

Nachmanides, Moses (son of Nahman) (1194–1270) Also known as Ramban, talmudic scholar, philosopher, kabbalist, biblical exegete, physician, born in Gerona (Catalonia). From his teachers he received talmudic traditions of both northern and southern France and succeeded in training the next generation of halakhists. While critical of some of Maimonides' views, Nachmanides worked for a compromise in the Maimonist controversy. Although victorious in his public disputation with an apostate in Barcelona in 1263, he was advised to leave the country and in 1265 arrived in the land of Israel, where he helped rebuild a Jewish community in Jerusalem and Acre. His place of burial is not known. Nachmanides' halakhic work consists mainly of novellae on the Talmud and halakhic monographs on specific subjects in which he exhibits a lucid style, logical presentation, and independence of judgment. In his biblical commentary he seeks out the broader message of both the laws and narratives and when citing earlier authorities treats their views critically.

Neo-Kantianism, a movement within German speculative thought, flourished from about the 1870's to 1920, associated with Friedrich Lange, Hermann Cohen and Paul Natorp, based on the Kantian understanding of the structure of rational thought. They saw the mathematical sciences as the model of knowledge in general and true Being as identical with thought, feeling and will. Ethical and aesthetic values were seen as real and valid. Unlike Kant they did not see the world of experience as a manifestation of a metaphysical reality beyond knowledge.

Neo-Platonism, the eclectic system of thought developed by Plotinus (born around 204 B.C.E. and active in Alexandria and Rome) based on a special version of Plato's philosophy in which he combined a speculative description of reality with a religious doctrine of salvation. The true reality is the one unknowable, unchanging God who can be reached by man only in a mystical ecstasy. Rejecting the idea of creation-ex-nihilo, Plotinus taught that the material world came from God in a process called emanation, that is a sort of flowing from God by necessity. These teachings had a major influence on Augustine and became an important strand in almost all of medieval religious philosophy.

Nietzche, Friedrich (1844–1900) most prominent rebel against the European culture of his time, its morality and its theology. Appointed professor of philosophy at University of Basel at age 24. His writing is characterized by a lively style and intense passion. Known for his proclamation that "God is Dead," accused Christianity and Judaism of having imposed upon Europe "a slave morality." In its place he advocated the ideal of the "Superman," one who would represent the full and free expression of the human physical intellectual and emotional will to power.

Noetic, pertaining to the intellect or matters intellectual and abstract.

Noumenal, Kant had distinguished between phenomenal reality, the world as we experience it and noumenal reality, a nonsensual reality ("the thing in itself") that exists independently of us, that we can know only as it appears to us, as organized by the a- priori categories of the mind.

Ontic, relating to aspects of being.

Ontology, the branch of philosophy that deals with the nature of being.

Ontological proof, an argument claiming to prove by logic the existence of God. Formulated by Anselm, reformulated by Descartes and debated ever since. The essence of this approach is that the existence of God follows necessarily from the idea of God. Since our idea of God is of one who is Infinite and Perfect and since there is nothing in our experience which is so, our idea could only have been caused by God Himself. (Descartes)

Pascal, Blaise (1623–1662), brilliant mathematician and physicist, considered precursor of modern existentialism, because he begins with the human situation as considered from within. A religious Roman Catholic who had a transforming mystical experience which impelled him to write the following on a piece of paper found sewn into his jacket after his death: "God of Abraham, God of Isaac, God of Jacob, not of the philosophers and scholars." Remembered for his statement: The heart has reasons which the reason does not know; and for an argument known as Pascal's Wager whose real value lies in the realization that religious faith involves "inescapable decisions in the face of inescapable uncertainty" (D.E. Roberts).

Plato (428 B.C.E.–348 C.E.), founder of the Academy in Athens, an actual school with a curriculum in science and philosophy. One of the first and most successful to engage in what we call "philosophy": a sustained and systematic rational inquiry into the world around us: what do we know and how do we know it, the effort to get behind the visible particular things to that which is the truly real, the world of "ideas." Plato's metaphysics was heavily influenced by his regard for mathematics. His teachings have come down to us in the form of his Dialogues (more than 20) which are in themselves literary treasures.

Ravitsky, Aviezer (b. 1945) Professor of Jewish philosophy, Hebrew University, has written widely on different areas of Jewish philosophy including some insightful articles on R. Joseph Dov Soloveitchik.

Rosenzweig, Franz (1886–1929) Theologian, born in Kassel, Germany, to parents whose Judaism was minimal, studied in various universities. In 1912, after an intense spiritual struggle, was about to convert to Christianity when he had a transforming religious experience during an Orthodox Yom Kippur service in Berlin as a result of which "he knew himself to be a Jew." He set out to return to Judaism and recover its meaning. While a soldier in the German army in World War I, he worked out his philosophy, which eventuated in his important book *The Star of Redemption* (1921). He associated with Hermann Cohen and Martin Buber, collaborating with the latter in producing a new German translation of the Torah, founder of the famed Lehrhaus in Franfurt in 1920. Rosenzweig's view of Judaism and of general philosophy was unique and independent. His view that all philosophy must begin with the fact of human individuality and subjective experience places him among the existentialists. He contracted a rare disease leaving him with a slow and creeping paralysis. He remained creative and spiritually serene until the very end.

Russell, Bertrand, (1872–1970) English philosopher and mathematician, leading exponent of analytic realism. Contrary to the Idealism of the time, he held that the duality of mind and matter, universals and particulars, reflect ultimate reality as are relations which are external. He believed that mathematics, which is to say logic, can serve as a model for the analysis of language and understanding of philosophy in general.

Saadia Gaon (son of Joseph) (882–942) Talmudic scholar, prolific author, leader of Babylonian Jewry, born in Egypt acquired comprehensive knowledge of Torah and of Greco-Arabic philosophy. Was involved in the stormy calendar controversy between the rabbinic authorities of Babylon and Eretz Yisrael, moved to Baghdad, where in recognition of his profound scholarship and forceful leadership in 928 was appointed head of the famed Yeshiva of Sura (then in decline) with the title of gaon. He restored the yeshiva to its former glory, punctuated by bouts of controversy with the exilarch, the political head of Babylonian Jewry. The contribution of Saadia to the development of Judaism was immense in every field, giving it the direction it has followed ever since. He came at a pivotal period, toward the end of the talmudic gaonic period, with its center in Babylon, and the beginning of the medieval period, with its center in Spain; was the first to write "books" in the modern sense, giving his halakhic works the form of monographs, i.e., a separate one on each section of the halakhic law logically organized; wrote several works on Hebrew grammar in which he was a pioneer, made an Arabic translation of the Bible and a partial commentary, produced the first *siddur* (prayerbook), a methodical compilation of the prayer service in Arabic for the whole year, wrote original *piyutim* (Hebrew religious poetry). His philosophic work *Emunot ve-deot* (*Book of Beliefs and Opinions*), written in Arabic, was the first to attempt to reconcile the Bible and philosophy, reason and revelation, believing it a religious obligation to find a rational basis for one's faith. The work was designed to help people refute the aggressive charges of the Karaites, and remains a primary source for an authentic philosophy of Judaism.

Scheler, Max (1874–1928) taught philosophy at the Universities of Jena and Munich. Believed that the spiritual life is the final reality and that "phenomenology" which states that "reality is to be realized and described by being brought to self givenness in immediate intuitive evidence;" can give us insight into that reality, has been called an "intuitive philosopher." In his writing, religious themes such as concept of man, repentance and evidence for the existence of God are analyzed with great insight.

Scholastics, theologians who indulged in the intellectual activity called scholasticism which was carried on in the medieval cathedral schools. This was a systematic fusion of Christian theology with the philosophy of Plato and Aristotle using a special dialectical (question and answer) method relying chiefly on strict logical deduction and based upon the work of Thomas Aquinas.

Stoics, a name given to the followers of the philosophy of Stoicism (sometimes called the Stoa) whose founder was Zeno of Citium (4th century B.C.E.) Although developed in Athens this philosophy became very popular through out the Roman Empire and whose chief representatives were Seneca, Epictetus and Marcus Aurelius (said to be the friend of Rabbi Judah Hanasi) Stoicism was originally a complete systematic account of reality but in time was reduced to a popular moral philosophy in which the Wise Man is he who knows how to free himself from the sudden ups and downs in his life and the effect it has on his emotions. One can and must by one's own will power control the effects that these external events have on one's nature and attain an inner serenity.

Syllogism, a form of deductive reasoning in which a conclusion is drawn from two assumed propositions (premises), one being a universal and one a particular.

Tillich, Paul, (1886–1965) German-born Christian theologian who taught at Union theological Seminary and Harvard. Much of his writing done in the modern temper is relevant to the philosophy of religion in general. He wrote, "That which is based on ultimate concern is not exposed to destruction by preliminary concerns and the lack of their fulfillment. The most astonishing proof of this assertion is the history of the Jews. They are in the history of mankind, the document of the ultimate and unconditional character of faith" (*Dynamics of Faith*, p. 119)

Teleological proof, see Five Ways

Theocentric, having God as its center

Tremendum, mysterium, a term given by Rudolf Otto (1867–1937) in his classic work, *The Idea of the Holy*, to the feeling that is distinctive of the religious experience. Otto goes on to give a very detailed and insightful analysis of the components of both the mysterium and the tremendum drawing on material from Scripture.

WORKS BY THE RAV CITED

IN THE NOTES

Divrei Hagut ve-ha-Aracha (Jerusalem: World Zionist Organization, Dept. of Torah Education and Culture in the Diaspora, 1982).

Divrei Hashkafa (Jerusalem: World Zionist Organization, Dept. of Education and Torah Culture in the Diaspora, 1992), p. 242.

Ha-Adam ve-Olamo (Man and His World: Essays and Talks by Rabbi J.D. Soloveitchik) (Jerusalem: World Zionist Organization, Dept. of Education and Torah Culture in the Diaspora, 1998).

Halakhic Man, trans. L. Kaplan (Philadelphia: Jewish Publication Society, 1983).

The Halakhic Mind (New York: Free Press, 1986).

Kol Dodi Dofek, trans. David Gordon, ed. Jeffrey Woolf (Hoboken, N.J.; Ktav 2006); Hebrew version in *Ish ha-Emuna, me'et ha-Rav Yosef Dov Soloveitchik* (Jerusalem: Mosad Harav Kook, 1968).

"The Lonely Man of Faith," *Tradition 7, no. 2* (Summer 1965).

"Mah Dodeikh mi-Dod," in *Be-Sod ha-Yachid ve ha-Yachad* (Jerusalem, 1976).

Out of the Whirlwind: Essays on Mourning, Suffering, and the

Human Condition, ed. David Shatz, Joel Wolowelsky, and Reuven Ziegler (Hoboken, N.J.: Ktav, 2003).

Purim Lecture of the Rav, אדר תש"ל, *transcribed by Baruch David Shreiber, pp. 138–139.*

The Synagogue as Institution and Idea," in Thoughts and Appreciation (Jerusalem, 1981), pp. 102–103 (Hebrew).

"U-bekashtem Misham," Hadarom 47 (1979) and also in *Ish ha-Halakha: Galui ve-Nistar* (Jerusalem: World Zionist Organization, 1979); In English: "From Thence Ye Will Seek."

Worship of the Heart: Essays on Jewish Prayer, ed. Shalom Carmy (Hoboken, N.J.: Ktav, 2003).

 Aspects of Rabbi Joseph
Dov Soloveitchik's
Philosophy of Judaism
An Analytic Approach